MODI MANDATE
2019

Praise for the Book

'Pradeep Bhandari's latest book provides a rare analysis of the 2019 verdict. It is penned by the person who, since his arrival less than a decade ago, has changed the grammar of psephology and indeed represents a generational shift among psephologists who engage with India's elections. This book offers the reader insights on both the mandate itself and the drivers of voter choice.

It is a must read for all who want to engage with the world's largest democratic exercise.'

—**Samir Saran**, President, Observer Research Foundation

'Pradeep Bhandari is a new age psephologist who has perfected the art of mixing quantitative and qualitative analysis. His extensive travels through India's heartland and intense interaction with voters lend credibility to his election forecasts. This book is compulsory reading to understand how politics works in New India and why Narendra Modi has triumphed against all odds.'

—**Kanchan Gupta**, Distinguished Fellow, Observer Research Foundation

'Pradeep Bhandari developed unique insights into the election process, based on his ground-up reach and research in various constituencies. The accuracy of his predictions certainly sets him apart.'

—**Mohandas Pai,** Chairman, Manipal Global Education

'Pradeep Bhandari has advanced the art of psephology by bringing in high science in the form of video interviews. This is why his record of forecasting is among the best.'

—**Surjit Bhalla**, Executive Director for India, Bangladesh, Bhutan and Sri Lanka, International Monetary Fund

'A trailblazing journey into the heart and soul of India, at once humbling and enthralling, this book is a must-read.'

—**Anand Ranganathan**, author and scientist

'In his uniquely rigorous way, Pradeep Bhandari changed the grammar of psephology in 2019 in India. He was the first to predict the BJP would cross 300 seats.'

—**Chitra Subramaniam**, award-winning journalist

MODI MANDATE 2019

DISPATCHES FROM GROUND ZERO

PRADEEP BHANDARI

RUPA

Published by
Rupa Publications India Pvt. Ltd 2020
7/16, Ansari Road, Daryaganj
New Delhi 110002

Sales Centres:
Allahabad Bengaluru Chennai
Hyderabad Jaipur Kathmandu
Kolkata Mumbai

Copyright © Pradeep Bhandari 2020

The views and opinions expressed in this book are the author's own and the facts are as reported by him which have been verified to the extent possible, and the publishers are not in any way liable for the same.

All rights reserved.
No part of this publication may be reproduced, transmitted, or stored in a retrieval system, in any form or by any means, electronic, mechanical, photocopying, recording or otherwise, without the prior permission of the publisher.

ISBN: 978-93-5333-997-5

Second impression 2020

10 9 8 7 6 5 4 3 2

Printed at Parksons Graphics Pvt. Ltd, Mumbai

The moral right of the author has been asserted.

This book is sold subject to the condition that it shall not, by way of trade or otherwise, be lent, resold, hired out, or otherwise circulated, without the publisher's prior consent, in any form of binding or cover other than that in which it is published.

This book is dedicated to my mother and father who are my biggest strength and inspiration.

CONTENTS

Foreword by Meghnad Desai	*ix*
Foreword by Arnab Goswami	*xi*
Introduction	*xiii*
1. Where the Opposition Blew the War Trumpet: Uttar Pradesh	1
2. The Battle between Regionalism and Religion: West Bengal	33
3. The Power of Women Voters: Bihar	61
4. Hindi Heartland: Rajasthan, Madhya Pradesh, Jharkhand and Chhattisgarh	79
5. Strategic Wins: Maharashtra and Gujarat	99
6. AAP or Not: Delhi	127
7. The Outliers: The Northeast and Odisha	143
8. Modi's Magical Captaincy: The Hilly States of Uttarakhand, Himachal Pradesh, Haryana, Punjab and Jammu & Kashmir	168
9. Unconquered So Far: South India	190
Conclusion: The Way Forward	212
Acknowledgements	219
Index	221

FOREWORD

I got to know Pradeep Bhandari a few years ago. We met on TV programmes, often with Arnab Goswami laying down the law from his anchoring position. Pradeep was totally focused on elections and voting behaviour. He was on a one-man mission to track voting behaviour wherever he went across India.

Pradeep's interest and his talents soon began to be appreciated. His business began to grow slowly but surely. After a while he was not just a one-man show but he had a team of young workers who were devoted to him. His predictions began to be quoted. In the fiercely competitive business of election forecasting, Pradeep not only survived but began to be distinctly visible. His brand, *Jan ki Baat*, is now a recognized part of the electoral polling game.

This book is the culmination of Pradeep's efforts. For the 2019 elections, he prepared well and built up a team to travel around the country and see for himself how the nation was going to vote. He has probed below the surface, learnt to draw conclusion from even the silences of frightened voters as in West Bengal. He knows the permutations of parties and their frequent couplings and divorces in Maharashtra and Bihar, Uttar Pradesh and Gujarat. The 2019 elections were thrilling as much because of the wild predictions made about the likely outcome but also uniquely it was an election about one man—Narendra Modi. The results, when they came, surprised everyone. But not Pradeep. Read why and learn how he did it.

I recommend *Modi Mandate 2019* as the best account you would get from anybody who has pursued the voters and gauged their intentions.

Meghnad Desai
Member, House of Lords,
United Kingdom

FOREWORD

It is my privilege to write this foreword for Pradeep Bhandari, whose magical journey in less than two years I have been witness to and a partner of. Pradeep is a rare mix of academic rigour, tremendous hard work and impeccable fieldwork—a combination that no other psephologist in India can match. What makes him special is that his true love—his political analysis—is based upon micro-level interactions and observations on the field when he travels to constituencies. He observes not just the local candidates, but also local customs, habits, demography and trends. This allows him to circumvent the boring and predictable pure number-based analysis of others in his field. No psephologist can ever claim to get all elections right, but only one person in India today can claim to have travelled to over 400 constituencies for the coverage of the 2019 general elections.

The Modi magic that defined the 2019 elections will be fully understood with what Pradeep writes in this fantastic description of the elections along with the videos of his groundwork heading the *Jan ki Baat* team and shooting some of Republic network shows. At 28, Pradeep has decades of Indian political analysis ahead of him and I am confident that many years from now this book will be re-read to understand how his career, travelling and reporting about our great nation started. I can't wait to get my hands on the 2024 edition!

Arnab Goswami
Managing Director,
Editor-in-Chief and Co-Founder
Republic TV

INTRODUCTION

'IT WAS LIKE A CRICKET WORLD CUP FINAL!'

That's my standard response whenever anyone asks me about my experience with the 2019 Lok Sabha elections. I recall how just like a cricket world cup final match, with every passing over, the Indian electoral match was becoming all the more unpredictable and unexpected. The last few overs literally kept the spectators on their toes, gasping for air at every delivery and the outcome stunned them all. These elections, unlike the 2017 Uttar Pradesh elections, went right down the wire.

Everything about the 2019 Lok Sabha elections was unique, which is why it became all the more imperative to collect all conflicting perspectives at one place. These elections were set against the backdrop of peculiar alliances and saw the staunchest of adversaries joining in union against one person, one party and one united ideology. For the first time in the political history of India, all parties virtually came together as a united opposition, rendering the electoral battle to be an anti-Modi vs pro-Modi fight at the macro level.

On paper, the 2019 Lok Sabha elections were the most exceptional of ballot battles our country had ever seen. These were the first elections which saw the Samajwadi Party (SP) and the Bahujan Samaj Party (BSP), the most ardent opponents of Indian politics, coming together to fight the general elections. Theoretically, this gathbandhan (alliance) was sweeping the elections, and what happened at the end was absolutely unexpected.

These were the elections that saw the state of West Bengal transitioning completely from a Trinamool Congress (TMC) vs Left fight, to the Left completely sliding into a state of oblivion and then turning into a direct fight between the TMC and the Bharatiya Janata Party (BJP).

These elections saw the BJP as a strong force fighting a frontal war in Telangana where in the assembly elections they were out for the count. These elections saw historical rivals, the Congress Party and the Janata Dal (Secular) [JD(s)] coming together in Karnataka, and their culmination indicating a strong vote share in theory. These elections stirred up all conjectures with regard to a possible alliance between the Congress Party and the Aam Aadmi Party (AAP). These were the elections where guessing games were lagbhag (almost) at peak.

This was the electoral battle which the BJP was entering with the burden of loss in the Hindi heartland region. These were the elections where, despite everything, a fresh new WhatsApp forward or TV channel survey would predict the BJP winning 200 seats.

These were the elections where the public was of the view that the Goods and Services Tax (GST) and demonetization would be the end of the BJP despite the Balakot air strikes. At the same time, these were the elections where people were of the opinion that whatever votes BJP landed in their kitty would be only because of the Balakot air strikes.

These were the elections where people thought the National Register of Citizens (NRC) would be responsible for wiping out the BJP from Assam. These were the elections where for the first time the BJP was fighting with full glory in the Northeast (of India)—a region where they did not even figure in back in 2014.

These elections were taking place when speculations of a new prime minister were rife on social media as well as mainstream media. These were the elections where women were the local spokespersons of the BJP. These were the elections which saw India's youth selflessly campaigning for Narendra Modi.

These were the elections where nobody could sense a wave and even the internal surveyors of the storm billowing the saffron party were biting their nails. These were the elections which made all the difference in Indian electoral history.

What happened? And most importantly, why did it happen?

Modi Mandate 2019 dissects all perspectives and opinions with the help of analysis from ground zero.

1
WHERE THE OPPOSITION BLEW THE WAR TRUMPET: UTTAR PRADESH

I lowered the pace of my treadmill, placed my phone on the dashboard and logged on to YouTube to watch the historic press conference that had compelled journalists from across the country to reach Lucknow at a rate of knots.

'*Aaj Bahujan Samaj Party aur Samajwadi Party ke national president ke beech ye sanyukt press conference ya khaaskar pradhan mantri Modi aur BJP ke rashtriya adhyaksh Amit Shah ki neend udane wali press conference hai!*' (This press conference between the SP and BSP national presidents will turn out to be a political nightmare for Prime Minister Modi and BJP President Amit Shah.)

These words by the BSP Chief Mayawati on 12 January 2019 marked the inception of the first major alliance to counter Narendra Modi, seemingly altering India's political scenario for the upcoming general elections. In 2014, the BJP had won 71 seats in the state, comprising a vote share of 42.3 per cent whereas the SP and the BSP had a vote share of 22.2 per cent and 19.6 per cent, respectively. Simple arithmetic suggested that SP–BSP together were now set to win a sizeable number of seats. If only elections in India were this simple!

In order to prove that this alliance would result in a success, it was necessary for both the SP and BSP to transfer their respective vote shares to each other in entirety. This test of transferability was the imperative factor that would determine the fate of the alliance.

It was the first time the SP and BSP were coming together for the Lok Sabha elections. Even in the bypolls held earlier when the SP and BSP seemed to have made huge gains by coming together, the voting percentage was still quite low (around 33 per cent) and more importantly, it did not account for 'Modi in Campaign' mode.

Exactly 25 years ago, in the 1993 assembly elections, the then SP Chief Mulayam Singh Yadav and BSP Chief Kanshi Ram had joined hands to counter the BJP juggernaut. In a four-cornered contest between BJP, SP–BSP, Congress Party and Janata Dal (JD), the BJP had won 177 seats with a vote share of 33.3 per cent whereas SP and BSP won 109 and 67 seats respectively, with a combined vote share of 29.06 per cent. The important thing to realize here is that these numbers were achieved despite caste being a dominant factor and BSP–SP's core strength in Uttar Pradesh (UP) back then.

A state with 80 Lok Sabha seats, which has given the country seven prime ministers and which plays the most important role in deciding the country's electoral fate, was posing a difficulty for psephologists and political pundits who couldn't predict the way the electoral wind was blowing. With the SP led by Akhilesh Yadav and the BSP led by Mayawati coming together to form a gathbandhan, experts who were earlier in the dark had now started having lopsided views which were not in favour of the BJP.

'Vote share has no direct correlation with seat share,' I asserted during a debate with Republic TV's Arnab Goswami, which happened soon after the SP–BSP alliance made the headlines. Every political analyst claimed this alliance as Modi's end game. While many believed the SP and BSP together had an edge over the BJP, I not only refused to accept it but also kept reiterating how the alliance had never passed the test of transferability. The two parties had long been each other's rivals. Who could forget the famous 'Guest House episode' of 1995?[1]

During the Gujarat elections too, I was cornered in a debate when I contended that the BJP would come back to power despite the famous trio of Hardik Patel, Jignesh Mevani and Alpesh Thakor coming together in alliance. Even at the peak of the Patidar reservation

---

[1] In 1995, an unruly mob of SP workers had marched into the guest house where Mayawati was in a meeting with her MLAs. According to reports, her room was vandalized, casteist and sexual slurs were thrown about and she was physically assaulted.

movement, when the odds were against the BJP, I stood by my unfaltering claim in its favour. And I was not just being intuitive; my assertion was based on ground realities. I had visited Mehsana, the region dominated by Patidars and the place where the Patidar reservation movement had its inception, over 13 times during the Gujarat assembly elections. In a strategic move, the BJP fielded independent candidates to cut into Patidar votes that were expected to go against the party. Each independent candidate individually helped take off at least 2,500 votes from the Patidar list, thereby helping the BJP to defy all odds. Nitinbhai Patel emerged victorious to the surprise of many. At that point of time, a leading activist-turned-politician-cum-psephologist who people like to colloquially refer to as a 'Gamcha Politician' predicted BJP's loss in all possible scenarios, but we know what became of it.

Geographically, there exists a distinctive demographic divide between the politics of the western and the eastern parts of UP. The western constituencies have a relatively higher Muslim population base while caste plays a dominant role in the political discourse of the eastern regions. Moreover, it is a recognized phenomenon that whenever caste plays an upper hand in any election, it ends up dividing Hindu votes, thereby adversely impacting the vote share for the BJP, a Right-leaning Hindu nationalist party. In fact, empirical evidence suggests that the BJP stands to lose when elections in UP move from the caste-dominated east to west and vice versa. This theory passed the test of time in the 2012 UP assembly elections where the phases moving from the east to the west ultimately became a significant contributing factor for the SP's clear majority. On the other hand, in the 2014 Lok Sabha elections and again in the 2017 assembly elections, both of which moved from west to east, the gains made by the BJP in the earlier phases where caste did not play an important role, resulted in the consolidation of Hindu votes to a large extent, thereby helping the BJP land a record margin. One of the key points to note in the 2019 general elections, overlooked by many, was how UP was set to undergo elections that phased from west to east.

My 2019 Lok Sabha elections journey began from the third week of January. My team was divided to cover all 543 constituencies with the aim of bringing out the ground realities of this election campaign to the general public and also, more importantly, to underline how the Lutyens' media was keeping the unwitting voters separated from actual realities on the ground. Moving with the political wind of the state—from western to eastern constituencies—let me evoke some ground realities which helped my team conclusively predict yet another election with accuracy.

KAIRANA

The Kairana constituency garnered the national media's attention only after the Kairana migration row (or the Kairana exodus) around the mass migration of Hindu families from Kairana during 2014–16. Since then, Kairana had been branded as 'New Kashmir' and turned into a definite mascot for winning UP. The party winning Kairana had a better—if not absolute—chance at winning UP.

Before we dissect the election outcome of Kairana, it is important to know that the constituency comprises five assemblies, namely Nakur, Gangoh, Kairana, Thana Bhawan and Shamli, among which the Kairana assembly has a relatively higher Muslim vote base. Although the BJP lost the 2018 bypolls, it was still leading in the Kairana assembly, which was a source of relief to the party. In 2019, BJP member Pradeep Kumar Chaudhary, who hails from the Gangoh assembly, contested from the Kairana constituency, spurring a sense of enthusiasm among Thana Bhawan and Gangoh voters who had been wondering why a Kairana Member of Parliament (MP) had to be specifically from the Kairana assembly.

Standing at a stall near the Shamli bus stand and sipping a hot cup of kulhad chai, I was all ears to the ongoing discussion between three old men who were talking about how Modi was dealing national security with a strict hand. Although, initially it gave me a sense of an emerging trend, it was too soon to presume anything, as my day had just begun and I had miles of experiences to bear witness to.

In Kairana it was a close contest between BJP's Pradeep Kumar Chaudhary and SP's sitting MP, Tabassum Hasan. The aftermath of the 2013 Muzaffarnagar riots resulted in a major demographic shift in several areas of the Kairana constituency. Any prediction at this stage was nearly impossible unless backed by a considerable sample base. I realized that it was going to be a hectic day, as I had to talk to as many people as I could. After refilling my water bottle from a pyaau (public drinking water tap), I boarded a bus to Kairana which is around 14 km from Shamli.

Throughout my election journey, I consciously chose to travel by public transport to get a better grip of ground realities. After reaching the Kairana bus stand, the first thing I noticed was a nearby masjid. Walking towards the masjid, my cameraman and I approached a group of Muslim men.

'*Namaskar, Bhai Saab!*' (Greetings!), I said with a smile.

'*Bataiye kya lagta hai aapko chunao ka...kiska palra bhaari hai?*' (Who, according to you, seems likely to win the elections?) I asked.

'*Lagna kya hai, ab jo hoga so hoga...*' (Let us see, whatever is to happen will happen...) said one of them.

'*Gathbandhan ko denge vote...*' (We will vote for the gathbandhan) said another.

'*Toh aapko lagta hai gathbandhan jeetega?*' (So, do you think the gathbandhan will win?) I pushed to get more insights.

'*Ab jeete koi, bhi hum toh gathbandhan ko hi vote denge,*' (Whatever be the result, we will vote for the gathbandhan) one of them replied.

I sensed a hesitation in his response, which reflected only one thing: although the core voters of the SP were intact even after the SP–BSP alliance, they weren't too sure about a definitive win for the alliance. The equation was rather simple to understand: the SP was the first preference for Muslim voters across UP, with the Congress Party second in line and the BSP being their last resort. Unwittingly enough, it was here that the Congress Party did more damage than good to the gathbandhan's cause. It cut into the gathbandhan's votes in places like Saharanpur, Sant Kabir Nagar, Basti and Badayun.

The interaction we had with the group outside the masjid had all the perfect elements to make it to *Lalkar*, a show I was working on with Republic TV, which aimed at presenting diverse public opinion from the ground. Conversations such as these were a definite hit among our audiences. But this one became so interesting at such a pace that we just went with the flow and ended up not capturing it for the show.

In our travels, it is usually our equipment or camera crew or even the simplest thing like a microphone that attracts a swarm of people towards us. However, when the election fever was at its peak this time, political conversations did not need a catalyst. More and more people started gathering around, which helped me get a wider view within a short span of time.

A middle-aged man mounted on his bicycle, with one foot on the pedal and the other on the ground, looked at me intently. He had an inquisitive expression on his face. It seemed he wanted to say something. So, I approached him.

'*Kya lagta hai kiski hawa hai yahan, Bhai Sa'ab?*' (Who do you think is set to win from here?)

'*Lagna kya hai, Modiji hi aayenge fir se!*' (Modi will make a comeback!) He sounded like he had been waiting all this while just to say this.

'*Aisa kyon lagta hai aapko?*' (Why do you feel so?)

'*Arey bhai, vishv mein desh ka naam kiya hai. Iske pehle humko kaun jaanta tha? Pakistan ki toh puri tarah se hawa hi nikal di hai...*' (He has put India on the world map. Who knew us earlier? He has given Pakistan a befitting reply...)

Before he could even complete his sentence, several people around him started nodding their heads in approval and soon the chants of 'Modi! Modi!' filled the air.

My eyes instantly wandered off and fell on an older woman. Her composure set her apart from the others in that enthusiastic crowd. She seemed hesitant at first, but when I removed my sunglasses and greeted her, she finally opened up.

'*Namaste Mataji, aap kya chaahte hai pradhan mantri kaun*

banna chahiye iss baar?' (Who would you like to see as the prime minister this time?) I enquired.

'Bhaiya, humko toh Modiji hi thik lagte hain...' (Modi is fine for us...) she replied.

'Kyon? Aisa bhi kya kiye hain Modiji?' (Why? What has Modi done?) I asked cynically.

Little did I know then that her response would turn out to summarize my entire day's journey.

'Kya nahi diye...gas chulha diye...ghar diye...paikhana diye... Itna koi nahi kiya hum gareeb logan ke liye. Unko upar wala bheja hai hum logan ke liye!' (What has he not given us—gas stove...a house to live in... toilets... No one else has done so much for us poor. God has sent him for us!) she said, with tears welling up in her eyes.

Evidently enough, the widely acclaimed 'Modi magic' had cast the right spells here.

My first question 'Who is going to win?' was always followed by a 'Why?' Voters without a rationale behind their choice are unpredictable, much like a box of frogs. I did not accept a 'Who?' that wasn't backed by a strong 'Why?' because in the absence of a solid reasoning, one couldn't be sure that people would act on the very preferences they had shared.

After meeting a plethora of people, the three things that I always found consistent to any conversation were: (i) people wanted Modi to stay; (ii) Hindu consolidation which arose during the 2014 campaign was pretty much intact and (iii) people were not only riding on the nationalism wave after the Balakot air strikes but also recognized and appreciated the government's welfare schemes.

While the Yogi Adityanath government's failure to solve the menace of animals on the loose was a matter of concern, the voters intelligently differentiated a state-level issue from the issues at the centre. I remember one of them saying:

'Awara pashu se dikkat hai...magar uske liye Yogiji ko bolenge... desh chalaane ke liye vote toh Modiji ko hi denge!' (We have problem with stray animals, but for that we will talk to Yogi [Adityanath]. For the country, we will vote for Modi!)

After the Kairana exodus, polarization was evident, which, clubbed with a fervent nationwide Modi wave, gave BJP's Pradeep Kumar Chaudhary an edge over the gathbandhan candidate Tabassum Hasan. In the end, Chaudhary emerged victorious with a comfortable margin of more than 92,000 votes. The Congress Party once again ended up cutting into the gathbandhan's votes, swinging away 72,000 votes from their kitty. This made the contest in Kairana, which had once looked neck-to-neck, a comfortable victory for the BJP.

MUZAFFARNAGAR

Muzaffarnagar, one of the most talked-about constituencies, with Muslims constituting over 40 per cent of the population, was about to witness a direct contest between BJP's sitting MP Sanjeev Balyan and Chaudhary Ajit Singh, the founder and chief of the Rashtriya Lok Dal (RLD). Jat voters, who form the second-largest community, were going to play a key role in deciding the fate of the candidates. Theoretically, Ajit Singh's Jat origins gave him a definite leg up in the game, even though Sanjeev Balyan was also a popular Jat face. In 2014, apart from riding the huge Modi wave, Sanjeev Balyan had won the Lok Sabha elections with over four lakh votes owing to the decision made by the SP, BSP and the Congress Party to contest separately. However, this time the game came down to only one thing, which in itself is a huge political divide in India—those with Modi and those against him.

'*Bhaiya, idhar toh sau prateeshat Ajit Singh hi jeetega!*' (Here, Ajit Singh will win 100 per cent!) I exclaimed loudly as I saw a group of Jat men crouched atop khatiyas (charpoys), circled around a hookah. In response to this, a man dressed in a pagdi (turban) and baniyan (vest) said something which would discredit poll experts across the nation who go about predicting the election results without paying as much as a single visit to the ground.

'*Arey kyon jeetega Ajit Singh...wo jeet gaya to jaa kar baith jaayega Dilli mein...humein kuch kaam karwana hoga to kya Dilli jayenge?*' (Why would Ajit Singh win? If he were to win, he would stay put in

Delhi. Would we travel all the way to Delhi if we have some work?)

Before I could interrogate any further, he added: '*Sanjeev Balyan to 3–4 saal se reh raha hai humare saath...bacche bacche ko naam se jaanta hai wo... Ajit ko khada karwa do...do naam na bata paye... jab tak ye Ajit tha to ek sadak bhi na banwaya...*' (Sanjeev Balyan has been living here for the past 3–4 years. He knows every person by name. Make Ajit stand in his own constituency and he won't be able to tell the names of even two people in our village. When Ajit was here, he did not get even one road built in the constituency.)

His companions, the group of Jats, looked intently as he spoke, nodding in assent.

This was news to me. I was expecting a certain connection between the Jat community and Ajit Singh. This initial interaction itself made it clear that this is not how the system runs anymore.

The long-running rotten caste dynamics had undergone a change and had, in fact, somewhat overturned. People no longer identified with a candidate only on the grounds of his/her caste; they sought more.

Now it was time I moved to Muzzafarnagar's marketplace where I was expecting to gain some more interesting insights. As I walked a few steps, I spotted a large black kadai (wok) simmering with sugarcane juice, which was on the brink of turning into gur (jaggery). I asked one of the workers emptying a basket full of sugarcane waste:

'*Kya lag raha hai, bhaiya, kaun aayega idhar?*' (Who do you think will win from here?)

'Modi!' he replied in a convincing tone.

Much like how a vat full of sugarcane juice ultimately ends up turning into the sweet-bitter jaggery, Modi's return seemed quite inevitable to these people. But was it enough to guarantee a win? One careless drift of the eye and one could miss a deeper trend altogether.

As I treaded along the market, I saw three Muslim men on a bike headed in my direction. I held my mic tight and instantly ran towards them.

'*Aap teeno ko kya lagta hai, Muzzafarnagar mein kiska chance hai?*' (Who, according to you three, stands a chance in Muzzafarnagar?) I asked.

'50–50', one of the pillion riders replied.

A core voter of gathbandhan predicting a 50–50 prospect was certainly not a positive sign for Ajit Singh who, as I had discovered earlier that day, seemed to have lost appeal with Jat voters. Going strictly by the statistics, Ajit Singh needed to get 70 per cent Jat and 90 per cent Muslim votes in his favour for him to finish first.

One of my questions always received a vague response, irrespective of whether I asked the voters or the party cadres themselves: Who is the gathbandhan's prime ministerial candidate? No one seemed to have any clarity whatsoever. While I was picking the brains of the local leaders for the show, a peculiarly enthusiastic young man walked up to me and said with absolute conviction: *'Bhaiya, agar idhar se Balyan nahi jeete na to meri ungli katwa dena.'* (Chop off my fingers if [Sanjeev] Balyan doesn't win from here.)

It was this level of undeterred faith that was missing in any of the gathbandhan supporters.

After this debate, I realized that it was not as easy a trail for Ajit Singh as a few Delhi-based journalists had so confidently marked out for him. As I visited more and more villages in the constituency and spoke to people, especially women, I could see the trail diminishing.

The premise that western UP will root out the BJP, which was the basis of the SP–BSP alliance, was fundamentally flawed. This was apparent from the fact that two of the most important western UP constituencies, Kairana and Muzzafarnagar, were seen going the BJP way.

BAGHPAT

It was getting dark already. After travelling for more than 4 hours, I got off the bus to join Arnab Goswami for a televised news debate. I took out my tripod stand and fixed a camera on it. Suddenly, I realized there was no place for me to sit. I searched my bag, shuffling its contents to find the newspaper I had picked up two days ago. I spread the newspaper across a vacant footpath and sat on it. A passer-by who had stopped to see what I was doing helped me arrange my set up. I then switched on the flashlight of my phone and requested him to aim it at my face. The debate had begun. Several onlookers, most of whom were tall, well-built Jats, surrounded me. Many others started chanting 'Modi! Modi!' while some of them took out their phones to take selfies with me.

'*Achcha bhaiya, yahan to Jayant Chaudhary ki seat pakki hai aur aap Modi Modi kar rahe ho!*' (Brother, everyone is saying that Jayant Chaudhary will win, but you are chanting Modi's name!)

'*Satya Pal nikalega ye seat. Aap aao gaon ke andar, hum aapko sab batate hain!*' (Satya Pal [Singh] will win this seat. You come to our village, I will tell you everything!) declared a sturdy Jat.

My entry to Baghpat itself managed to shake all my preconceived notions and left me wondering if the Jat factor would prove to be irrelevant here too.

Soon after the Election Commission of India (ECI) announced the dates, various political leaders criticized it for scheduling the elections during Ramzan, the Islamic holy month when a majority of Muslims fast from dawn to dusk. This decision was seen as an act to deliberately dissuade Muslim voters, which would indirectly amount to benefitting the BJP.

There was an apparent sense of reluctance among Muslim voters, but Ramzan was not the only reason. Muslims had realized that the significance of their votes had considerably gone down and they were no longer the only deciding factor in the elections, especially after how Hindus had consolidated in support of the BJP and how the Modi factor was taking over. The 2018 bypolls in Kairana had also been held during Ramzan, but Muslim voters had still come out with much enthusiasm and in large numbers to seal the deal for the gathbandhan. They were conscious of the value of their votes, mainly because the BJP's core voter base had eluded these bypolls owing to the absence of an active campaign by Modi and a cognizance of the fact that these results weren't going to change things at large.

Moving along, I arrived at the town's square which harboured statues of freedom fighters aplenty. I spotted a tiny eatery nearby, and chose to dine in it. To get a fresh perspective, I walked up to the rasoiya (cook), who was busy making tandoori rotis.

'*Arre Maharaj, kya haal? Raajneeti ki bhi kuch khabar rakhte hain?*' (How are you? Do you keep track of politics?)

He nodded in the affirmative and I came straight to the point.

'*Aapko kya lag raha hai, Maharaj, kaun aayega?*' (Who do you think will win?) I asked.

A few seconds of silence, a reassuring smile, and the words: '*Aayega to Modi hi!*' (Modi will return [no matter what who says]!)

In the run-up to the elections, '*Aayega to Modi hi*' had been the standard conclusion in almost every political debate. This simple line had resonated with the masses, and it was only natural that it was later picked up by the BJP as its official campaign slogan. Nothing could be more reflective of the people's emotions and the imminent mandate that would end up changing the course of India's electoral history.

Moreover, while many in UP believed that the BSP chief, Mayawati, was confident of getting majority Jatav Scheduled Caste (SC) votes, in her speech in the Muslim-dominated Deoband which comes under the Saharanpur constituency, she appealed to the Muslims, '*Musalmaano ko saath mein vote karna padega!*' (Muslims would have to vote in tandem!) It signalled that perhaps she had sensed Jatav SC votes weren't going entirely into the gathbandhan's kitty.

GAUTAM BUDDH NAGAR

A high-profile seat that covered assemblies like Noida and Dadri, Gautam Buddh Nagar was a direct battle between Dr Mahesh Sharma of the BJP and the gathbandhan's candidate Satveer Nagar. Barring 2009–14, when the constituency was under BSP rule, Gautam Buddh Nagar had always been the BJP's stronghold.

Several rumours doing the rounds at that time suggested how the sitting MP, Mahesh Sharma, was not getting a ticket from the party this time and these rumours were fuelled when Sharma was met with black posters and flags on his arrival at a village called Raina. Despite all odds against him, I made an unflinching assertion in a debate on Republic TV: If someone from the BJP was getting a ticket again, it would be Mahesh Sharma, owing to the absence of any other contender stronger than him or, for that matter, even equally strong.

The presumption that Mahesh Sharma would be on the losing side of things was logically fallacious because, for him to lose, Brahmins and Gujars had to vote against the BJP. That seemed very unlikely, as the Brahmins who were earlier against the BJP due to the imposition of GST, had come out to support Modi after the GST relaxations. A majority of Bhati Gujars too backed Mahesh Sharma after one of their leaders, Narendra Bhati, joined the BJP.

At a conclave in New Delhi's Talkatora Stadium to address the traders' community that was miffed with the GST's impact, Modi announced a slew of measures that, according to him, were to be implemented if the National Democratic Alliance (NDA) government was sworn into power for a second term. Modi also greeted these traders as his brothers, the impact of which was instantly seen in the form of widespread support from the traders' community right after the event concluded.

In Gujarat's assembly election, which took place approximately five months after the introduction of GST, it was popularly believed that the traders' community was going totally against the BJP. However, the BJP managed to win 13 out of 16 seats in Surat, a well-known traders' hub. At that point of time too, I had insisted that while the traders might have faced issues, they didn't doubt Modi's intent and were going to vote in his favour.

The proposed airport in Jewar, an assembly in Gautam Buddh Nagar constituency, and Mahesh Sharma's Kailash Hospital, where a large number of people received free treatment, were some governance touchpoints which only strengthened the case in BJP's favour.

AMETHI

'Bhaiya, thoda tez chala sakte hain?' (Can you drive a bit faster?) I asked the driver taking us from Rae Bareli to one of the most talked-about constituencies—Amethi.

'*Aap dekh hi rahe ho road ki haalat...*' (You can see the condition of the roads for yourself...) He answered as I zoomed in my camera lens to record a short on-the-road video. We were in Jais, a city with a municipal board in Amethi district, with Muslims constituting over 30 per cent of the population. Interestingly, the car's speedometer never for once crossed the 20 kmph mark from the time we entered Amethi.

Was Rahul Gandhi, the Congress Party's president, going to get crushed in the Gandhi bastion? This question was boggling the minds of many. One major contrast between the 2014 and 2019 elections was that Smriti Irani was no longer an outsider in Amethi, and this was enough to predict a definite downfall in the Congress Party's vote share, if not a complete loss. Even at the time of the previous general elections, when Smriti Irani was considered an outsider, the winning margin for Rahul Gandhi had decreased from 3.7 lakh in 2009 to a little over a lakh in 2014—the lowest ever winning margin for a Gandhi scion.

The five assemblies of Tiloi, Salon, Jagdishpur, Gauriganj and Amethi that form the Amethi constituency were ruled by the SP back in 2014. However, after the 2017 UP assembly elections, a majority of these constituencies came under the BJP and observed exceptional step-ups in the law and order situation. Under the Yogi Adityanath government, a zero-tolerance drive towards crime and criminals was launched to beef up the rule of law and order in UP. The state police was directed to register FIRs in all cases, with no exceptions. As a result of this, around 3,065 wanted criminals were arrested, 45 killed and 1,294 encounters took place between the police force and criminals in less than a year. In popular public perception, the law and order in UP had improved under Chief Minister Yogi Adityanath.

Until 2019, Rahul Gandhi had been getting votes in Amethi in the name of Sanjay Gandhi and Rajiv Gandhi, but it was no longer the poll plank.

After travelling for almost 45 minutes we came to a Hanuman temple across which was a *kachori ki dukaan*, next to which was a mobile phone shop. It was in the latter where I unexpectedly ran into the person who curated the social media account of Amethi+.

'*Kya lag raha maahol, bhaiya...dekho sach sach batao...* (What does it look like...tell me honestly...)' I asked him.

'*Bhaiya, mandir ke saamne khada hun jhooth nahi bolunga... Modiji wapis aayenge,*' (I am standing in front of a temple, so I won't lie... Modi will return to power) he said with conviction.

'*Uttar Pradesh mein Modiji kaam kiye hain...aur desh ke liye Modiji hi bestum best hain!*' (Modi has worked for UP and there is no one better than him to run the country!) He added further, even before I could ask.

This man belonged to the Jatav SC category. There were no anti-Modi sentiments even in Rae Bareli.

Sitting on a charpoy, blowing on hot cups of tea in their hands, some middle-aged men were talking politics. I couldn't stop myself and straightaway went and crouched near the charpoy, in order to fit in the crowd.

'*Aur kaka, kya baatien chal rahi hain? Maahol toh zordaar takkar wala lag raha hai!*' (What are you conversing about? It seems there is going to be a stiff political battle!) I said.

'*Kaahe ka takkar. Lag toh raha hai Modi hi aayega fir se. Magar dekho aage aage hota hai kya!*' (There is no fight. It is evident that Modi would return to power. But let's see what the final outcome is!) one of them said.

This was the general view throughout the nation. But I was curious about the specificities with regard to Amethi.

'*Haan magar Amethi mein Rahulji ko harana namumkin hai!*' (Yes, but it is impossible to defeat Rahul [Gandhi] in Amethi!) I teased them. With this, I hit the bull's eye. All of them seemed to disagree with me in unison.

'*Namumkin to bhaisaab kuch bhi nahi hain...aur humein to lag raha hai iss baar na ho payegi Rahul bhaiya ki naiyya paar!*' (Nothing is impossible, and we feel Rahul [Gandhi] would have a tough time winning in Amethi this time!)

Ironically enough, it was in that moment that I realized that we were seated right behind a piece of barren land that held immense significance. This was the very land which was allocated for Samrat Cycle Factory in 1984 as a part of the promise to generate jobs for the local people. Allegedly, in the run-up to the elections, the Gandhi family had distributed portions of land or pattas to the people of Amethi. Maybe it was easier than keeping the promises they had made.

'*Rahul bhaiya kuch na karenge...wo aate bhi hain to Gauriganj Guest House mein rukte hain...aur hum log se muh chipa ke bhaagte hain,*' (Rahul [Gandhi] doesn't do anything substantial. He just comes to Gauriganj Guest House and leaves without meeting us) said one.

What further cemented my belief that the BJP had a decent chance in Amethi was my discussion with the people outside Hindustan Aeronautics Limited (HAL) factory. The company had come in the limelight when the Congress president accused the Modi government of a scam in the Rafale defence deal. The Gandhi scion vehemently opposed the government's decision to not extend the Rafale contract to HAL, an Indian PSU.

Wearing an *angocha*, we reached the HAL factory's gate. I had made up my mind and was expecting severe criticism against the Rafale deal and the Modi government. I set up the tripod and camera and began recording for my show.

'*Namaskar, main Pradeep Bhandari swagat karta hun aapka mere show Lalkar mein...*' (Hello everyone! I, Pradeep Bhandari, welcome you all to my show *Lalkar!*)

'*Rafale ke baare mein aap kya kahenge?*' (What is your take on Rafale?) I asked, almost sure about the response.

It was quite shocking to learn that seven out of ten people gathered outside the HAL factory were of the opinion that Rafale would prove to be an important addition in strengthening the country's national security. Before I could delve in further, we were surrounded by Congress workers who started chanting 'Rahul! Rahul!'.

Another thing that stood out in Amethi was Smriti Irani's regular presence in the constituency over extended periods of time. Despite not being an MP, she conducted several small meetings in order to understand local issues, travelled booth to booth and alleviated the miseries of the residents. In sharp contrast to her, Rahul Gandhi had outsourced his campaign to his sister Priyanka Gandhi Vadra, perhaps because he wasn't too confident about facing the people of Amethi. By now I realized that it was not just the Modi factor but sentiments against the Congress Party that would help Smriti Irani cut back on the vote margin, if not land a victory in Amethi. Furthermore, Rahul Gandhi's decision to contest from Wayanad took away with it any possibility of the Congress giving a fight in what had erstwhile been strong seats for the party, such as Dhaurahara, Kushinagar and, of course, Amethi. This decision had grave bearings on the chances of the Congress Party in Madhya Pradesh, Rajasthan and Chhattisgarh which had incumbent Congress governments.

VARANASI

'*Aap kya keh rahe hain...yahan bhi aur kendra mein bhi aayega to Modi hi...*' (What are you saying? Modi will emerge victorious here as well as get a majority at the centre...) said a Banaras Hindu University professor, as he chewed paan masala.

This was in response to my question: '*Kya lag raha hai...sarkar badal jayegi iss baar? Idhar to Priyankaji aa jayengi log keh rahe hain...*' (What does the situation look like? Will there be a change in government this time? People are saying Priyanka [Gandhi] would come to power...) We were at 'Pappu ki Adi', a famous tea shop in Banaras whose display board reads '*Bharat ki rajneeti ko disha dene wala vishwa prasidh Pappu ki Adi*' (The tea stall that has given direction to politics in India—Pappu ki Adi). The tagline read '*Kashi ke sangeetkaron, professoron, patrakaron, kulpatiyon, acharyon aur rajeentigyon ka buddhi sanwardhan sthan*' (The meeting point of Kashi's professors, intellectuals, journalists, philosophers and politicians for intellectually stimulating conversations).

The gathbandhan had fielded Shalini Yadav, who had not even won a mayor election in the past, against Modi. It was clear they knew they didn't stand a chance against Modi, and all they wanted was a scapegoat. After making a lot of noise, triggering debates and stirring up political discussions, Priyanka Gandhi Vadra, who once expressed interest in contesting against Modi, also decided not to contest, supposedly choosing to give time to handling party responsibilities rather than focusing on only one seat. The Congress, as a part of their usual modus operandi, chose Ajay Rai as a scapegoat. UP was peculiar in this sense. While Modi's staunchest rivals in UP—Mayawati and Priyanka Gandhi Vadra—were themselves not contesting elections, they maintained claims regarding an anti-Modi current in the state. It was also evident from the fact that even Akhilesh Yadav, former UP chief minister and president of the SP, couldn't afford wagering by contesting from any seat other than Azamgarh.

It was in this city of the Ganges that I realized it was not Modi's election but more of a mass public movement by the people who were campaigning for him. Banaras [also Varanasi] surprised me. In my entire journey, I had not encountered a reasoning as rational as I did in Varanasi.

'*Modi! Modi! to kar rahe ho magar kuch vikas bhi hua hai yahan par?*' (You are chanting Modi's name, but has any development taken place here?) I asked, trying to imitate the renowned jibe often picked up by the Opposition. The man started chanting 'Modi! Modi!' the moment he realized I was shooting for a political show. I was about to write him off when to my surprise he started reciting Modi government's schemes from A to Z.

When we reached the ghats, I couldn't help noticing they were cleaner than ever before. My eyes fell on a poster which made a rather bold claim: '*Kachre ka dibba maatr 50 kadam mein*' (The next garbage bin is just 50 steps away.)

My sceptical mind sought proof. I asked one of my team members, Abhinav, to check and confirm if this was indeed true. Lo and behold, the results answered another burning question I had had for long: Why do people in Varanasi blindly trust Modi? The dustbins were placed within 50 steps, exactly like the poster claimed. And what was more, there were portable toilets too, placed in short distances near the ghats to ensure additional cleanliness. I could see vikas (development) right in front of me.

Modi had become synonymous with development, and I realized this soon after a well-learned man in his late sixties said this to me: '*Modiji ko Banaras se nahi ladna chahiye, Banaras ka to kaafi vikas kar diye wo paanch saal mein...kahin aur se ladenge to wahan bhi vikas hoga*' (Modi shouldn't contest from Varanasi. He has done enough development here in the past five years. If he contests from another place, that place too will get developed).

While the elders identified with Modi's vikas, youngsters were drawn to him because what they saw in Modi was a ray of hope. I particularly remember what a young boy said to me: '*Modiji ne desh ka naam uncha kiya hai...duniya bhar ke deshon ne Modiji ko inaam diya hai...aur aaj jab Modiji kisi vishwa stariya meeting mein jaate hain to unko bahut samman milta hai...ye desh ke liye bahut badi baat hai. Hamaare desh ki chavvi inn pichle paanch saalo mein bilkul hi badal gayi hai...*' (Modi has made India proud globally. And whenever he goes to any international-level meet, he is shown respect. This is a big thing for our country. The country's image has really changed in the last five years...)

While voters with a BJP leaning always backed their answers with reasoning, supporters of the gathbandhan and the Congress Party seemed to lack confidence in their leadership. They probably knew the outcome already.

To get diverse opinions, I sought out a famous dosawala opposite Vishwanath Mandir. He hailed from Andhra Pradesh and his opinion would mean a lot. However, his evaluation wasn't any different from the majority in Banaras. He said: '*PM pad ke liye to* Modi *hi sahi hain*! (Modi is suitable for the prime minister's post!)'

'If you permit me, I shall file my nomination from the holy city tomorrow. I will then return to thank you all after winning the polls!' Modi had said amid a sea of people chanting his name during his roadshow in Varanasi which traversed from Lanka Gate to Ganga Gate. Wherever he went, Modi was showered with flower petals apart from the unconditional love he received from the crowds. His roadshow was a festival in itself, its sheer opulence having the ability to overshadow Holi or even Diwali. Varanasi was shut voluntarily and people were on the streets to confer their unconditional support to the man who was now a part of their family and more.

KUMBH EFFECT

The largest religious gathering in the world, a congregation of Hindus in millions, a sangam (confluence) of spirituality and knowledge of people from across the globe, the Kumbh Mela was unmistakably an electoral salvation for the BJP and the Yogi Adityanath government.

This time the scale and grandeur of the Kumbh Mela hosted in UP's Prayagraj was very different from the Kumbhs held earlier. The Yogi Adityanath government allocated a whopping ₹4,236 crore, which was thrice the budget of the Maha Kumbh that took place in 2013, thus making it one of the world's biggest organized festivals ever. Be it the employment of world-class technology, the emphasis on cleanliness or measures to ensure public safety, this Kumbh definitely stood out.

Though the BJP leaders refrained from admitting it openly, it was clear since May of the previous year that the Yogi Adityanath government would leave no chance to milk the Kumbh festival for extracting political nectar. However, whatever the intent behind it might have been, nobody was even questioning it. It was for the very first time that millions of Hindus were made to feel important. This meant that they would naturally incline towards the BJP.

I was lucky to be part of the festival, not only because of its sacredness, but also, where else could I get to talk to so many people from different parts of the country in one location.

On the boat ride to take a holy dip, I was accompanied by a family of six. I asked the mother: *'Kaisa lag raha hai sarkar ka saara prabandhan, behenji?'* (How are you finding the arrangements made by the government?)

'Adbhut. Hum pehle bhi aaye hain Kumbh snan karne, lekin iss baar kuch alag hi anubhav raha. Bhagwan bahot raaji-khushi rakhe Yogi ji ko' (Wonderful! We had come to Kumbh in the past too, but this time, the experience has been different. May God bless Yogi

Adityanath [for giving us this experience at Kumbh]),' she said, as if almost blessing him.

On my return trip, as I chatted with the boatmen, I was taken aback by how nationalism mattered so much even to someone who most likely barely managed to make a living. *'Pakistan ko ghar mein ghus ke maare hain Modiji...ye hota hai mard ka jigra...aisi hawa tight ki hai inki ki ab Bharat ki ore aankh utha ke bhi nai dekhenge...',* (The Indian forces entered Pakistan and gave it a befitting response. Modi has done what a strong leader would do. He has taken them to task. Next time they will think twice before attempting to disturb peace in our country) said a boatman, his hands tightly gripping the oars as he spoke.

'Aur Rahul Gandhi? Uska kya?' (And what about Rahul Gandhi?) I asked casually.

'Uska kya, bhaiya? Kuch aata jaata toh hai nahi. Aap hi bolo, kya usme itna kaleja hai ki dushman ko maar giraaye?' (What about him? You tell me, does he have the courage to defeat our enemy the way Modi has?)

With this he had me speechless. While the BJP had not spared any chance to remind the public about the Congress' lack of action after the 26/11 Mumbai attacks, the Congress' statement questioning the armed forces had also added fuel to the fire. As evident from people's reaction to the slightest mention of Rahul Gandhi, he had no credibility and the Congress Party too had lost any of what had remained so far.

GORAKHPUR

When the BJP lost Gorakhpur in the 2018 bypolls—a seat which the party had not lost since 1989—many started believing that the 2019 general elections were also slipping out of its hands. However, there were many factors that accounted for the loss in the bypolls.

The Nishad community is the second-largest demographic group (consisting of around 25 per cent voters) in Gorakhpur. Earlier, the

Nishad Party had led protests in demand for reservation, and during one such protest, some Nishad workers tried stopping a train, which had stirred a major unrest. The UP Police was forced to intervene and carry out a lathi charge. Nishad candidates had landed tickets from the gathbandhan, thus splitting Nishad votes. The SP–BSP alliance fielded Praveen Kumar Nishad against BJP's Upendra Dutt Shukla from Gorakhpur. Shukla, unlike Yogi Adityanath, wasn't Gorakhpur math's choice.

The Gorakhpur math was much more than just a religious spot—it was a place where people from across Gorakhpur came together. Since the Gorakhpur constituency was huge in size, it became difficult for one candidate to cover its entire geography in the last leg of the election campaign. This is why the math's support has always been an important factor in the election. The math attracts people—and elections eventually are a game of numbers. Low voter turnout was also one of the main reasons for the BJP's defeat in the bypolls, which however wasn't the case in the 2019 election.

In 2019, BJP resolved all the underlying issues which had led to its defeat in the bypolls. They fielded the successful Bhojpuri actor–singer Ravi Kishan in the general elections. Because of his closeness to Yogi Adityanath, he automatically received the math's support.

Before the 2019 elections, Praveen Kumar Nishad had formally joined the NDA after the SP led by Akhilesh Yadav asked him to contest again with its symbol. Nishad, however, was clear that he wished to fight as a Nishad Party candidate. He instead supported Ravi Kishan from the outside, even though the actor–singer did not belong to the Nishad community. Against Kishan, the SP fielded Ram Bhuwal Nishad, a former BJP leader who rebelled after he was denied a ticket in the 2017 assembly election.

On 21 March 2019, when Gorakhpur was celebrating Holi, I was there as a part of my election tour. There was bhang, celebrations and people dancing on the streets to the chants of 'Jai Bhole Baba'. I spoke to one such person who, though dancing, seemed relatively sober to me.

'Holi ki badhai, bhaiya...kya lag raha hai aapko chunav ka?'

(Wishes for Holi! What do you think about the upcoming elections?) I asked merrily.

'*Bhole baba ki kasam... Modiji ko wapis layenge bhaiya...pichli haar ka badla lenge...*' (I swear to God. We will ensure Modi's return. We have to avenge the loss in the bypolls) he answered even as he continued dancing.

Winning back Gorakhpur was now a matter of prestige for the lakhs of devotees of the Gorakhpur math and I had observed the same concern on Yogi Adityanath's face during one of his *Lok Sunwayis*, where he interacted with the local people.

I remember speaking that day to a man selling peanuts. According to him, no matter what the results come to be, Modi had tried his best and did not give up. He had tried to deliver everything he promised and his intent was always right.

Back then, when I was presenting my exit poll in a debate with Arnab Goswami, Ravi Kishan was also on the panel. I had announced he was about to win comfortably and that had brought a smile on his face.

SHRAVASTI

A northern UP constituency, the BJP won in Shravasti owing to the huge Modi wave of 2014 with a margin of less than a lakh. Daddan Mishra of the BJP had defeated the SP's candidate Atiq Ahmad and the BSP's Lal Ji Verma.

Shravasti was earlier under Balrampur constituency, the place from where the former prime minister of India Late Shri Atal Bihari Vajpayee lost by a small margin of 2,052 votes to Shubhadra Joshi, the woman who had proposed marriage to him. Vajpayee had declined citing how he was an asset to the Rashtriya Swayamsevak Sangh (RSS) and could not spare time for someone.

Rizwan Zaheer, a popular Muslim leader and the secretary of the Peace Party of India (PP), had contested the 2014 elections, receiving more than one lakh votes. He ended up dividing Muslim votes, which had benefitted the BJP. Zaheer decided not to contest in the 2019 elections, which meant that anti-Modi votes were consolidated, making the contest real tough.

As a part of my election tour, I went to a village in the Bhinga assembly, where I had the opportunity to meet the gram pradhan, a very learned and courteous person. After exchanging greetings, I asked him about the current political scenario in the constituency.

'I wouldn't tell you anything about it. But I will show you,' he said.

He took me for a bike ride through the village. We crossed around 200 pucca houses. But why was he showing me these houses?

These houses were constructed with the aid of the central government under the Pradhan Mantri Gram Awas Yojana. Thirty-five of them housed Dalit families and 15 had Muslim families residing in them.

The question was whether the consolidation of Muslim votes and an anti-incumbency wave against the BJP's sitting MP Daddan Mishra could put a dampener on the Modi factor and vikas.

MACHHLISHAHR

The contest in this constituency was between BJP's B.P. Saroj and the gathbandhan's candidate Tribhuvan Ram. An interesting point to note here was that in the 2014 elections, B.P. Saroj had contested on a BSP ticket against SP's Ram Charitra Nishad. While he had lost by around 1.7 lakh votes, he still had an edge, as he was not beginning from zero and was already a popular face among Dalits and BSP core voters.

I spoke to a barber whose shop was near the village. He said: '*Hum toh chahate hai Modiji wapis aaye. Hum toh BJP ko hi vote denge. Hum Patel OBC jaati ke hain. Hamara log sab BJP pe mohar lagaega!*' (We want Modi to return to power. We will vote for the BJP. We are from the Patel OBC community. All our people are supporting BJP this time!) I sensed a positive swing towards the BJP. Maybe the Patel OBCs were not entirely with the BSP.

Most of those belonging to the Patel OBC community were rallying behind the BJP. Despite not being too happy with the UP state government, Patel OBCs could not view anyone except Modi as their prime minister. For them, it was a fight to defend their *varchasva* or dominance over the other communities. For the BJP, on the other hand, the support from the Patel OBC community was their only chance at emerging victorious. It was the support of the Patel OBC that had got them in the race in Machhlishahr in the first place.

However, my interaction with a middle-aged man in the village made me realize that the caste equation could not be entirely scrapped. '*Modiji kaam to kiye hain…pucca ghar bhi banwayein hain… magar samaj rahega to hi hum rahenge…*,' (Modi has done a lot of work. He has given us a house. But we can live with dignity only as long as our caste and community survives…) he said. He was a Jatav Dalit, a core voter of BSP. Caste-based politics was still alive here, at least to some extent.

As I moved on, I bumped into a woman dressed in traditional ghoonghat. As she was rushing out of her house, wiping the corner of her eyes with the edge of her pallu, I approached her.

'*Kaisa chal raha hai, kaki? Raajneeti ki khabar rakhti hain aap?*' (How is everything? Do you keep track of politics?)

My microphone and camera intimidated her. She was a little hesitant at first, but started conversing once I removed the camera setup.

'*Idhar toh Mayawati hi aayengi, hae na?*' (Mayawati would win from here, correct?) I asked.

'*Nahi Modi sarkar aayegi,*' (No, Modi government will win) she replied.

During our brief conversation I noticed something which didn't let me sleep that entire night. She had injury marks on her arms, most likely a sign of physical assault.

Pretending I did not notice, I asked her further: '*Kyon, Modiji kyon aayenge? Kya kiye hain wo?*' (Why will Modi win? What work has he done?)

'*Kya nahi kiye…ghar diyo, sauchalaya diyo, bijli diyo, gas chulha diyo…Mayawati kya diyo? Kuch bhi nahi…sirf baata!*' (What has he not done? He has given us a house, toilet, electricity, gas… What has Mayawati given us till now? Nothing, except empty promises!) This woman too belonged to a Jatav Dalit family.

The BJP had slim chances of winning in Machhlishahr. They were in an edge-to-edge competition, as most middle-aged Jatav Dalit men preferred the gathbandhan over the BJP. However, old-aged Jatav Dalit men, despite being the benefactors of Mayawati's schemes, did not consider her as their first choice. Moreover, the BJP could finish in front only if the votes of Patel OBCs were consolidated and Jatav Dalit women voted in its favour. Evidently, Jatav Dalit votes were divided and it was difficult to get a clear picture on who would be the winner.

Another significant factor besides the caste equations was how two classes of people were emerging as the core strength behind the BJP's rise to victory. These were the women who had received the benefits of the Modi government's welfare schemes and youngsters who viewed Modi as a ray of hope. If I were to make an educated guess back then, this was true of not only this constituency but the entire country. Women and youngsters were engulfed by the Modi wave. In the end, the BJP won in the constituency by less than 200 votes.

KUSHI NAGAR

A constituency adjacent to Gorakhpur, Kushi Nagar has over 80 per cent voters in the general category. The Brahmins and Thakurs combined comprise over 30 per cent of the total vote share, which gives them a decisive role in elections. Yogi Adityanath had always been a formidable Thakur face of the BJP in Gorakhpur and his presence impinged upon nearby constituencies too. As much as it worked in favour of the BJP to have a strong Thakur candidate in their nest egg, it was also a matter of growing concern for them. Imposing Thakur supremacy could lead to a substantial slip in the Brahmin vote count of their pool. Therefore, to ensure the party registered Brahmin votes, the BJP was forced to switch candidates at the last moment. Vijay Kumar Dubey was given a ticket to attract Brahmin votes. Yogi Adityanath, meanwhile, would ensure the Thakur votes.

An eastern constituency of UP, the BJP won in Kushi Nagar in 2014 with a margin of around 85,000 votes. However, this time, media and poll experts were putting the BJP at third place in a tripartiate contest between the BJP, the gathbandhan and the Congress Party.

The Congress nominated Kunwar Ratanjit Pratap Narain Singh. One of the tallest Congress leaders, he was referred to as Raja-Rajwada Neta by the people of his own constituency, but he managed to rebrand his image to a pro-poor leader by conducting multiple discussions and holding one-to-one talks with the locals. The media appreciated his approach of personal connect. People called this outreach activity as *'Modi ka khauf'*!

There's a much-storied shop near the Kushi Nagar bus stand whose owner keeps abreast of the politics of the constituency. Interviewing him gave us a broader idea of how the BJP not only had a fair chance at winning but also of increasing its vote margin. Kushi Nagar constituency had built the highest number of toilets, which was a clear sign of development.

The general secretary of the All India Congress Committee (AICC), Priyanka Gandhi Vadra, attended several meetings in Kushi Nagar and formulated a good momentum. She had grabbed the interest of the national media and viewers alike. While the entire ecosystem was pulling out all the stops to project her as someone who would make a huge difference in UP's election, these sentiments were never to be heard, seen or felt at the ground level.

Priyanka Gandhi toured eastern UP extensively during the election season, but she could not prove to be a vote-puller for the Congress. As it turned out, the party lost its deposit in a majority of those places. There was a time when star campaigners could swing entire constituencies in their party's favour, but in modern polity of aware voters, their relevance has been largely reduced to being mere crowd-pullers at best. In the absence of a strong party worker base, and the time constraint and lack of commitment towards eastern UP, the Priyanka effect did not hold.

In retrospect, Rahul Gandhi's decision to outsource the campaign to his sister was probably not the best of his decisions. Here, just as in Amethi, voters proved that they preferred continuous and consistent engagement of their leaders, with turnarounds expected by political parties through airdropping of new faces right before elections being a massive miscalculation.

One point to note, particularly in this constituency, was the mighty existence of Brahmanwad and Thakurwad. Vijay Kumar Dubey, the BJP candidate, is a Brahmin and the Congress' candidate, former Union Minister Kunwar Ratanjit Pratap Narain Singh, is a Thakur. While Brahmin voters tended to incline towards the BJP, Thakur voters were divided between Kunwar Ratanjit Pratap Narain Singh and Yogi Adityanath, who is also a Thakur, which gave a clear edge to the BJP.

FATEHPUR SIKRI

A northern constituency of UP, Fatehpur Sikri is dominated by the Jat SC community, who have always played a decisive role in the constituency's political fate. In 2009, BSP candidate Seema Upadhyay won by a narrow margin of around 9,000 votes owing to the Dalit voters and some upper-caste voters extending their support to the BSP. Owing to the Modi wave, in 2014, the BJP won by more than 1.7 lakh votes.

To repeat the 2009 theory, the gathbandhan fielded Shribhagwan Sharma (Guddu Pandit) in 2019, ignoring the Modi undercurrent. Rajkumar Chahar, a very popular Jaat leader, was fielded by the BJP in an attempt to pull Jatav voters who were no less than 2.5 lakh in number. The Congress candidate, Raj Babbar, could not pull Jatav votes and ended up giving an overall edge to the BJP.

Raj Babbar hails from the Brahmin community, who are in considerable numbers in the constituency. Babbar has been a four-time MP, having won on both Congress and SP tickets. However, this time the Brahmins and non-Jatav SCs in the constituency preferred the BJP over the Congress, with the BJP ending up with a 64 per cent vote share.

A very interesting thing to note here is that UP's politics has been majorly centred on the SP and BSP. The core voters of SP are Yadavs, who have a reputation of being Dalit oppressors, and the BSP's core voters are Dalits. A failure on the part of the BJP to field a strong candidate would result in the Brahmins and other upper castes having to decide between the SP and the BSP. If they choose the SP, Yadavs will have a coign of vantage over the Brahmins, who in turn would automatically choose the BSP, especially given the fact that the BSP almost always fields a Brahmin candidate from such constituencies.

Political analysts often incorrectly connect the rise of BSP with Jatav SC votes. While the support of Jatav SC voters was essential for a win, it was not sufficient. For any party to be successful, both necessary and sufficient conditions need to be fulfilled. The sufficient condition for a BSP victory was the support of upper-caste voters. Traditionally, the BSP was the party of the oppressed, and the SP was of the Yadavs or the oppressors (as called by BSP supporters). The state of the BJP in UP was often used to decide the relative performance of BSP. When BJP was weak in the state, the upper castes rallied behind the BSP, which is why they were given a good weightage in the ticket distribution of BSP, as in 2012. In 2019, however, with the BJP emerging strong, none of the upper castes drifted towards the BSP.

En route Mainpuri, the constituency which includes Agra, from where Mulayam Singh Yadav was contesting, I found the time to speak to a few people at a bus stand. I asked a local: *'Idhar kya hisab kitab hai, bhaiya?'* (What are the political equations of this place?)

Instead of answering my question, he counter-questioned: *'Aap kahan ja rahe ho?'* (Where are you heading to?)

'Mainpuri,' I answered.

He came closer to me and whispered, *'Humein to lag raha iss baar Mulayamo nipat gaya.'* (I feel Mulayam Yadav is also gone this time.)

If this happens it will be one of the biggest news of 2019, I thought to myself as I boarded the bus. After two-and-a-half hours I reached Mainpuri, from where I proceeded to a village. There were these potato fields where I spoke to a few men and women. A Yadav man claimed that he will vote for Mulayam since he had worked for them, whereas women unanimously supported Modi. A microanalysis carried out by my team found one common trend emerging this time: women at large were voting for Modi, which, while it may not be enough to defeat Mulayam Singh Yadav in his bastion, was certainly sufficient to reduce his margin of victory.

The BJP not only won the Fatehpur Sikri constituency but also succeeded in increasing its vote margin—a clear indication that the party had done quite well across caste and community lines and people had reposed their faith in the BJP. It also signalled a shift of Jatav SCs to the BJP, which had not been the case in 2014.

GHAZIPUR

Ghazipur was hit by the Modi wave in 2014, with BJP emerging victorious, albeit with a small margin of 32,000 votes. In 2019, according to the public and workers on the ground, BJP's internal politics would overshadow vikas and the Modi factor, thereby leading to its fall.

Despite speaking to a multitude of people, it was quite difficult to conclude anything on the election outcome of the constituency. Even within BJP supporters, there were diverse opinions on the candidate. People at large, however, appreciated the work done by Manoj Sinha, the party's sitting MP.

A person who I met in a khet said: '*Manoj Sinhaji ko jitana hi padega kyonki agar Ansari jeet gaya to wo aur uska bhai maahol kharab kar denge.*' (We need to help Manoj Sinha win because if Ansari wins, he and his brother will spoil the situation in our area [in terms of law and order].)

Afzal Ansari, the gathbandhan's candidate, was all set to secure the Muslim votes that stood consolidated in his favour. Mukhtar Ansari, Afzal's brother and a gangster-turned-politician, was considered a nuisance in the area. People feared that if Afzal got hold of the constituency, it would result in a poor law and order situation.

Thakur votes were the key to win this constituency. Due to the BJP's high-level internal politics, these votes got divided, which proved electorally fatal for Manoj Sinha, despite Rai (Bhumihar) votes consolidating in his favour. If locals are to be believed, after the BJP received the historic mandate in the 2017 assembly elections, the sitting MP, Manoj Sinha, was slated to take over as the state's chief minister. However, BJP's top leaders chose Yogi Adityanath over him. Both Yogi Adityanath and Manoj Sinha have their loyal vote base. As per reports on the ground, some locals said that Sinha's win would be registered as a back-to-back victory, thus escalating him to the position of a tall leader in the region. Some even saw him as a prospective chief minister in the next assembly elections. This might have been the reason why Thakur votes did not go to Manoj Sinha in their entirety.

FARRUKHABAD

This north UP constituency was in the news primarily because Salman Khurshid, a popular Congress leader, was contesting from here. Khurshid, who conceded to the Modi tsunami, was in the Ministry of External Affairs during the United Progressive Alliance (UPA) rule.

Unlike media houses, people on the ground neither viewed Khurshid as a winner nor did they want him to win. In fact, they felt that by fielding him, the Congress Party had damaged the gathbandhan's chances too. Many people believed that if the Congress had paid heed to the larger picture and had fielded another candidate—preferably not a big name—the gathbandhan would have stood a better chance. By nominating Khurshid, the Congress Party had diverted Muslim votes from the gathbandhan's kitty, unwittingly working as a vote cutter. The party had lost sight of the overall grand scheme and was bent on defeating Modi in an individual capacity. It highlighted the main problem with the Opposition's campaign: it revolved around the erroneous philosophy of leading an 'anti' campaign. Such campaigns generally have been unsuccessful in Indian elections. The Opposition had failed to provide an alternate vision, an agenda or even a reason to the public to not vote for Modi—something that could have triggered public anger against Modi. In its absence, the negative campaign nosedived.

Journeying to Farrukhabad from Shahjahanpur, I decided to travel by auto-rickshaw in order to connect better with people. Conversations with people on the road can turn out to be unique. Stopping the auto next to a field, I spoke to the workers.

'*Kaise hain, bhaiya?*' (How are you, brother?) I asked.

'*Kaun hai aap...aur ye auto mein kaahe ghoom rahe hain?*' (Who are you and why are you travelling in this auto?) I was asked.

I explained how travelling by an auto gives me the luxury to stop and talk to local people whenever I wanted. He quite candidly told me: '*Dekho bhaiya, rajneeti wagerah toh samajh nahi aati hai humein... magar (pointed finger to his left) ye jo road dekh rahe ho wo pehle khadanja thi!*' (See, I don't understand politics, but the road you are seeing in front of your eyes, it wasn't there earlier!)

Mukesh Rajput, the sitting BJP MP, had undertaken exemplary public work, and it was not any marketing gimmick but real work, which the local people vouched for. This was one of the main reasons why he got a ticket again in 2019.

Throughout my journey, I spoke to countless people and held innumerable debates. From all that I gathered, the trend was more or less the same: gathbandhan supporters were not too sure about the the alliance's ability to defeat the BJP. Even when someone expressly said that they were going to vote for the gathbandhan, they were not too confident about a win. Very few people were displeased with the sitting MP, Mukesh Rajput, and those rare instances too was clearly overtaken by the Modi factor.

As I edged through the last few constituencies in UP, it was now time for me to pack my bags and head to another high-profile campaign battleground—West Bengal.

2

THE BATTLE BETWEEN REGIONALISM AND RELIGION: WEST BENGAL

The best soldiers the Britishers have are recruited from the peasantry of India. Death is a thing of no importance to them. If you rob them, murder them, tax them, do anything to them, they will be quiet and gentle, so long as you leave them free to practice their religion. Britishers touched them there and that is when the 1857 mutiny started.

—Swami Vivekananda

This is exactly what Mamata Banerjee was doing in West Bengal, the land which gave us Swami Vivekananda. This is perhaps what will go down in history as the beginning of an uprising in West Bengal. The contest in the state was between fear, apparently created by the TMC, and the glimmer of hope that the public was seeing in Modi.

The perception of Hindu voters that Mamata's politics completely revolved around minority appeasement drove them to take a firm stand with the BJP. Rural voters were seemingly scared of foul play by TMC workers and urban voters might not have been quite vocal with their support for the BJP, but a silent pro-Modi undercover campaign was in the works in West Bengal.

The state, with its 42 constituencies, was going to play a very important role in the 2019 Lok Sabha elections. With BJP facing the gathbandhan (SP–BSP alliance) in UP, making it difficult for them to match their previous tally of 71, it was essential for them to significantly improve their tally in West Bengal to obtain a majority at the national-level once again.

The rally at Brigade Parade Ground in Kolkata on 19 January 2019 was the Opposition's first united rally. It was attended by political stalwarts such as Akhilesh Yadav, Chandrababu Naidu, Mallikarjun Kharge, M.K. Stalin, Farooq Abdullah, Sharad Pawar, Tejashwi Yadav and many more. The then Congress Party president, Rahul Gandhi, also extended his support to the Opposition's exercise in displaying unity. According to Mamata Banerjee, the rally would sound the 'death knell' for BJP in the Lok Sabha elections.[2] A few days later, Modi held a rally at the same Brigade Parade Ground, brimming with a crowd so huge that it was nothing short of historic.

Soon after winning the 2014 Lok Sabha elections, Amit Shah, the BJP president and current home minister, had identified the West Bengal constituencies as green pastured seats and the BJP started actively working on a plan to make inroads into the state. The most pressing inflexion point came during the 2018 panchayat polls, when the BJP gained a foothold into Maoist bastions—in districts such as Purulia and Jhargram. This happened despite TMC reportedly unleashing a reign of terror, in which at least 12 people were killed and more than 43 got injured.[3] It is believed that TMC party workers prevented members from other parties to file nomination papers and as a result, won without any contest. More than 20,000 gram panchayat villages, zila parishads and panchayat samitis remained uncontested in the violence-marred local polls. Ballot boxes were set ablaze, booths captured and political killings committed. It was then that the ECI scheduled elections in such a way that West Bengal saw polling in five of the seven phases of the Lok Sabha elections.[4]

---

[2]https://www.deccanherald.com/lok-sabha-election-2019/tmcs-mega-rally-will-sound-bjps-death-knell-713629.html, last accessed 27 December 2019.
[3]https://timesofindia.indiatimes.com/city/kolkata/widespread-violence-during-rural-polls-in-west-bengal-12-killed/articleshow/64164622.cms, last accessed 27 December 2019.
[4]https://www.cpiml.net/liberation/2018/06/tmc-terror-west-bengal-panchayat-polls, last accessed 27 December 2019.

If we rewind a little back in time, we will acknowledge that it was the TMC which decimated the Left in West Bengal to a point where it now faces an existential crisis across India. In the 2009 Lok Sabha elections, TMC increased its tally from 1 to 19, and then from 19 to 34 in the 2014 Lok Sabha elections. Some of the biggest factors that had helped TMC gain ground in West Bengal were the Singur Tata Nano controversy,[5] the Nandigram violence[6] and Operation Sunshine.[7] The three incidents led to gains for Mamata, such that for the next few years she and her party members arduously touched on these issues, coining their famous political war cry—*'Ma Mati Manush'* (Mother, Motherland, People) in their election campaigns. But nobody could have guessed that those once oppressed would soon be perceived as the oppressors themselves.

Prime Minister Narendra Modi blew the conch shell of BJP's political campaign in the camel-shaped state of West Bengal from the northern tribal areas and the party emerged victorious in seven of the region's eight Lok Sabha seats. A major part of the western region, which has a sizeable Hindi-speaking population, was also engulfed in the Modi wave, clearly proving that the BJP was not just an alternative to millions of poor but also a ray of hope for the entire state citizenry. It was easier to get BJP's development programmes through the eye of a needle, as Mamata continued banking on Muslim votes

---

[5] In 2008, the then TMC opposition revolted against the CPI (M) government for handing over the most fertile portion of land in the whole of the Singur to the Tatas. Later in the same year, after a brief meeting with the then Chief Minister Jyoti Basu, Ratan Tata confirmed his decision to move the Tata Nano project out of West Bengal. Tata mentioned his frustration with the opposition movement against the Singur Project led by TMC Chief Mamata Banerjee. This made Mamata look like a winner.
[6] The Nandigram violence, in the aftermath of a failed project to acquire land for a Special Economic Zone (SEZ) by the government of West Bengal under the erstwhile Communist rule, strengthened Mamata's political grounds.
[7] Operation Sunshine, the communist party's drive to remove illegal hawkers from the streets of Kolkata, ended with a whimper after strong protest by Mamata. These illegal settlers, who formed a part of the largest refugee sectors in the capital city of Kolkata, had exponentially grown in numbers, encroaching on the pavements of the city. By mobilizing these hawkers against the ruling party's decision to evict them, Mamata increased the numbers in her favour.

and Muslim votes alone. While the TMC won Muslim-dominated constituencies, overall the issue of development gained impact and emerged as the winner in the electoral battle.

Throughout the 2019 Lok Sabha elections, there were allegedly innumerable instances of poll rigging and violence by TMC workers.[8] As the election progressed, the contest got bitter, with Mamata going from 'not accepting Modi as PM' to the extent of saying 'Modi should be thrown out of the country'.[9] This galvanized TMC workers into action—they were apparently looting ballot boxes, vandalizing polling booths, attacking opposition workers and committing excesses that had not been heard of before.[10]

Be it Mamata Banerjee's resistance to Yogi Adityanath's rally in West Bengal or what was perceived as her autocratic stance, even her core voters were going against her now. People were anguished and actively sought avenues to display their dissent with the incumbent government, and the electoral battle gave them that opportunity. As a result, West Bengal witnessed a historic voter turnout.

Journeying across West Bengal was a challenging experience for me, but I imagined it must have been as challenging for the voters to make the journey from their homes to the polling booths. People did not open up to me, many pushed away the mic and some even shushed me at the slightest mention of Mamata. If I had not seen it with my own eyes, I wouldn't have probably believed it: the majority of Bengal's public was engulfed in what could have been a fear of Mamata and her party workers.

The BJP was acutely aware of the undercurrents of public fear

---

[8]There were multiple news reports to this effect. See, for instance, https://www.hindustantimes.com/lok-sabha-elections/lok-sabha-election-2019-vandalism-rigging-reported-from-bengal-in-last-phase-of-polling/story-gL4RvdF04HppzGRhe15HzM.html, last accessed 27 December 2019.

[9]https://www.indiatoday.in/elections/lok-sabha-2019/story/mamata-banerjee-behaving-like-a-dictator-fear-of-losing-has-made-her-desperate-ravi-shankar-prasad-1526548-2019-05-16, last accessed 27 December 2019.

[10]https://www.indiatoday.in/elections/lok-sabha-2019/story/lok-sabha-elections-2019-violence-casts-shadow-over-west-bengal-in-last-phase-of-polls-1528659-2019-05-19, last accessed 27 December 2019.

in Bengal and they smartly turned it into a full-fledged political campaign: '*Chup Chaap Kamal Chhaap*' (Silently press the lotus button in the polling booth) resonated well with the voters, who were no longer willing to submit to what apparently was a life of constant fear and they supposedly wanted to root out the TMC from the state. BJP President Amit Shah's claim that their party was going to secure at least 22 seats in the state added fuel to the fire. Mamata was nervous and this was evident in her speeches. Her statements moved away from '*Ma Mati Manush*' to '*Modi Hatao Desh Bachao*' (Remove Modi, Save the Country).[11] On 2 May 2019 she compared the Opposition's campaign against Prime Minister Modi to the sepoy mutiny of 1857 to oust the British.[12] As the elections neared, there was a controversy regarding Mamata apparently having said she'd 'slap' Modi, which Mamata later denied, saying she had instead remarked about the 'slap of democracy'.[13] Modi had responded to the 'slap' remark saying he will take it as a blessing.[14] With every passing phase the BJP was picking up momentum, and Mamata's personal statements plateaued TMC's campaign.

NORTH KOLKATA

I was in the middle of memorizing a few lines in Bengali for the West Bengal election journey when the pilot's announcement caught my attention. We were about to land in Kolkata in a couple of minutes. I rolled back the paper in my pocket and chanted *Jai Shri Ram*! This

---

[11] https://www.business-standard.com/article/current-affairs/tmc-will-hit-streets-with-modi-hatao-desh-bachao-slogan-mamata-banerjee-116122200911_1.html, last accessed 27 December 2019.

[12] https://timesofindia.indiatimes.com/elections/lok-sabha-elections-2019/west-bengal/news/mamata-invokes-sepoy-mutiny-for-her-oust-modi-campaign/articleshow/69146045.cms, last accessed 27 December 2019.

[13] https://www.hindustantimes.com/lok-sabha-elections/why-should-i-slap-pm-mamata-banerjee-explains-slap-of-democracy-remark/story-E8ot2zWWPht8DxO9jOADAK.html, last accessed 27 December 2019.

[14] https://www.hindustantimes.com/lok-sabha-elections/your-slap-would-be-a-blessing-pm-modi-hits-back-at-mamata-banerjee/story-LuWAMTRdGrII3xZXSiZU8K.html, last accessed 27 December 2019.

had become a slogan of political and religious freedom in West Bengal, and as much as I wanted the gods on my side, little did I realize how impactful these three words could prove to be. Upon reaching Kolkata I met my team members, who had been on the ground for the past one month and had been keeping me posted about all the happenings in the state. Outside the airport I spotted a fleet of peeli (yellow) taxis, which made me feel I was back in the 1980s. 'No Refusal' sign was imprinted across the taxis and yet I encountered at least five refusals to take me to my destination! Finally, as I boarded a cab, I remember thinking to myself: this is not going to be easy.

Heading to the centre of the city, I was mighty impressed with the roads leading from the airport to Park Street, but my sense of delight was short-lived. Just like the 'No Refusal' signs on the cabs, this too was merely a show. My driver hailed from Jhargram and belonged to the Muslim community. When I initiated a political conversation with him, I realized I already had a deeply engraved prejudice in my tone. To my surprise he shattered all my prejudices with his views.

'*Mamata ki ati ho gayi hai!*' (Mamata has overdone it!) he said.

Here was a core voter of Mamata who held resentment towards her brand of politics. Further in the conversation I discovered that he was looking for better alternatives, and he considered the BJP as one of them. Not all Muslims in the state were against the BJP. At least 8–10 per cent who belonged to the western regions such as Jhargram, Medinipur and Purulia were likely to go the BJP way.

As I entered the city, I started getting a real picture of the state of things. The TMC flags flying high in almost every nook and corner of the city were telling me that Mamata was still the strongest leader in West Bengal. Some claimed that BJP posters and in fact posters of any central government schemes were forcibly ripped off the walls or painted over in black across the city by TMC party workers. However, my work there was to gather people's opinion without any preconceived notions.

The *Janta* segment of my show *Lalkar* had never been this dull. Despite people gathering around us in large numbers, including a large proportion of youngsters, I was unable to collect as many opinions as I would've liked. Just like the 'No Refusal' cabs, nearly all refused to speak to me on record. One middle-aged man said: *'Zyada politics samajh nahi aata hai humko'* (I don't understand much of politics). He was clearly avoiding me and that was apparently the kind of fear the TMC workers had instilled in the minds of the local people. Another said: *'Sab sahi chal raha hai!'* (Everything is fine!) as if indirectly implying—'wrap up the show'.

We moved on to the famous Jadavpur University, hoping to gather diverse opinions at the campus. I immediately noticed a middle-aged bespectacled man with a moustache, his appearance resembling that of a typical Bengali man.

'Aapni kemon aachen? Kya lagta hai BJP hara payenge Didi ko?' (How are you? Do you think the BJP would be able to defeat Mamata?) I asked.

'BJP ko koi vote nahi dega…wo bahar ka party hai…unko Bengal nahi samjh aata hai! (No one will vote for the BJP. It is an outsider party. They don't understand Bengal) he replied.

'Magar BJP bolti hai wo bahot kaam kari hai paanch saal mein aur janta khush hai unse…' (But the BJP says it has done much work in the last five years and that the public is happy with them) I remarked.

'Kuch nahi kiya hai… Notebandi…GST…sab fail ho gaya…janta ko pareshaan kiya hai bas!' (They haven't done anything [constructive]… Demonetization… GST…everything failed. They only troubled the public!) he answered, almost bursting with rage.

This was the overall opinion among anti-BJP voters.

I then interacted with more than 30 students and some locals. I still could not find one voice supporting Modi. Be it fear, anger or resistance to an alien political party, Modi was clearly not their choice.

I then moved to New Market area. Kolkata has a significant number of Marwaris, the creamy business class. Owing to their numbers, they could influence the election in North Kolkata constituency. In that small market I spoke to a few street vendors:

'Ki hocchhe, dada?' (How are things?)

'*Khoob bhaalo, aapni bolun...*' (I am good, what about you?) The puchka vendor replied.

'*Mamata didi ke baare mein kuch bolna chaahenge?* (Do you want to say something about Mamata?) I quizzed further.

'*Marvaaoge kya, sa'ab?*' (Do you want me to get into trouble?)' He folded his hands and waved me away from his stall.

After speaking to street vendors in New Market I realized that people were too scared to even speak against the TMC lest they go against the party or Mamata for that matter. It seemed that if TMC workers got the slightest hunch about a voice of dissent among these street vendors, they would make their lives difficult. The fear was so strong that even if a few of them had a leaning towards Modi, they wouldn't vote altogether. Nobody among them would as much as dare think about rebelling against Mamata and her workers. It was a tough choice between a life of misery and a life in constant shadow of fear. '*Jaan hai toh jahaan hai,*' (If there's life then there's world) I remember my team member joking at that time.

Rahul Sinha from the BJP was contesting against Sudip Bandyopadhyay of TMC. Many BJP workers believed that Sinha was not the right candidate. On speaking to one of the West Bengal BJP workers, I understood the reason behind Sinha not receiving ample support from the party workers: 'When we do padyatra, Rahul Sinha asks us to walk a few steps behind him and this has stirred feelings of resentment among several workers who have put up campaign posters across Kolkata without the image of Rahul Sinha and Modiji,' he said.

It was just a day prior to the ECI invoking Article 324 to bring all campaigning in West Bengal to a halt, 19 hours before the scheduled time. Parts of Kolkata were witnessing widespread violence after the massive road show in Kolkata by BJP president Amit Shah, during which a statue of Bengali icon Ishwar Chandra Vidyasagar in Vidyasagar College in North Kolkata was vandalized. Both BJP and TMC accused each other for the incident and the subsequent violence. However, as it turned out, the incident worked in Mamata's favour. The Bengali pride had been hurt, and the TMC left no stone unturned to project this incident as an invasion of some sort. Mamata jumped to the chance of invoking Bengali asmita or pride. And it worked. The TMC in Bengal rode the sympathy wave while BJP ended up footing the bill for being a non-Bengali party.

KOLKATA SOUTH

It is common knowledge that Kolkata, especially the northern and southern regions, is a TMC stronghold. With over 40 per cent of its population Muslim, Kolkata South constituency was an undisputable bastion of Mamata's TMC—and Mamata ascertained her victory here in advance owing to this very reason. However, when it comes to elections, despite everything, one can't be too sure of the outcome. While the scales may have been tipped in favour of TMC, the BJP was all set to give a good fight to them.

It just so happened that I had an opportunity to visit TMC's party office, the one where Mamata sits, a few years ago. I remember that her residence was well-guarded and after a thorough security check my phone was taken for submission. I was then led to her room through a narrow entry. I was appalled by what I saw. People were sitting crouched on the floor with their hands folded in submission. Outside the office, the entire vicinity was adorned with pictures of Mamata and in each one of these photos she could be seen dressed in a white scarf or burqa, gesturing almost as if she was performing namaz. It was a clear and unabashed display of her leaning for the minority voter base.

A few hundred metres outside Mamata's office is a small temple. At this Kalka Mandir I spoke to a few people. Although they were not quite vocal with their views, I could still sense a natural discontentment on their faces. A person inside the temple spoke in a very low voice: *'Mamata didi hum logon ke liye kuch nahi karti hain'* (Mamata does not provide us with welfare benefits).

Even though a large number of workers could be seen roaming around, Mamata maintains a very low profile at her residence. Hers is an ordinary house and she owns just one car. In striking contrast is her nephew Abhishek Banerjee, whose extravagant lifestyle is something that the eye cannot miss. He resides in a multistorey house with multiple car parking. Security arrangements too were more superfluous at Abhishek Banerjee's house than at Mamata's.

DIAMOND HARBOUR

Abhishek Banerjee, Mamata's supposed successor, contested from Diamond Harbour. It wasn't a tough contest for him. She would do anything to make her nephew win and with 30–40 per cent population being Muslims, there was a demographic advantage for the TMC.

While we were taking a short trip of the constituency, I spotted an army man riding a bicycle. Believing him to hold a rational reasoning, I hit up a conversation:

'*Jai hind, Sir!*'

'*Jai Hind*,' he replied in a firm voice.

'*Sir, kaisa lag raha hai yahan, kaun jeetega?* (Sir, who do you think will win from here?)' I asked.

'*Jeete koi bhi, mera vote Modiji ko jayega...national security aur OROP ke liye*,' (No matter who wins, my vote will go to Modi...and to national security and OROP [One Rank One Pension]) he replied.

He was probably the first one to voice his opinion loud and clear. Being an ex-army man, he was obviously not threatened by TMC workers.

We continued towards a shop right opposite the TMC office. The couple who managed the shop were about to pull down the shutters for a lunch break. It is quite common in West Bengal for shop owners to close down for a few hours for an afternoon siesta. Before they could close, we caught them in time and questioned them on their political views.

'*Mamata didi hi jeetega magar vote kam hoga... BJP jeet sakta tha magar TMC ka gunde nahi jeetne denge*,' (Mamata would win, but the vote share would be less. BJP could win, but the TMC goons wouldn't let that happen) responded the man in a subdued tone.

Before I could probe any further, his wife signalled him to silence, probably fearing trouble from TMC workers across the road.

We then went to meet a poor Hindu family who told us how one of their family members had been decoyed by the local TMC workers, but this was not even the saddest part of their story. I was appalled at the utter casualness with which they were narrating tales of political killings and kidnappings of people who did not conform to the political ideology of the ruling party in the state. Crime in the state was a routine affair and was made so by TMC workers, with the state police too seemingly knuckling under the Mamata government.

It was impossible for the BJP to win in a scenario where even a handful of those who expressly wished to vote for them would have to put their lives at stake to do so. What further frightened these voters was the passive-aggressive messaging in Mamata's speeches. I remember one in particular where she explicitly warned people of consequences if they dared to back the BJP. The voters were left with little choice. I remember how even post the election results of 23 May, Subhashish Chakraborty of the TMC issued a directive to the party cadres to restrict anti-TMC voters in South 24 Parganas to vote in future. The Bengali portal *ei bangla 24x7* had also reported it on 29 May 2019.[15]

'*Aap jaayenge vote dene iss baar?*' (Will you go to vote this time?) I asked a lady living in a hutment in Diamond Harbour.

'*Nai baba...jaan pe khel ke vote nahi dena...himmat karke jaayenge bhi toh aadha raasta se TMC ka maanush log baari wapis bhej deta...fir ghar aake tang alag karega...itna jhamela kaun paale? Humko rozi-roti kamaane se fursat nahi, vote dene kaha jayenge babu batao?*' (No Sir, we won't risk our lives in order to vote. Even if we gather strength and march towards the polling booth, the TMC workers would trouble us and send us back. Why should we take so much stress? We are busy trying to earn a living, how can we go vote?) she said.

Even those who would dare to step out to vote would be discouraged by TMC workers. I think Mamata sensed the silent

---

[15]https://www.opindia.com/2019/05/cannot-allow-hindus-to-vote-anymore-trinamool-rajya-sabha-mp-tells-party-workers/, last accessed 27 December 2019.

Chup Chaap Kamal Chhaap movement overtaking the city, despite the BJP trying hard to keep it under the covers. She was pulling out all stops to contain an uprising of any sort.

DUM DUM

The Dum Dum constituency, close to the Kolkata airport, has a huge influence of outsiders. Although anti-TMC sentiments were clearly visible there, the organization of TMC was quite impenetrable, which might have overshadowed the anti-TMC sentiments of the people. The TMC workers were very well-connected to the local residents of the constituency and regularly organized meetings and events with them. Every place we set out to, we encountered TMC workers, let alone TMC supporters, actively campaigning. Modi's rally here had made one thing clear—the contest wasn't going to be easy.

'Didi...' the prime minister had said in a sarcastic tone during his rally at Dum Dum.

The crowd went berserk for a minute and it felt as if the BJP was going to have a sweeping victory in Dum Dum. However, the question remained: Would all these people rooting for the BJP here actually translate into votes?

TMC had strengthened its organization and apparently its goons were more active than ever before.

After the Mamata government's unabated refusals for rallies and denial of permission to land choppers, Modi made it into a Mamata vs Modi battle. On the day of the Dum Dum rally, Narendra Modi said: 'I'm going to West Bengal for a rally in Dum Dum. Let us see if didi allows it. If she has her way, she will not allow my helicopter to land.' The Bengal elections that had been gaining momentum now reached its peak.

An interesting thing to note was that in Dum Dum and many adjacent constituencies where BJP flags were unfurled, TMC flags were found at the very same spots the next morning.

BARRACKPORE

Adjacent to Dum Dum is the Barrackpore constituency, with more than half of the voters hailing from the working class and around 35 per cent of them Hindi-speaking. This gave BJP a slight edge over Mamata. The BJP gave ticket to Arjun Singh, an erstwhile TMC member with a solid vote base in the region.

In Barrackpore, I had the opportunity to speak to someone who not only offered interesting insights but also managed to alter my perception regarding the real situation vis-à-vis how things appeared. He had been a TMC supporter for more than 20 years and was quite satisfied with the way the party was working in the state. It was only after a long chat and after my assuring him that I don't have any political affiliations did he eventually open up in front of me. He disclosed how everyone in Barrackpore was voting for Modi. This was when I realized the BJP's slogan *Chup Chaap Kamal Chhaap* was actually working wonders in West Bengal. There were several similar slogans that had not only found acceptance but were seemingly working quite well with the people on the ground. *'Iss baar half, agli baar saaf'* (This time half, next time chaff) is one such slogan that I can recall. Here, 'next time' probably referred to the assembly elections.

BASIRHAT

'Hum Mamata ko vote nahi dega... Durga Pujo nahi karni deti... Jai Shri Ram nahi bolne deti... Mamata ko harayenge', (We won't vote for Mamata. She does not allow us to do Durga Puja, she doesn't allow us to utter Lord Rama's name. We will defeat her) said the owner of a roadside shop in Basirhat as I stopped to grab a cup of tea.

Basirhat, with Muslims comprising over 50 per cent of the population, is a fitting constituency to understand the extent of what is ostensibly Mamata's politics of minority appeasement. Talking to the locals here I got my hands on an informal dossier of some sort. One person complained: *'Mamata didi 5 lakh baanti hai kabristan ke liye, Hinduon ke liye kabhi koi nahi socha itna!'* (Mamata gives 5 lakh [to Muslims] for cemetery, but doesn't think as much for Hindus!)

I was extremely pained to see the way Hindu families were forced to live a life of abject poverty here. Several families were living adjacent to nullahs and there wasn't even space to set down one's feet outside the doors of these houses due to the open sewers. One thing that these hutments had in common besides misery was the photo or idol of Durga Maa. As I tried to delve a little deeper into the conversation about Mamata and TMC workers, the eldest in the family said: *'Zyada baat mat karo...wo sun lenge to ye ghar bhi tod denge!'* (Don't talk so much. If they hear it, they will damage this house too!)

What kind of a gloomy existence were they subjected to? Had they completely given up hope?

I couldn't stop myself from asking: *'Is baar badlegi sarkar?* (Will the government change this time?)

None of them replied.

When I asked about Modi, I could spot a spark of hope in their eyes.

'Wahi aa jayein to shayad kuch bhala ho!' (If he comes, maybe we will be better off!) said one of them.

Later in the day, I went to a local market to understand the opinion of urban voters. Speaking to a Hindu man who had come to buy groceries, I found out that majority of Muslims in Basirhat were favouring the TMC over the BJP. Basirhat was the constituency that had marked the beginning of TMC's ascension to power and it was really tough for the BJP to defeat the TMC in its bastion.

Moreover, the TMC fielded Nusrat Jahan, a famous face in Bengali cinema, against BJP's Sayantan Basu who had contested from Purulia in 2009. Nusrat Jahan not only brought the glamour factor with her, but also the unflinching support of the Muslim voters.

BANGAON

Bangaon, the eastern constituency of West Bengal, witnesses a heavy influx of illegal immigrants due to its proximity to Bangladesh. Due to its demography—the presence of the Matua community in large numbers—BJP President Amit Shah had identified Bangaon as a green pasture for the BJP. The Matua community, originally hailing from East Pakistan and later Bangladesh, is a sect of Vaishnavite Hindus. The Matuas in Bengal, the second-largest SC community in the state, were staunch supporters of Mamata Banerjee till the time her politics changed tracks to what was ostensibly politics of minority appeasement. With an estimated population of 30 lakh in West Bengal, the Matua community has the capacity to influence the results of at least six Lok Sabha seats and over 60 assembly seats. Mamata Banerjee had promised citizenship and welfare schemes to the people of Matua community, but these promises have remained unfulfilled. The community was now looking at Modi with hope. With the announcement of NRC, the BJP had already promised that the Citizenship Amendment Bill (CAB) would cover all persecuted Hindus from Bangladesh.

Thakurnagar, which falls under the Bangaon constituency, is home to more than 60 per cent Matua voters and is called the 'Mecca of Matua'. Narendra Modi kick-started his West Bengal campaign with a rally in Thakurnagar, addressing a gathering primarily of the Matua community. Right before the Thakurnagar rally, Modi also met Binapani Debi, the Matua matriarch, also known as Bodo Maa. Modi touching her feet and asking about her health made headlines. The rally was a great success, with people turning up in large numbers. Reportedly, many villagers had to go back home due to lack of space to even stand.

Shantanu Thakur, Binapani Debi's grandson, was the BJP candidate and he was set against his aunt and sitting TMC MP, Mamata Bala Thakur.

WESTERN REGIONS

The western regions comprise of areas of Purulia, Bankura, West Medinipur and Jhargram. These places also have a significant non-Bengali population. This, like north Bengal, was considered a sweep region for the BJP. Neighbouring the state of Jharkhand, it also had border effect, where the population was positively impacted by the reach of the central government's welfare schemes in Jharkhand. The BJP's rise in Bengal started with the panchayat polls of 2018. The west was one region which gave BJP the first ray of hope.

Bishnupur

A key factor that emerges from the history of voting in West Bengal is consistency—not of the party in power, but of voters. As per the trends observed, voters in the state tend to re-elect the ruling party and for long terms. Before Mamata rose to power, CPI (M) had held the reins of the state for 34 years. The same trend can be observed in the case of Mamata Banerjee's TMC, which has been firmly in the saddle since it won the assembly elections in 2011.

Bishnupur was once the CPI (M)'s citadel until TMC swept the 2014 elections, bringing CPI (M) to a near existential crisis. With the contest now between TMC and BJP, religious polarization had become a key factor. In this fight, whatever was left of the CPI (M), allied with the BJP. *'Pehle Ram Fir Vaam'* (First Ram, then Left)—CPI (M) was clear with their allegiances and priorities.

After travelling for nearly 5 km in a Bolero with a malfunctioning air-conditioner, I was forced to ask the driver to halt near a small sattu shop for refreshments. I saw five or six men donning lungi and baniyan in a typical Bengali fashion standing outside the shop. After getting some sattu, I tried to initiate a conversation with them without taking out my mic and camera.

'Kya lag raha hai, bhaiya...Mamata didi fir se aayengi?' (What does it seem like... Will Mamata return to power?)

They exchanged looks with one other. After an awkward long pause, one of them asked: *'Aap kahan se aaye hain?'* (Where have you come from?)

If I had said Delhi, they would have immediately identified me as a person related to politics. So, I said: *'Bambai... Bambai se hun'* (Mumbai... I am from Mumbai).

We spoke for a few minutes, but the conversation was not political in nature. There was unrest in their eyes, which seemed to be a reflection of the sense of fright that Mamata and her workers had ingrained in their minds. I had heard of the TMC indulging in elaborate scaremongering in the state, but I was unfamiliar with the sheer extent of it.

'*Chaliye main jata hun...aage Purulia jana hai.*' (I will take your leave now... I need to go to Purulia).

After about 40 minutes, I saw a group of 40–50 rickshaw-pullers. We were still in Bishnupur. Rickshaw-pullers in West Bengal are among the worst off and would be the right people to tell me about the on-ground situation, or so I thought. I, along with my cameraman, approached them. People are often drawn to cameras like moths to a flame. Several people gathered around us. Inadvertently, I ended up driving them away with my first question. I had asked them about the TMC government, but as soon as they heard the words 'TMC' coming out of my mouth, hesitation spread across their faces. They did not have the luxury to be as casual about such conversations as I was.

This gave me an initial sense of a trend emerging in the election. It was going to be historic any which way. If people remained scared, TMC would sweep the elections and if people dared to overcome their fears and make it to the polling booths, BJP would gain grounds like never before.

Starting his career with the Congress and then switching to TMC, the sitting MP of Bishnupur, Saumitra Khan, joined the BJP in early 2019. He was already a renowned face among the public—one who could channelize people's anger against Mamata into votes for the BJP.

Purulia

Before reaching Purulia in the afternoon, I noticed a common service centre on the way. Believing it would provide me a good idea of the political scenario in West Bengal, I decide to enter it. Judging it to be the safest place for me to shoot, I quickly took out the camera.

A young boy in a red shirt and black pants—some sort of uniform it seemed—came running to me. With folded hands he requested me to not take any pictures or videos. I immediately switched off the camera and kept it back in my bag. I assured him that I was only taking a look around.

'*TMC wale ye sab tod denge. Please aap ye sab mat kariye,*' (TMC workers will vandalize all this, you please stop all this) said the scared boy.

He then told me that the common service centre was for the registration of people to avail the central government's Ayushman Bharat Yojana, but TMC workers had ordered him to shut it down. They had also warned him of consequences, if they happened to find out that it was still operational.

Medinipur

The constituency of Dilip Ghosh, the former West Bengal state president of the BJP, Medinipur has over 30 per cent Muslim population. As per ground reports, Hindus were largely siding with the BJP due to the nuisance created by TMC workers.

In Medinipur, TMC workers actively interfere in youth/student politics. I was passing by a college when I noticed a rising smoke surrounded by many students. I reached the spot to find Modi's effigy being burnt. It was the deed of a few youth members of the TMC. Upon speaking to some of the students present there, I was surprised to find that a majority of them did not approve of what was happening. These students wanted to keep away from all forms of politics due to its impact on their studies.

Another thing that I found surprising was that people here were not aware of the various central government welfare schemes, let alone benefitting from them. No local newspaper or channel would run the risk of publishing any central government welfare schemes, dreading trouble from the state. Local residents also told me how TMC workers tore down the posters and banners of central government schemes.

The very next day, Shivraj Singh Chouhan was about to hold a rally and BJP workers were enthusiastically putting up posters and flags. I spoke to one of the workers who was quite excited and yet a little scared as some of the posters had been torn down by the TMC workers.

'*Kiski taiyyari chal rahi hai, bhaiya?*' (What are the preparations for?) I asked him.

'*Shivrajji ki rally hai kal…to bas usi mein lage hain,*' (It is Shivaraj's rally tomorrow… We are busy with that) he replied.

'*Itni mehnat kar rahe ho… BJP jeet paayegi?*' (You are working so hard… Will the BJP be able to win?) I enquired further.

'*Bhaiya, Mamata didi se log trast hain…koi bolega nahi magar vote BJP ko denge!*' (People are frustrated with Mamata… No one will say anything, but they will vote for the BJP!) he said, almost convincingly.

I moved ahead, stopping at a shop where people were making clay idols. I spoke to the owner who was a moortikaar (sculptor).

'*Abhi kiski moorti ban rahi hai dada… Durga Puja mein to time hai.* (Whose idol are you making … There's still time for Durga Puja.)'

'*Ye to Saraswatiji ki hai,*' (It's a Saraswati idol) he replied.

'*Bahot sundar hai. Kuch photos le sakta hun?*' (It's beautiful. Can I take some photographs?)

The idols were indeed magnificent and I could not stop myself from taking a few selfies with them. Going back to conversing with him, I pointed at a huge idol and asked: '*Dada, ye wali moorti kitne ki hai?*' (How much does this idol cost?)

'*Ye 18 hazaar ki hai. Ye line wali 15 hazaar se 20 hazaar wali hain.* (This one is for ₹18,000. The idols in this row cost between ₹15,000 and ₹20,000.)'

'*Aur kitna samay lagta hai inko banane mein?*' (And how much time does it take to make these?) I asked, expecting the answer to be not less than a month.

'*Chaar kaarigar din raat lagte hain isliye 15 din mein ho jaati hai,*' (Four artisans work day and night to make it in 15 days) he answered.

I wanted to ask him something politically relevant but seeing the lukewarm response so far, I was a little hesitant. Finally, I could not hold back any longer: *'Dada, sarkar se koi madad hai?'* (Is there any help from the government?)

'Kya madad...hamari samasya tak nahi sunte...kuch milna to door ki baat...dusron ko jo maango mil jata hai...paisa milta hai... unka rally karne ke liye jagah milta hai...permission milta hai...' (What help? They do not even listen to our problems. Others get money, resources and place and permission to conduct rally...)

I had found my answer and could project a trend, even if it was bleak in the making. Medinipur had many Hindus who had been royally ignored by the Mamata government. This could change a lot.

En route to Kharagpur, I noticed a large number of trucks queued up on the right side of the highway. On talking to a few truck drivers, I learnt that Mamata had devised a new method to look after the law and order situation of the state—civic volunteers. Civic volunteers weren't police but were placed to aid the state's police force. They are usually young TMC supporters who get up to ₹8,000 per month to ensure people were complying with Mamata's orders. They are not governed by any service rules, which automatically grants them open-ended powers to act against people who oppose Mamata's policies or rules.

'Kya lag raha hai yahan par kaun jeetega?' (Who do you think will win here?) I asked a truck driver.

'Hum kuch nahi kahenge. Aap khud dekho aur samjh jao. Humara to kaam hai sarkar jaisa bole waisa karo' (We won't say anything. You see for yourself and understand. Our job is to do what the government tells us to do)

I wanted to get a holistic picture. *'Mamata ki laagche?'* (What do you think of Mamata Banerjee?) I asked another driver.

He replied in just one word: 'Modi'. After a long pause, he added: *'Mamata humein humara poora paisa nahi deti... 300 rupaye bola tha dene ko, din ka 180 hi milta hai!'* (Mamata Banerjee's government does not give us our money. We were promised ₹300, but we get only ₹180 per day!)

The BJP already had a good hold on this constituency and the Modi factor was proving to be the cherry on the cake.

It was time for me to move on to the next constituency, Jhargram.

Jhargram

'Jaaiye pehle per dho lijiye,' (First go wash your feet) said a man pointing towards a handpump after I posed my regular question *'Kya maahol hai yahan, dada?'* (How is the political atmosphere here?) to him.

I was in Jitusole village of Jhargram. My feet were soiled due to walking on muddy paths. Not even a drop of water came out from the handpump that he had pointed out to me. I walked to the next handpump which was about 30–35 metres away, but as luck would have it, there was no water here too. Before I could start looking for the next one, it struck me why the man had asked me to wash my feet. He wanted me to experience their living conditions first-hand. There was a deep underlying message in what he had said to me, and it was getting clear to me with each passing day: the people of West Bengal were deprived of the most basic necessities, but self-ridicule was not lost on them.

Jhargram, one of the two tribal areas in Bengal, the other being Alipurduars, is home to people leading miserable lives filled with never-ending tribulations. It was heart-wrenching for me to see how those people had almost given up on hope. They did not wish to exercise their right to vote. Their failure to derive any benefits from government welfare schemes had broken their will. They saw a last ray of hope in Modi. They believed he could change their destiny and prove to be a messiah of some sort.

I believe village voters are the sanest ones. They neither hand out votes in return for ideology nor do they have any prejudices. They vote for the party that works for their development, the party that can make their lives better. They don't overthink, nor do they vote by herd mentality, and that's precisely the reason why they have the potential to change any government in one go.

Hungry mouths don't understand elections; they know food—and it seems Modi came across as that morsel of hope for them.

It was around 8–9 p.m. It was pitch dark outside. After driving for about 40–45 minutes we spotted a source of light and some huts on the horizon. We were told that these belonged to tribals and we were advised to maintain a safe distance from them. Apparently, the tribals here were so frustrated that they could potentially attack us or our vehicles. But for me their opinion mattered.

The next day, I went to the hut of a farmer who earned ₹200–250 per day and supported a family of five on this meagre income. He offered me muri (puffed rice) for lunch. Muri was their daily lunch—and most times the only meal of the day. He told me how the government neglected them and how local leaders, MLAs and MPs paid absolutely no attention to their needs. He also informed me that their local MLA could often be spotted lying drunk on the streets. Such was the state of affairs!

The next house I went to was a little better constructed than the previous one but it was still not suitable for living. Two brothers lived here. Both were teachers and they also ran a small cloth shop in their free time. One of the brothers told me how BJP's performance in the panchayat polls had given them some hope and how they have decided to vote for the BJP.

Pointing to the road outside he said, '*Ye sadak bahut pehle bani thi...thoda barish mein paani bhar jata hai...koi ja nahi sakta.*' (This road was constructed long ago. Even a little rainfall leads to waterlogging, which renders it unfit for use.)

I didn't have any answers or solutions to address his concerns. All I was seeking was to gain a sense of the election swing and what would work for them.

A peculiar thing that I noticed in various parts of West Bengal was that lottery counters reflected how people had more faith on chance than on themselves. One would find it difficult to get their hands on a bottle of water but not a lottery ticket—a very sorry state for the people and very telling of the quality of governance.

This reminds me of Modi's interview with the Bollywood actor

Akshay Kumar, and particularly an answer to one of his questions which aptly fits West Bengal's situation where even youngsters placed more faith on luck than on themselves.

'What would be the three wishes you'd ask for if you get your hands on the fabled Aladdin's Lamp?'

'See, if I get "Aladdin ka Chirag" with magical powers then I'd ask all educationalists to stop narrating the story of "Aladdin ka Chirag". People should be taught to work hard. It is hard work that is important and not laziness,' Modi had responded. Every youth of the country should engrave those words in their mind forever.

One cannot bet lives on probabilities and possibilities. In the 2019 elections, Bengal was at an important crossroads: would the people of Bengal only sit and wish away their miseries or would they act to change their circumstances?

Jhargram has people belonging to the Mahato OBC caste and the Lodha tribe. While the Mahato caste constitute roughly 20 per cent of the total population and are entirely on the BJP's side, the Lodha tribe constitutes around 14 per cent of the population and, as a voter base, is divided between the BJP and TMC.

A villager took me to the site of Laxmi Cements, a company which the state government had given the permit to produce cement. Laxmi Cements was illegally dumping manganese ore waste near the site. Several village workers extracted manganese from this waste and contracted Parkinson's disease. They were now living with physical deformities. The state government, it seemed, couldn't care less, and never paid any heed to such health threats to the people. I was informed by the local people that there were many such illegal nexuses and organized corruption rackets around.

NORTHERN REGIONS

The northern part of West Bengal is famous for hill stations and tea gardens, and has a long history of neglect. The region has been denied welfare benefits by the Mamata government. En route to Darjeeling, the dazzling snow peaks of Kanchenjunga and the beautiful tea gardens on the hill slopes were a refreshing sight. I was all enthused to spend my days in the villages of Darjeeling, Jalpaiguri, Kooch Bihar and Alipurduars.

Darjeeling

Ahead of the Lok Sabha elections, the TMC entered into an alliance with the Binay Tamang-led faction of the Gorkha Janmukti Morcha (GJM) in Darjeeling. One of the two seats that the BJP won in the 2014 Lok Sabha elections had been with GJM's help. Five years had passed since then and now the dynamics had completely changed. During the Gorkhaland agitations, GJM split into two factions in 2017. While the Bimal Gurung-led faction of GJM remained with the BJP, the Binay Tamang-led faction of GJM went with the TMC. With the faction that chose to go with them having an upper hand, BJP had benefitted from this split.

If rumours on the ground were to be believed, the BJP had also tried to form an alliance with the GJM faction that ultimately went with the TMC; apparently, some horse trading had also taken place, but in the end the then BJP MP S.S. Ahluwalia couldn't manage it. This resulted in triggering internal politics and soon BJP workers and supporters started demanding a different candidate. The party decided to field Raju Bista, the managing director of Surya Roshni Limited, as its canditate for the 2019 elections.

While travelling from Darjeeling to New Jalpaiguri we made a short stop at Kurseong which, surrounded by many tea gardens, is a famous sightseeing spot. Our hectic election schedule did not allow us to enjoy the scenic views and we directly went to a house belonging to a man in his late sixties.

Quite aware of the politics around him, he spoke to me on the condition of anonymity. He revealed how illegal immigration was hampering their lives: '*Humari umar 68 ki ho gayi par aaj tak koi pension na mila...wahan Bangladesh se aaye 30–40 umar walon ko mil rahi hai pension.*' (I am 68 years old now but I am yet to receive any pension. And there are illegal immigrants from Bangladesh who are 30–40 years old and they are already receiving pension.)

When I mentioned how the government was working towards deporting illegal immigrants, he pointed out how the immigrants had more documents than Indian citizens and that it was too late to deport them. He had absolutely no hopes from the state government or from any authority for that matter.

Darjeeling was harbouring nothing short of a tempest in a tea kettle. Nobody could have guessed such turmoil was brewing amidst these beautiful tea gardens. Would the chaiwallah's promise to tackle immigrants be enough to blow off some steam here?

Jalpaiguri

During the panchayat polls, an entire village in Jalpaiguri constituency had been denied their voting rights. When people of the Phulbari village reached the polling booths, they were told that their votes had already been cast. It was claimed that TMC supporters had been behind this disruption of the polling process.

BJP's performance in the panchayat polls had instilled a sense of hope among people who could foresee the possibility of a change in their situation for the better. The panchayat election that had concluded in May 2018 showed that the BJP had made strong inroads into former Maoist bastions—districts such as Purulia and Jhargram. Though it trailed the TMC in both, the party won more than a third of the gram panchayat seats in these two districts with the backing of the tribal population.[16]

Through my interactions with people here I learnt that the assembly election in 2021 was all set for a big surprise.

Alipurduars

In the tribal constituency of Alipurduars, the on-ground realities that I came across had the potential to give sleepless nights to anyone. On our way to Alipurduars via Siliguri we had to break our journey at Jaldapara, known for its national park, due to an extremely bad weather forecast.

---

[16] https://www.livemint.com/Politics/hp3vudIsReCo7NjtaO2eoN/West-Bengal-panchayat-polls-Former-Maoist-bastions-now-BJP.html, last accessed 27 December 2019.

We resumed our journey the following day when the weather was relatively better. After travelling for about an hour, we stopped at a tea garden to speak to the labourers working there. We also visited a basti (hutment) nearby. There we saw a handpump, with more than 20–25 women surrounding it. There was only one handpump for every 40–50 families. There were no schools for the kids. There were no doctors in the entire basti and the nearest place where a doctor was available was more than 20 km away. That doctor too was available only once a week. What would happen if someone was in urgent need of medical assistance? That question and the general state of things there pained me. The labourers earned a meagre daily wage of ₹150 after slogging for 14–16 hours and it was never enough to meet ends. This isn't just a story of a bad day; it is what the lives of these people had been for the past several years.

Looking at their deplorable condition, I decided to speak with them, to understand their needs and to know their views. As they narrated their problems to me, perhaps hoping that I could somehow help, all I could do was to listen helplessly. Their struggles were very basic. How had they missed their ticket to the development bandwagon that the entire country was currently riding on?

As we approached Alipurduars, we noticed some tents on either side of the road. This was close to the Bhutan border. The people living in these tents are largely dependent on the state government, as the benefits of—or for that matter even information about—central government schemes do not reach them anyway. The state government controlled their lives.

We moved ahead to Kalchini via Nimti Domohani, a very isolated place which is almost at the edge of India. These places also had basic living problems that we earlier saw in the bastis in Jaldapara. However, despite being isolated, we were surprised to find people in Kalchini were extremely angered with what was viewed here, and elsewhere in the state, as Mamata's politics of minority appeasement. The fact that illegal migrants now had valid ID proofs and more government documents than an actual Indian citizen was a sign of the corruptibility of government officials.

Cooch Behar

The last constituency in the northern region of West Bengal, Cooch Behar also reflected the anti-Mamata sentiments. News of Phulbari villagers being denied their voting rights in the panchayat polls had reached places such as Sitai and Sitalkuchi, thus adding to people's resentment against the TMC. The performance of BJP in the panchayat polls gave people hope and they were likely to turn up in large numbers for the Lok Sabha elections. However, despite all this, one has to realize that the condition of a state's public can improve only if the state government notices them or there's a way for the centre's scheme to reach the remotest regions of West Bengal.

After talking to many people in the northern constituencies of West Bengal, I realized that the BJP was going to sweep the elections. If I had to summarize the key issues that were going to swing the public towards the BJP, I would say it was Mamata's apparent tilt towards the minorities and how she was seen as standing between central government schemes and the people of Bengal, forcing them into a life of misery.

The northern and western regions of West Bengal were considered a stronghold of the BJP. With Cooch Behar and Alipurduars swinging in full favour towards the party, 50 per cent of the vote share in the northern and western regions of the state was leaning towards the saffron party. A closer look would reveal that the welfare schemes of the central government had not reached the northern regions. In the western parts, which were in close vicinity of Jharkhand, people were benefitting from these schemes and roughly 4–5 seats were expected to land in the BJP's kitty. However, the capital city of Kolkata would not so shockingly enough turn out to be a dampener for them, as was evident from the hollow or negligible presence of the BJP there. It was the eastern region of Bengal that helped the BJP, a national party, to make inroads the state which had long been in the hands of regional parties. With the Muslim regions heavily polarized in

TMC's favour and the remaining regions reduced to a neck-to-neck battle, it was difficult to predict a clear number.

Besides geography, language too played a significant part in Bengal's politics. TMC continued to sweep among the Bengali-speaking section of society while almost 70 per cent of the Hindi-speaking public supported the BJP. While TMC received the forthright support of the Muslims, BJP was able to sway the Matua community in their direction. Above all, the Modi factor combined with Mamata's communal and anti-welfare stance contributed significantly to an undeniable electoral dynamic surfacing in the state.

In 2009, TMC had won only 19 seats, but in 2014, it had recorded a thumping victory by landing 34 out of 42 seats in the Lok Sabha, routing the entire Left from West Bengal. The party had made momentous inroads in the Left bastion in north Bengal back then, seizing four seats—Cooch Behar, Jalpaiguri, Alipurduars and Balurghat. The same trend was observed in the case of the BJP. Like the TMC, the BJP too changed the game in 2019 by working on cadre expansion. In 2019, the party made stunning inroads in Bengal by jumping from a mere two seats in 2014 to an astounding 18 seats in 2019, while the TMC bagged 22 seats. The seats which were once the debut seats of TMC in the previous elections were now being won by the BJP. The fact that TMC could not hold its first-time seats was quite telling.

3

THE POWER OF WOMEN VOTERS: BIHAR

Bihar is arguably the Indian state with the most dynamic politics. With the Janata Dal-United (JDU) first getting into an alliance with the Rashtriya Janata Dal (RJD) for the assembly elections and then parting ways to form an alliance with the BJP made, it became quite difficult to predict the outcome of the Lok Sabha elections in Bihar. Chief Minister Nitish Kumar had, however, realized quite early on that choosing to be part of the gathbandhan for the Lok Sabha elections would result in massive losses for him and his party in the electoral game. Opposition reached its nadir and the BJP was at its crest. In such a scenario, Nitish Kumar was left with little choice but to go with the BJP. There was, however, interdependency between the two. As much as Nitish Kumar was banking on the BJP, the latter also needed him. A survey revealed that Nitish Kumar had a strong hold on over 30 per cent of the extremely backward castes (EBCs) and 5 per cent Kumris, without the support of whom no party could win.

One thing that stood out as distinct when compared to the politics of the olden days was that the BJP was now an equal partner. Unlike the times of Atal Bihari Vajpayee and L.K. Advani, when the BJP used to have a lesser seat share in regional alliances, JDU and BJP shared 17 seats each to contest in the 2019 Lok Sabha elections.

Bihar, a state with 40 constituencies and reputed to have shades of caste politics, was ready to witness a head-on contest between the NDA led by the BJP (which had got into a pre-poll alliance with JDU and with the Lok Janshakti Party [LJP] led by Ram Vilas Paswan) and the mahagathbandhan, which included the Congress, Rashtriya

Lok Samta Party (RLSP) led by Upendra Kushwaha, RJD led by Tej Pratap Yadav, Vikasheel Insaan Party (VIP) led by Mukesh Saini and Hindustani Awam Morcha (HAM) led by Jitan Ram Manjhi.

One of the most interesting things to see in Bihar was that the BJP, JDU and LJP trio was shattering the caste composition, thereby putting together an electoral chess spread which was not solely based on caste permutations. 'Take-off votes' or the core voter base with which a party begins its contest is an important point of assessment to start with. Chandravansi, Mallah and Dhanuk communities together constituted around 30 per cent, Bhumihars and Brahmins constituted 12–15 per cent, Kurmis, 3 per cent; Mahadalits and Paswan Dalit, 5 per cent; Manjhi, 3 per cent; and Baniya OBC, 7–8 per cent of the population. When put together, these constituted more than 55 per cent vote share, which could be termed as the take-off vote percentage for the NDA. Eighty per cent Yadavs and Muslims were inclined towards the RJD and Congress. Kushwahas, who constituted 6 per cent of the total population, were not entirely with Upendra Kushwaha, which meant that the Congress and RJD had 30 per cent vote base and the remaining 15 per cent were sway voters.

Both RJD and Congress were majorly dependent on Yadav voters, who belong to Gaya, Muzzafarpur, Samastipur and Patna, and wherever Yadavs are in majority the voting percentage has never been more than 50 per cent. In fact, if electoral history bears any evidence, only around 20–30 per cent of Yadavs have preferred to vote on nationalism. This time too the Yadavs were divided. While the educated ones were siding with the BJP, those who identified more with their caste were siding with the RJD.

In the 2015 assembly elections, JDU pumped in oxygen into a moribund RJD by forming an alliance with it. However, RJD leaders did not want Nitish Kumar to be the chief minister. Two years later, in 2017, they parted ways and JDU formed an alliance with the BJP and later became a part of NDA for the 2019 Lok Sabha elections as well.

As in several other states, women in Bihar too were siding with the BJP and JDU. Apart from the Modi factor, another emerging dynamic that helped women to make up their mind was the Nitish Kumar factor. By banning liquor in the state, Nitish Kumar had struck a good chord with womenfolk.

Modi, on the other hand, had a much larger than life image in Bihar. He was known here not just for the Statue of Unity or for his welfare schemes but for what he did to strengthen the country's internal security, and for teaching Pakistan a lesson. *'Ye naya bharat hai, ghar mein ghus ke maarega'* (This is a new India that will cross into enemy territory and retaliate) and *'Wo teen ko maarenge hum teen sau ko maarenge'* (If they kill three of our soldiers, we will kill three hundred of theirs) echoed well as sentiments among the youth. Modi had an unsurmountable image of a strong leader capable of leading the country with an iron hand.

Although the issue of dwindling jobs was a matter of concern for the youth, they still decided to repose their faith in Modi. The realization that Modi deserved another term to tame unemployment, as it was not something which could be resolved in a short span of five years, pushed the youth to vote for him.

One thing that I found consistent throughout my journey in Bihar was how people had reposed an unwavering faith in Modi. The election was undisputably going to be Modi-centric, with development agenda, various welfare schemes for the poor and keeping national interest at the fore ensuring an upper hand to him.

PATNA SAHIB

After landing at the Jay Prakash Narayan Airport, I took a cab to the historic Gandhi Maidan from where in 1974, Jayaprakash Narayan had launched his fight against the Emergency. Towering over Gandhi Maidan, towards the northwest, stands the statue of Mahatma Gandhi, under which I spent my night. In a corner of the maidan a wedding was taking place and people could be seen dancing joyfully. At around 11.45 p.m., upon looking closely, I found out that both the bride and the groom belonged to the lower caste. I tried speaking to a group of young boys who were dancing a little away from the crowd and the main stage. They saw me but did not stop. I took out my camera and mic to take some interesting shots. I even indulged in some dance moves. After some time, I asked one of them about the political scenario in the city. They started chanting 'Modi! Modi!' even as they continued dancing.

Later that same night I spoke to a few more people at the wedding only to realize that while the Pulwama attack had consolidated voters across caste lines, the Balakot air strikes had reinvigorated confidence in Modi.

However, a key factor that was working against the NDA here was the new sand mining policy. In 2017, after forming an alliance with the BJP, the Nitish Kumar government came up with a novel sand mining policy named the Bihar Minor Mineral Rules, 2017, which was enacted with the aim of suppressing the sand mafia and removing middlemen from the system but which ended up impacting the entire sand mining business. Yadavs, who constituted 80–90 per cent of people in the sand mining business, were filled with resentment against Nitish Kumar. However, there were some core voters of RJD who branded it as a state-level issue and continued to support Modi in the Lok Sabha election while choosing to go with the RJD in the assembly elections.

While the RJD–Congress alliance lacked solid leadership, traditional voters of RJD weren't ready to accept Tejashwi Yadav as their leader and went to the extent of labelling him as an overhyped politician. People missed Lalu Prasad Yadav and his inimitable style of canvassing for votes. Though Lalu Prasad sought bail to carry out 'essential responsibilities as a party president' ahead of the election, his appeal was rejected. Not only was he missing in the campaign this time, there were no photos or statues of him either. The RJD and Congress leaders together struggled to fill the vacuum created by Lalu Prasad.

Patna Sahib was about to witness an interesting contest between the sitting MP Shatrughan Sinha and Union Minister Ravi Shankar Prasad. A two-time MP from BJP, Sinha joined the Congress in 2019 when the BJP didn't give him a ticket to contest the Lok Sabha elections. Sinha grossly miscalculated the Modi wave, choosing to fight against the undefeatable simply because he was fixated on getting a ticket. The Kayastha community, which is the demographic majority in Patna, has a natural inclination towards the BJP. Yadav and Rajputs are second and third in the demographic line. Ravi Shankar Prasad has the image of a well-learned person which, in addition to having Modi on his side, was keeping him far ahead of Shatrughan Sinha in the competition. Sinha's rebellious attitude towards his own erstwhile party rendered a loss of his credibility. Even core voters of the Congress and RJD weren't taking him seriously. It wasn't a tough fight for Ravi Shankar Prasad and BJP's margin from the seat was also expected to increase substantially.

DARBHANGA

The Darbhanga constituency had a story similar to Patna Sahib's. Kirti Azad, who won the 2009 and 2014 Lok Sabha elections on a BJP ticket, rebelled to join the Congress Party. In 2019, Kirti Azad contested from Dhanbad and lost by a margin of over 4 lakh votes.

Soon after leaving the BJP, Azad made various damaging remarks about BJP leaders, which harmed him more than anyone else. He lost his standing among the public and the BJP became the obvious choice for voters. I spoke to a few people on-ground about Kirti Azad. One of them said: '*Ye bagawat karne wale hamesha aisa hi karte hain…dusri party mein jayenge to bhi aisa hi karenge…inko jeeta kar koi fayda nahi!*' (These rebellious kinds always rebel. Even in another party, they'd follow the same pattern. There is no point in helping them win.)

Another reason for the mahagathbandhan's failure was Md Ali Asraf Fatmi, who represented Darbhanga for over 13 years. Expelled from the RJD by Tej Pratap Yadav for showing disrespect, he joined the BSP to contest from Madhubani. However, his association with the BSP didn't last long. He disassociated himself from the party and withdrew his candidature saying 'I am a free bird now. My joining BSP was just a formality. It was a one-day affair.'[17]

---

[17] On 29 July 2019, Md Ali Asraf Fatmi joined JDU.

VAISHALI

Vaishali is an ancient city that goes way back to the times of the Mahabharata. References to Vaishali can also be found in ancient Buddhist and Jain texts. It was here that Lord Buddha announced his Nirvana and delivered his last sermon. Democracy is said to have originated in Vaishali around 600 BC.

The contest in Vaishali was between RJD's Raghuvansh Prasad Singh and LJP's Veena Devi. While Veena Devi was contesting a Lok Sabha seat for the first time, Singh had tremendous experience, having served as a people's representative in the legislature for over four decades since 1977. Rajputs and other upper-caste voters had been unanimously supporting Singh over the last 25 years. This time though they were supporting Veena Devi because she was backed by Modi. While the mahagathbandhan was banking on the name and work of Raghuvansh Prasad Singh, the NDA was contesting on the issue of development which seemed to have resonated well with people.

In a sweet shop called Nirmal Sweets, I spoke to a few people. A youngster who was there to buy some sweets said he liked Modi because Modi had opened several medical and engineering colleges in the state. A middle-aged man seemed happy with Modi's work, especially for providing non-stop electricity. The shop owner himself was a Modi supporter and saw in him an honest leader.

While in Vaishali, I convened an episode of my show *Lalkar* near a Gautama Buddha statue. Representatives from RLD, BJP and LJP joined me for the '*Target Pe Neta Ji*' segment of the show. Ironically, earlier the same day, Singh, who is known for implementing the Mahatma Gandhi National Rural Employment Guarantee Act, 2005 (MGNREGA), gave a scandalous statement that got the Congress on the backfoot. He compared Nyuntam Aay Yojana (NYAY)—a minimum income guarantee scheme—with MGNREGA, criticizing the very scheme on which the Congress was contesting elections. He called out the NYAY scheme for giving money to people in exchange for no work. On my show, the local leader acted completely ignorant of Singh's statement.

One thing that became apparent on the show was that while the Opposition parties seemed to be united on the outside, the core people of those very parties weren't clear about a prime ministerial candidate. I asked the RJD leader: '*Aapke neta Tejashwiji keh rahe hain ki Rahul Gandhi ko pradhan mantri banaya jayega. Aap ka kya kehna hai iss par?*' (Your leader Tejashwi is saying that Rahul Gandhi would be made the prime minister. What do you have to say on this?) He was baffled and he responded: '*Hum nahi maante isey! Aur fir jo high command bolenge wo hi hoga!*' (We don't agree with this. But then whatever the high command says we will follow.)

This lack of clarity contributed to making the election campaign difficult for them—how do you fight an election without a definite face, especially when you are pinned against someone who is a public sensation? Even if you do, winning would be a remote possibility. Maybe overlooking this crucial factor was where the gathbandhan erred.

KISHANGANJ

Muslims comprise around 56 per cent of the population in Kishanganj constituency. The constituency had been the Congress' stronghold since 2009. The BJP had managed to win this seat only once, when in 1999 Syed Shahnawaz Hussain emerged victorious by a small margin of 8,648 votes.

However, this time, the elections turned into a triangular contest after the All India Majlis-e-Ittehadul Muslimeen (AIMIM) fielded Akhtarul Iman, a popular Muslim face who is also known as the Owaisi of Bihar, drawing parallels with the AIMIM president Asaduddin Owaisi. Akhtarul was pitted against Congress' Mohammad Jawed and JDU's Syed Mahmood Ashraf, which resulted in a division of Muslim votes between the Congress and AIMIM.

While the Congress was banking on Muslims as its core voters, the JDU was banking on development work undertaken by Nitish Kumar. Muslim women, in all probability, were going to support the JDU, as they could relate well with Nitish Kumar's social welfare initiatives.

On the day the election results were declared, Kishanganj emerged as the lone Bihar constituency won by the Congress. The vote margin though had reduced from nearly 2 lakh to a mere 30,000.

GAYA

A city of historical significance and a holy place for Hindus, Gaya's population comprises around 79 per cent Hindus, 20 per cent Muslims and 1 per cent split between Christians, Jains and other religions. Gaya is the place where Lord Rama, with Sita and Lakshmana, offered pind-daan for his father, Dasharatha. Bodh Gaya, 16 km from the main city, is one of the holiest sites of Buddhism. It is here that Lord Buddha attained enlightenment. Gaya has always been a citadel of the BJP and the party hadn't lost the seat in the past three decades.

En route to Gaya we stopped at a basti. Four or five women were sitting just outside their houses. I spoke to them about the political scenario:

'Mataji, kya lag raha hai...suna hai sharab bandi se bahot nuksan hua hai jaan maal ka?' (People are saying the alcohol ban has caused a lot of financial loss to families. How do you feel?)

With a stern look on her face one of them responded: *'Kaahe ka nuksaan hua hai! Paise bach jaate hain...bacchon ki padhai ke kaam aate hain...aur pati log ghar mein aa kar maar-peet nahi karte...sab accha hua hai!'* (What loss? We save money, which can be used for our children's education. And the husbands don't come home and beat up their wives. What has happened is good!)

Although she initially looked at me firmly, the lady turned out to be far more generous, offering me litti chokha (a stuffed whole wheat dough ball served with a mashed potato relish) made in pure ghee.

After having litti chokha I entered Gaya and the first thing I noticed was a small chai shop where a destitute man was having tea. I reached out to him and spoke with him while sipping a cup of tea. He was a rickshaw driver. I asked him if the government had done anything there and who he thought should win. He replied that he now had a bank account and received money directly into that account from the government. I realized that Modi's schemes were not just on paper but the benefits were reaching the ground level, transforming the lives of many.

KARAKAT AND UJIARPUR

A few months before the 2014 Lok Sabha elections, the RLSP led by Upendra Kushwaha had entered into an alliance with the BJP-led NDA. As per the alliance, RLSP contested from three seats from Bihar in the 2014 general elections, namely Sitamarhi, Karakat and Jahanabad. They won all the seats, riding on the Modi wave. However, the party could not replicate the same performance in the 2015 assembly elections, winning only two of the 23 seats they contested from.

For the 2019 Lok Sabha elections, RLSP wasn't given a ticket as per its demand, due to which, despite being a part of the NDA, Upendra Kushwaha was holding backdoor talks with the RJD for a pre-poll alliance. On 20 December 2018, the RLSP entered into an alliance with the Congress-led UPA.

Although the UPA gave RLSP three seats to contest from, it became difficult for Upendra Kushwaha to find candidates who could contest. In the end Kushwaha himself contested from two seats—Karakat and Ujiarpur. He lost both.

SAMASTIPUR

Samastipur, the constituency which the BJP had won with just 10,000 votes in 2014, had many factors working against the NDA in 2019: caste composition with Yadav and Muslim voters together constituting more than 50 per cent of the population and anti-incumbency for the sitting LJP MP Ram Chandra Paswan, brother of Union Minister Ram Vilas Paswan, being significant reasons.

Upendra Kushwaha, who left the NDA to join the UPA grand alliance, had a strong influence over Samastipur and nearby Lok Sabha constituencies and was assumed to be capable of creating a dent in

NDA's total tally. However, JDU's return to NDA compensated for this loss and, above all, the Modi wave was likely to overcome all these factors combined together. This was evident on the ground. For the first time in a Lok Sabha election, voters were ignoring the candidate and were voting solely in the name of Modi, with Nitish Kumar acting as a catalyst.

Riding the Modi wave, Ram Chandra Paswan managed a comfortable victory against Congress' Ashok Kumar. On 21 July, Ram Chandra Paswan died due to a heart attack, bringing the victory celebrations to an end.

AURANGABAD

Aurangabad has for long served as an example of winning elections based on development work. The sitting MP, BJP's Sushil Kumar Singh was contesting against the Hindustani Awam Morcha candidate, Upendra Prasad. Singh's work formed a part of his core campaign dialogue, as during his tenure the constituency witnessed development like never before. Frequently in the news for droughts, Aurangabad was revitalized after Prime Minister Narendra Modi and MP Sushil Kumar Singh ensured the completion of the remaining 20 per cent work on the North Koel Reservoir, also known as the Maithon Dam Project in Jharkhand, which would irrigate Aurangabad and Gaya districts of Bihar.

According to an official of the Water Resources Department, 'The project had started in 1972 and continued in a piecemeal manner till 1993, after which the work was stalled due to objection from union forest and environment ministry. Only after the NDA took over, the project not only got completed but also the water of the dam is going to Bihar.'[18]

After talking to the local people, I got to know that Sushil Kumar Singh had used his Members of Parliament Local Area Development Division Scheme (MPLADS) funds to develop roads which

---

[18]https://timesofindia.indiatimes.com/city/patna/jharkhand-dam-to-boost-irrigation-in-abad-gaya/articleshow/67387270.cms, last accessed 27 December 2019.

interconnect national and state highways in Bihar and Jharkhand. He also passionately expressed the need to expedite construction and conversion of the Sherghati–Imamganj–Salaiya State Highway in Bihar into a national highway.

Development work done by the BJP government was substantially visible on the ground and voters had made up their mind about who they were going to vote for. Singh comfortably defeated Prasad to become the MP from Aurangabad for a second time.

VALMIKI NAGAR AND WEST CHAMPARAN

The BJP had emerged victorious in the Valmiki Nagar constituency in the 2014 Lok Sabha elections. However, in 2019, after the JDU–BJP alliance culminated, the ticket was given to JDU. Baidyanath Prasad Mahto, the JDU candidate, came third in a three-cornered contest between the BJP, Congress and JDU in the 2014 elections, but in 2019 he was riding on the huge Modi wave. In a constituency where people were kept devoid of basic infrastructure and an environment conducive for business, development was the main agenda. I talked to the owner of a small business, who said that while there's a river from Valmiki Nagar to Nepal, there was no infrastructure to do anything and one had to travel at length on a daily basis.

People here still held resentment against the Congress Party and claimed it hadn't done a single thing in 70 years. Under the BJP rule since 2014, the region had seen some development, which made the locals hopeful of a brighter future under the saffron party.

'*Pehle ye sab jungle tha, koi rasta nahi tha...humein poora ghoom ke jana padta tha, magar ab ek road ban gayi hai, usse kaafi aasaani ho jaati hai...*' (Earlier it was all a jungle. There was no path [through it]. We had to go around it, but now we have a road, which has made it easier...) said a local resident.

Although Bihar is infamous for caste-based politics, even those who attached a lot of importance to their caste identity were looking at development as a prime factor on which to vote in the 2019 elections. Most of them wanted to vote for Modi who had ensured that development reached areas that had long stood ignored.

Similar to Valmiki Nagar, development work had also taken place in the Paschim Champaran constituency. Dr Sanjay Jaiswal of the BJP, who hailed from Patna, had been representing the constituency since 2009 and had made several efforts to deliver development in the remotest corners of the region. His developmental work overshadowed the caste and religion demographic factors. Despite the region comprising over 35 per cent Dalits and Muslims, who the Congress Party believed to be their core voters, Jaiswal managed a comfortable win for the consecutive third term.

As I spoke to more and more people, I learnt that Jaiswal had a very good connect with the public and he often conducted public meetings and events. While women majorly benefitted from Modi's welfare schemes such as the Pradhan Mantri Ujjwala Yojana, youngsters were happy with the work done by Jaiswal. The Modi factor worked as an added cherry on the cake.

KATIHAR, ARARIA AND SHEOHAR

These three constituencies are very crucial to analyse the overall voting pattern in Bihar. The popular Congress leader, Navjot Singh Sidhu, had appealed to the Muslims in the Katihar constituency to vote unitedly in order to defeat Prime Minister Narendra Modi in the elections. The words he used were *'Agar sab Muslim ekjut ho kar vote karenge to Modi salat jayega.'* (If all Muslims come together to vote in tandem, Modi will lose.)[19] Sidhu's statement invited heavy criticism across party lines and an FIR was registered against him. But a bigger impact was the counter-polarization which happened on the ground. Even though Katihar has around 50 per cent Muslims, Congress' Shah Tariq Anwar lost the seat to JDU's Dulal Chandra Goswami.

Similarly, in the Araria constituency with more than 40 per cent Muslims, the Congress' attempt of polarization resulted in counter-

---

[19]https://www.business-standard.com/multimedia/video-gallery/general/agar-muslim-ekjut-hoke-vote-dala-to-modi-sulat-jaega-navjot-singh-sidhu-82648.htm, last accessed 27 December 2019.

polarization, and ended up glueing Hindus of different castes together against the Congress' divisive strategy. Nitish Kumar's image among the Mahadalits further helped the situation.

Sheohar is one of the constituencies which, due to Naxal influence, needed the central government's intervention to restore a normal public life. In the last 10 years, the constituency witnessed unprecedented development and action against Naxalites. While BJP's Rama Devi wasn't a very strong face, the Modi wave combined with Nitish Kumar's popularity among women made Rama Devi look all set for victory. At the same time, RJD's Syed Faisal Ali wasn't even popular among Muslims and voters were calling him an outsider. Rama Devi eventually won the contest with more than 3.4 lakh votes.

JAMUI AND KHAGARIA

Jamui was another constituency which was affected by the Naxals. It was a high-profile seat because LJP's Chirag Paswan was contesting from here. Ground reports suggested that voters weren't very happy with the sitting MP, Paswan, but were reposing full faith in Modi. Kisan Samman Nidhi Yojana and pension for the elderly would ensure that the elderly population would vote for the NDA whereas the Pradhan Mantri Ujjwala Scheme made sure that women would again root for Modi.

Upon speaking with the populace, I got to understand that a few years back it was almost impossible to step out after sunset because of the Naxalites. However, their influence had considerably declined since Modi became the prime minister.

'*Ab naxaliyon ka khauf bahot kum ho gaya hai...kisi bhi samay bahar ja sakte hain...ab jo hume suraksha diya hai vote usi ko na denge?*' (Now the fear of the Naxals has reduced greatly. Now we can go out anytime. Won't we vote for the one who has given us this feeling of safety?) said a middle-aged man.

Chirag Paswan was famous among the youth for having worked in Bollywood, but that wasn't enough to win the elections. However, the

Modi–Nitish popularity came to his rescue and managed to persuade unhappy voters to cast their votes in his favour.

In Khagaria the sitting MP, Mehboob Ali Kaiser, was contesting against Krishna Yadav of the RJD. Modi's popularity can be reckoned from the fact that even after fielding a Muslim candidate during a time of religious polarization and with the anti-incumbency factor at play against him, he still had the voters' support.

Initially, voters were reluctant and Nitish Kumar had to hold rallies where he tried to explain how their vote for Mehboob Ali would actually be going to him or Modi. Voters followed his word.

A middle-aged man with whom I spoke at length told me an interesting line which was his rationale for voting for Mehboob Ali. He said: *'Engine sahi ho to dibbe bhi aage badh hi jaate hain!'* (If the engine is good, then the coaches too end up moving forward.) By this he meant he had faith in Modi and Nitish Kumar and that they would ensure development took place irrespective of who the MP is.

BEGUSARAI

A high-profile seat, Begusarai was among the most talked-about constituencies of the country. It was going to be a three-cornered contest between Giriraj Singh of the BJP, Kanhaiya Kumar of CPI and Tanveer Hassan of RJD.

My first interaction with the people of Begusarai was at a bus stop. I spoke to a group of 4–5 people. When asked if they saw Kanhaiya as a strong leader, one of them said: *'Arey wo gol gappa jeet bhi gaya to kya karega...kahan jayega?* (Even if he wins, what will he do? Where will he go?)

The biggest mistake a party can make is to underestimate the intelligence of voters. While the Congress tried to lure voters with the NYAY scheme, by fielding Kanhaiya, the CPI yet again proved that while the Opposition parties claimed to be united against Modi, they were not. Voters were smart enough to understand this.

A person who must be in his forties said, *'CPI se khade hain Kanhaiya...ab jis party ka astitva hi khatam ho gaya hai usey jitakar kya fayda...hum logon ki koi baat to aage pahunchegi nahi.* (Kanhaiya is representing CPI. What is the point of voting for a party that has nothing left of it? Our concerns will not reach anywhere [if such a party wins].)

Begusarai has over five lakh people from the Bhumihar caste, who identify themselves as hardcore nationalists. Kanhaiya—who, in some quarters, was called an anti-national after the JNU *tukde-tukde* controversy—was hoping Bhumihars would vote for him. In contrast, Modi had established himself as a nationalist leader who believed in the 'nation first' theory. Modi thus became the first choice for the Bhumihars. Kanhaiya's candidature had stirred a bigger sense of nationalism among voters, who were now adamant at ensuring the BJP's win at any cost.

I spoke to a few people while journeying through the constituency. A few saw a ray of hope in Kanhaiya; he was after all a young leader with a doctorate degree. The majority, however, wanted Modi back.

A young man who I met at a small shop, when asked about his choice of candidate, replied: '*Modiji ko hi denge...wo desh ko jodne aur aage badhane ka kaam kiye hain... Kanhaiya desh ke tukde-tukde karne ki baat karta hai...agar wo sansad mein chala gaya to Kashmir ko alag karne ki bhi maang karne lagega!*' (We will vote for Modi. He has worked for the integration and the development of the country. Kanhaiya talks of breaking up India into pieces. If he reaches the Parliament, he may start demanding a separate nationhood for Kashmir.)

After the announcement of the Balakot air strikes by the Indian Airforce, many opposition leaders started demanding evidence of it, which further added fuel to the fire. In Begusarai, around 70 per cent of the Muslims and 50 per cent of the Yadavs found the Opposition's demand for proofs justified.

Women, who were one of the biggest beneficiaries of Modi's welfare schemes, were completely on his side. The Triple Talaq Bill also played a crucial role and a huge chunk of Muslim women too ended up siding with Modi.

Nationalism, religious polarization, Modi wave and the Nitish–

Modi popularity among women were the main factors in the constituency where Giriraj Singh defeated Kanhaiya Kumar with a record margin of over 4.2 lakh votes.

MUNGER

In Munger it was a direct contest between JDU's Rajiv Ranjan Singh alias Lalan Singh and Congress' Nilam Devi, wife of MP Anant Singh who had been debarred from contesting due to his conviction in a murder case. Surajbhan Singh is one of the tallest leaders of Bihar and is popularly known as the Bahubali of Munger. However, his popularity stands to diminish outside the Munger assembly.

Lalan Singh didn't hold a very positive image and Surajbhan Singh's popularity was likely to beat him comfortably. The Modi–Nitish factor totally overshadowed all these local names and voters were expected to vote with the larger picture in mind. As I spoke to the local public, I realized that the Congress was very strong in the Munger region. However, in other assemblies it seemed to have lost the plot.

Continuing my journey, I went to a house that was being whitewashed. I was told that the daughter of the house was set to get married. I spoke to a few women in the house, trying to gather their political opinion. They didn't watch television and were not much aware about politics. I asked them if any government scheme had made their lives better. They told me that water crisis had been an issue but was getting resolved. One of the ladies pointed her finger to show me a paani ki tanki (water tank) that was getting installed and told me that water pipelines were also getting laid.

Nitish Kumar and Modi were complementary to each other with their image, work done and popularity among women owing to welfare schemes. When I asked these women about sharab bandi (alcohol ban), they told me that it was the best decision made by any government in a long time. *'Ye sabse achcha kaam kiye hai Nitish sarkar...ab maradana pi kar nahi aate...gharon mein maar-peet bhi nahi hoti...paise bhi bachte hain...aur kabhi peete bhi hain to chup chupa ke peete hain!'* (This is the best thing done by the Nitish government. The men don't come home drunk now. There are no beatings at home. Money is also saved. And even if they do drink, they don't do it openly).

SITAMARHI

This constituency close to the Nepal border was witnessing a contest between JDU's Sunil Kumar Pintu and RJD's Arjun Rai. Here too the BJP candidate was overshadowed by bigger political faces like Modi and Nitish Kumar. I had some interesting interactions here and will not especially forget a particular one.

I was in a khet when I saw a person returning to his home in his bailgaadi (bullock cart). On seeing him I quickened my pace and boarded his bailgaadi—the act reminding me of my childhood when we'd run to get on passing bullock carts like this. I asked him: *'Bhaiya, iss baar kise jitaoge?'* (Who will you help win this time?) His response would probably make even Gulzaar saab speechless. *'Bhaiya, ab bijli aane lagi hai to laalten ki kya jarurat hai?'* (Who needs a kerosene lamp now that we have electricity?) It took me a few seconds to comprehend his metaphorical answer. Laalten (lantern) is the RJD's symbol, and Modi's rural electrification had made laaltens or kerosene lamps obsolete.

An interesting thing that I observed was that the alcohol ban imposed by the Bihar government had pushed men to cross the Nepal border to get drunk. The wives of these men were still happy as they drank less often, less openly and did not come home drunk regularly.

MUZZAFARPUR AND GOPALGANJ

In Muzzafarpur, BJP's sitting MP, Ajay Nishad, was contesting against VIP's Raj Bhushan Chaudhary. As evident on the ground, it wasn't going to be a tough contest for the BJP.

I was en route to Muzzafarpur from Patna when I saw a small temple on the side of a road and immediately stopped my car. I went inside the temple to pray and while coming out I saw a big poster of Lalu Yadav's elder son Tej Pratap Yadav. Some RJD workers were also there. I spoke to them.

'Kya bhaiya, har jagah aap ka hi prachaar chal raha hai...lagta hai iss baar bahut seat aane wali hain!' (Your canvassing is in progress everywhere. It seems this time you are going to win a lot of seats!) I said smilingly.

One of them responded: *'Prachaar to hum kar rahe hain magar andar se janta ka pulse to Modi wala hai.'* (We are canvassing, but deep down inside we know that the mood of the people is with Modi this time.)

This was huge, especially coming from the horse's mouth! It not only showed how the RJD workers were themselves not too confident about their party, but was also proof of the magnitude of the Modi tsunami. Similar sentiments were observed in Gopalganj too. An SC seat with a considerable number of Brahmins, Gopalganj was the birth place of Lalu Prasad Yadav and an RJD bastion. However, JDU and BJP won this seat in 2009 and 2014, respectively.

While conducting a debate among the ground leaders of the contesting parties in Gopalganj as part of the *'Target Par Neta Ji'* segment of my show *Lalkar*, I noticed that the audience was defending Modi vociferously. I have seldom seen such euphoria for any political leader. When the RJD leader asked what Modi had done in the past five years, the audience bursted with replies: surgical strikes, Balakot air strikes, Awas Yojana, Ujjwala Yojana—the list was endless.

In the debate when the RJD leader commented, *'Modi ne Rafale mein paisa khaya,'* (Modi had taken money in the Rafale deal) the audience not only laughed but accused the Opposition of deliberately delaying the defence deal to harm the interests of the nation. Such was their faith in Modi.

4

HINDI HEARTLAND: RAJASTHAN, MADHYA PRADESH, JHARKHAND AND CHHATTISGARH

Spread across a quarter of India's total geographical area, the Hindi heartland is home to almost one-third of the country's population. The spoken language in the area through different dialects is Hindustani, which is a mix of Hindi and Urdu.

The BJP had received an overwhelming response in the Hindi heartland in the 2014 Lok Sabha elections, with the party emerging victorious in 190 of the 225 seats across 10 states in the region. The Opposition was left with merely 15 seats, with other parties and independent candidates winning the remaining 20 seats. Three of the Hindi heartland states—Madhya Pradesh, Chhattisgarh and Rajasthan—slipped from the BJP's hands in the state assembly elections held in 2018, raising genuine doubts over the party's ability to replicate its 2014 performance. The party had won 62 of the 65 seats in these three states in the 2014 Lok Sabha elections.

Repeating the outcome of the 2014 elections seemed a far-fetched possibility for the BJP, but only until we surveyed thousands in these states. We found that the voters' trust in Modi was very much intact and that there were several factors that contributed to a different voting pattern in the assembly elections.

In this chapter we will talk about four states, namely Rajasthan, Madhya Pradesh, Chhattisgarh and Jharkhand.

RAJASTHAN

The story of Rajasthan's 2019 Lok Sabha election kicked in a few days ahead of the 2018 assembly elections. In 2014, the BJP had won all 25 seats in Rajasthan, reducing the Congress' tally to zero. However, a huge anti-establishment wave against the Vasundhara Raje government made Modi and Amit Shah realize that they would be unable to save the state in the 2018 assembly elections. In a rally Amit Shah had said: '*Vasundharaji par aashirwaad banaye rakhiye un par vishwas rakhiye!*' (Please continue keeping faith in and blessings on Vasundhara!)—which can be read as a reflection of this sentiment.

With the Opposition's popular slogan '*Modi tujhse bair nahi, Vasundhara teri khair nahi,*' (Modi, we have no enmity with you, but we will not forgive Vasundhara) the BJP was all set to lose the state, but its margin of loss was still in question. This margin would decide the fate of the BJP and the Congress in the 2019 Lok Sabha elections. The only thing that was etched in stone was that the BJP would not be able to repeat its 2014 tally.

Another trend that was against BJP retaining the state was the fact that no party had ever won consecutive elections in Rajasthan. There is a famous saying in the state, '*Roti dono taraf se senko, tabhi acchi banti hai,*' which in political terms translates into both BJP and Congress being given an equal chance to ensure that the state grows. The BJP had had its turn, and going by this logic, it was the Congress' turn now.

Before the ticket distribution in Rajasthan, there was an internal tussle within the BJP. While Amit Shah wanted Gajendra Singh Shekhawat as the state president of the party, Vasundhara Raje chose her close aide Madan Lal Saini. Vasundhara had her own faction of supporters which constituted roughly 100–110 MLAs and so Amit Shah had to agree with her choice.

Another factor that resulted in the BJP's loss was the khanan mafia, people who were close to the BJP and promoted more in comparison to local civil workers, labourers and mistris who costed the latter group their jobs. In the name of environmental clearances, several construction works were stopped, which resulted in huge job loss in the construction sector, thereby affecting the labour class. However, illegal construction work kept progressing.

Moreover, strictly with respect to the history associated with Rajasthan, the state can be broadly divided into seven regions, and this division conforms to its geography and demography as well.

Marwar: The Marwar region is in south-west Rajasthan. Marwar or Marwad is formed from two words: 'Maru' which means desert and 'Wad' which means area. It includes Jodhpur, Barmer, Nagaur and Pali. People who belong to the Marwar region are called Marwaris and mostly belong to the business class.

Shekhwati: The northeast region of Rajasthan, Shekhwati is basically a large portion of the Thar Desert. It includes Jhunjhunu and Siker. Known for their valour and bravery, the Shekhwats are driven by a sense of patriotism.

Jangla Pradesh: Less populated than other regions, Jangla Pradesh includes Bikaner, Hanumangarh and Ganganagar.

Matsyanagar: Historically known as the Matsya kingdom, the people of Matsyanagar are known to be descendants of Lord Krishna, Lord Rama and Arjuna. People in this region practice syncretic Hindu–Muslim religion and many of them are Hindus who converted to Islam. Matsyanagar includes Alwar and Bharatpur.

Mewar: The land of the Rajputs, Mewar is a south-central portion of Rajasthan and includes the present-day districts of Udaipur, Chittorgarh, Bhilwara, Rajasmand, Pirawa tehsil of Jhalawar district along with a couple of districts of Madhya Pradesh and some parts of Gujarat.

Hadoti: The region near the Chambal River, Hadoti includes Kota, Baran and Jhalawar. This region is a BJP fortress and even in the 2018 assembly elections, when there was a huge anti-incumbency wave against Vasundhara Raje, the BJP managed to win maximum seats from this region.

Dhundhar: Dhundhar, also known as the Jaipur region, is a historical region of the state of Rajasthan. It includes the districts of Jaipur, Dausa, Sawai Madhopur, Tonk and the northern part of Karauli district. This region is the citadel of Congress leader Sachin Pilot.

Local parties here, as elsewhere, have greater influence over area-specific elections rather than statewide or national elections. In state-level elections, regional parties play an important role and in Rajasthan particularly, independent candidates—with around 60 per cent of them being rebel candidates who had been denied tickets by parties—hold significant influence. These rebel leaders enjoy enough power to make or break the election results and could reduce the vote margin of a party to such extents that it could even lose the election.

Jats, Rajputs and Gujars dominate the political narrative in Rajasthan. The general category constitutes around 18–20 per cent of the demography, with the rest being ST, SC or Muslim communities.

Even after being fairly cognizant of the fact that the Congress Party had a good chance of winning the assembly elections, an internal tussle was brewing in the party's state unit. Both Sachin Pilot and Ashok Gehlot wanted to be Rajasthan's chief minister, but the way to achieve that was to have the maximum number of MLAs on their side.

Sachin Pilot being a Gujar had a defined region that includes Dausa, Sawai Madhopur and Tonk. He also had the young voters in his kitty due to his age. Ashok Gehlot, on the other hand, was respected by people across caste and religious lines. He and his schemes were appreciated by all and since he had already been the chief minister once, the race to the chair was any day far easier for him.

During campaigning, the Congress realized that Gujars were the biggest community in the region, and declaring Ashok Gehlot as a chief ministerial candidate was not in their best interests. So, they let people believe that Sachin Pilot could also be their chief minister. Ashok Gehlot expressed his displeasure at the Congress' decision of not declaring him as the chief ministerial candidate and in a rally, pointing at himself, said: *'Ye jo aapke saamne hain ye bhi CM ho sakte hain.* (The one standing in front of you can also be your CM.)

If the Congress were to win with a record number of seats, it could choose between Pilot and Gehlot as the chief minister. However, Gehlot could only benefit if the Congress was to get close to majority seats. The Congress winning less than 100 seats would mean that Ashok Gehlot would have to seek the support of independent MLAs with whom he shared good relations, and only then could he become the chief minister. This was the reason why Gehlot interfered in Pilot's region during the ticket distribution process. The process of ticket distribution had resulted in a lot of disturbance within the party, with several leaders who had been denied tickets coming forward to rebel.

The 2018 assembly election results had been a major setback for the BJP and its supporters. But despite the gloom, there was also hope that the party would perform decently in the Lok Sabha elections–due to vote share. While the Congress with 100 seats had a vote share of 39.3 per cent, BJP with 73 seats had a vote share of 38.8 per cent, which was only 0.5 per cent less than that of the Congress.

The Lok Sabha elections differed from assembly elections in many ways: the issues were different, the choice of leadership was different and people were ready to rise above caste lines to make their favourite national party win.

One member from almost every other family in Rajasthan is serving the nation at the border, and with the surgical strikes, Balakot air strikes and a stern stand against Pakistan, Modi had struck the right chord with the people of Rajasthan. Making the election campaign about nationalism was likely to prove effective.

There was a huge Modi wave and despite the BJP losing the state elections six months earlier, they still had a good hold on the Lok Sabha contest. Except for a few seats where it was going to be a close contest owing to several reasons, the BJP was set for a comfortable win across the state. The contest was going to be difficult in Nagaur, Jodhpur, Barmer and Tonk–Sawai Madhopur due to tall leaders contesting, caste composition, independent rebel leaders joining back the parties and several other factors.

Let us analyse these constituencies one by one.

Nagaur

This constituency holds historic importance as it was here that Jat politics originated in the country. With Rajasthan's demography comprising around 25 per cent Jats, winning the confidence of voters from the community was an essential condition to win the elections.

Across Rajasthan, the Jat and Rajput communities are always locking horns with each other. From Nagaur, the NDA had fielded Rashtriya Loktantrik Party (RLP) founder Hanuman Beniwal against Dr Jyoti Mirdha of the Congress Party. It became a Jat vs Jat contest, with Dr Mirdha enjoying an advantageous position since her family had had six MPs from the region and hence was very popular among the Jats. It was said that the Rajputs were majorly supporting the Congress despite Gajendra Singh Shekhawat campaigning for Hanuman Beniwal.

The Congress had the support of the Muslims, SCs and Rajputs, while the Jats were roughly equally divided between the BJP and the Congress. However, this was as per caste composition and an assumption that the voters would follow the leaders of their respective castes or religions. The factor which absolutely overshadowed this equation was a huge nationalism wave—in addition to an unsurmountable Modi wave—that was sweeping the state, bringing together voters from across caste divides. My interactions with as many as a thousand people belonging to different castes revealed the same. As Hanuman Beniwal said in a rally: *'Dushmani Vidhan Sabha mein nikal li, ab desh ka socho.'* (You've had your revenge in the assembly elections, now it's time to think about the country.)

Jodhpur

With the removal of Pali from the Jodhpur constituency after delimitation, Rajputs and Jats are now equally impactful in Jodhpur. The contest between Gajendra Singh Shekhawat and Vaibhav Gehlot, the son of Chief Minister Ashok Gehlot, was the most awaited contest in Rajasthan.

Rajput, Bishnoi and Jat are the three main castes in Jodhpur. It was only after visiting Rajasthan that I came to know that the word 'Bishnoi' comes from bees (20 in Hindi) + nau (9 in Hindi), which refers to the 29 commandments that are central to the Bishnoi philosophy. The Bishnoi community has always been a core voter base of the Congress but the Congress' stand on the army in the aftermath of the surgical strikes led them to rethink their stance. The leaders of the Opposition not only questioned surgical strikes but the Opposition's ecosystem had also called it 'Farzical Strike' ('farzi' in Urdu means fake). All this while, almost every family—irrespective of whether they belonged to the Bishnoi, Rajput or Jat community—had members serving at the border. Unlike the Congress, the BJP had very smartly customized their leaders' speeches depending on the place they were being delivered. In Jodhpur, Modi talked about nationalism, Balakot air strikes and BJP's strict position against Pakistan.

In families with a member serving in the armed forces, the common sentiment was against the Congress Party. A member of one such family said: *'Congress bolti hai sab farzi hai...aur jab hum apne bete se baat karte hain to wo batata hai yahan to roz goli baari ho rahi...'* (The Congress says it's all fake. But when we talk to our son, he tells us there's firing every day on the border.) This anti-Congress sentiment around the 'fake' strikes then translated into communities, villages and finally entire districts turning against the Congress.

Another factor that played an important role was the Congress' failure to understand caste composition and its importance. Gajendra Singh Shekhawat had all the Rajput voters with him whereas Jats, who always tend to vote against Rajputs, were expecting a Jat leader to contest against Gajendra Singh Shekhawat. However, Congress leaders' 'putra moh' seemed to render them blind to the party's bleak future. Congress' cadre too went against the party and that was the point when they lost the battle. Further, Ashok Gehlot came from the Mali caste and could only get the votes of a few Jats for his son, based solely on his goodwill.

Hanuman Beniwal campaigned for Gajendra Singh Shekhawat, asking voters to think beyond caste lines and vote for the nation, eventually persuading them to vote for the BJP. This shifted some of the Jat voters to the BJP.

Barmer

Barmer was a prestige fight for the Congress, as it had fielded Jaswant Singh's son Manvendra Singh against BJP's Kailash Choudhary. Manvendra had joined the Congress ahead of the assembly elections where the party had used him as a scapegoat against Vasundhara Raje. Manvendra, however, had joined the party aiming to win the Lok Sabha elections and hence was given a ticket.

Barmer and Jaisalmer together constitute one Lok Sabha seat. Barmer has more Jats than Rajputs. Jaisalmer, on the other hand, has SCs, Muslims and Rajputs constituting the majority of the population, all of whom tend to lean towards the Congress. With Kailash Choudhary being a Jat, Manvendra Singh was going to be the obvious choice for the Rajputs.

Gajendra Singh Shekhawat and Hanuman Beniwal held many rallies, trying their luck with sway voters. Here again, the nationalism wave became a big factor and people voted for the BJP and Modi. The Balakot air strikes, avenging the death of 44 jawans martyred in the Pulwama attack, had cemented Modi's image as a strong leader.

Tonk–Sawai Madhopur

Tonk–Sawai Madhopur, one of the 25 Lok Sabha constituencies in Rajasthan, was Sachin Pilot's bastion. Gujars, Meenas and Muslims are the three most dominant communities of this constituency. In 2014, not less than 70 per cent of the Meena community voted for the BJP. However, in 2019, the figure decreased when the Congress fielded Namonarayan Meena.

The seats were expected to go to the Congress, with the following composition: Muslims were going to support the Congress, as the BJP had always projected itself as a staunch Hindu party. The Meenas, one of the largest communities in this constituency, were also going to support the Congress because of Namonarayan Meena.

However, despite all these equations, Gujar youth were supporting the BJP. Gujars identify themselves as a nationalist community and hence were inclined more towards the BJP, even though Sachin Pilot belongs to the same community.

Yet again, Hanuman Beniwal got a majority of the Jat voters to the BJP, thus ensuring the BJP wins even the most difficult seats.

MADHYA PRADESH

The 2018 assembly elections had been a major setback for the incumbent BJP government in the state. One of the most popular BJP chief ministers, Shivraj Singh Chouhan, couldn't save the state. The BJP won 109 seats and the Congress, 114 seats. The majority mark was 115. Even with fewer seats, the BJP had managed to get a slightly higher vote share than the Congress. There are some political analysts who project election results assuming a direct correlation between vote share and seats, which doesn't always hold true. While the BJP had 41 per cent vote share on their side and the Congress had 40.9 per cent, the Congress still emerged with more seats under its belt. Interestingly, there were more than 15 seats where the vote margin was less than 1,000.

There was a natural anti-incumbency factor against Chouhan due to his 15-year-long tenure even though it witnessed development and progress in the state. However, Chouhan made things worse for himself by making certain unnecessary statements that worked against him, even among his core voters. During a rally, Chouhan, in order to please Dalit voters, claimed that nobody could remove the SC/ST Act. The fact was that nobody had even thought about repealing the Act, but the mention of it resulted in the voters from the general category–his core voters—drifting away from him. Another problem that could have led to Chouhan's defeat was him not taking the sangathan (organization) into consideration while disbursing tickets. The BJP lost some seats which had been its forte—Vidisha and Gwalior being two such constituencies.

The anti-incumbency against Chouhan, however, did not imply a sentiment against Modi or the BJP, and the vote share bears witness to the same. A myth portrayed as truth by mainstream media was that the BJP lost the state due to farmers' protest, which was not true. Farmers' uprising happened in the Neemach region, which is a rural belt, where the BJP had won the majority of seats.

Since Chouhan took up the weight of the election campaigning entirely on his shoulders, Prime Minister Modi didn't do as many rallies as was expected. Chouhan, on the other hand, alone held more than 150 rallies. In the end, the BJP fell short of the majority mark by six seats in the 2019 assembly elections. But what changed over a period of only 7–8 months that led to the BJP winning a record 28 seats out of 29?

In a village near Gwalior city, I spoke to a tribal man who was happy with the Modi government. I cynically mentioned how the Congress had defeated the BJP and how the same shall repeat itself in 2019. The man not only disagreed with me but took me to the house which he had received under the Pradhan Mantri Awas Yojana. In a similar instance in a village in Bhind, a family received a new toilet under the Swachh Bharat Abhiyan. An even more interesting story was that of a Muslim family. The husband, the sole breadwinner of the family, had recently gone through a life-saving operation as a beneficiary under the Pradhan Mantri Ayushman Yojana. I spoke to his wife, who said: *'Main toh Modiji ko hi vote dungi warna aaj itna paise kahan se laate inke ilaaj ke liye... mere shauhar kisi ko bhi vote dein, main Modiji ko hi dungi.'* (I will vote for Modi. How would we have managed money for the medical treatment? Irrespective of who my husband votes for, I will vote for Modi.)

If nationalism was the driving factor in Rajasthan, various central government schemes had worked their way into the hearts of voters in Madhya Pradesh—the Pradhan Mantri Awas Yojana and the Pradhan Mantri Ayushman Bharat Yojana having the most impact.

Women and youth were unanimously voting for Modi and there was a general perception that the BJP had been punished once during the assembly elections and Modi should not be punished again.

We will now analyse a few constituencies which everyone had their eyes on and which would define the future course of Indian politics.

Guna

Guna was Jyotiraditya Scindia's home and citadel. He had not lost a single election here in the last 17 years. However, 2019 was a different case altogether. Scindia had lost ground and he too realized it. This was the reason why his wife and even his son came out to campaign for him, trying all means to save the seat and guard the family's prestige.

Against Jyotiraditya Scindia was BJP's Krishna Pal Singh Yadav. Yadav had worked as Scindia's MP-representative before he parted ways with Scindia ahead of the 2018 assembly polls because of a dispute over being denied a ticket from Mungaoli.

Assemblies such as Chanderi and Mungaoli, which had always been anti-BJP, went with the BJP this time as Jyotiraditya remained away from ground and had almost no interaction with the local people. Moreover, assemblies such as Shivpuri, Ashok Nagar and Kolaras, where the BJP usually leads, gave them an extended margin this time, thus leading to a huge defeat for Jyotiraditya Scindia with over a lakh votes in margin.

Unlike in the assembly elections, the Lok Sabha elections were managed by the sangathan and hence it was ensured that local leaders reached out to voters and made them aware of what all had changed in the last five years. The sangathan had identified local leaders who then conducted various small-scale meetings where they patiently explained to voters about the BJP's manifesto and all the work done by the party.

Bhopal

Sadhvi Pragya vs Digvijay Singh—one of the most awaited contests of the 2019 elections—wasn't just a BJP vs Congress fight. Rather, the RSS was trying to send out a message to the world through this symbolic gesture—that there was no concept of saffron terror or Hindu terror. Prime Minister Modi himself defended Sadhvi Pragya Singh Thakur's candidature, saying the 'Hindu terror' accusations against her were a malicious attempt to tarnish India's age-old legacy.

With the fight being to protect the Hindutva ideology from getting defamed, the RSS was more active than ever before. The Sangh workers conducted more than 5,000 small meetings and left no stone unturned to ensure BJP's victory here. The result was to give a strong message to the Congress and the rest of the Opposition that voters had rejected the term 'saffron terror' that had been coined by them. It was all about voting for Modi and the RSS.

Bhopal constituency has eight assemblies, with Huzur, Govindpura, Uttar Bhopal and Dakshin–Paschim Bhopal being the most important ones. The Huzur region has a mixed population in terms of caste and religion and it has never been tough for the BJP to win. Govindpura is the region from where BJP leader Babu Lal Gaur, a former chief minister of Madhya Pradesh, hails, and hence voters of this region had a natural inclination towards the BJP. Uttar Bhopal has around 60 per cent Muslim voters and Arif Aqueel of the Congress had never lost an election from here since 1998. Digvijay Singh was likely to receive maximum votes from here. Dakshin–Paschim Bhopal had considerable number of jhuggi voters who also favoured Digvijay Singh. Sehore sided with the BJP during the time of the assembly elections and was poised to be a catalyst region in the Lok Sabha elections as well. In terms of the polling percentage, Sehore emerged as the frontrunner with 76.3 per cent, while 66 per cent of the voters polled in Uttar Bhopal. The high voting percentage in both these assemblies indicated that the voters were coming out for the BJP in their stronghold and there was a visible polarization in Dakshin–Paschim assembly.

It is also to be noted that historically Bhopal had been the BJP's fortress. Even when the party was defeated in the 2009 Lok Sabha elections, it won in Bhopal with over 45 per cent vote share.

During my travel I always make it a point to exercise regularly. I remember running past the statue of Raja Bhoj beside the Bhopal Lake early one morning when I saw two burqa-clad women. I was curious about their views on the election.

'*Iss baar Bhopal ka chunao garma raha hai?*' (Do you think the elections in Bhopal are picking up?) I asked.

They were initially reluctant to respond, but later whispered: '*Garma toh raha hai...par vo Sadhvi Pragya Modi ke naam par jeet jayegi...agar kisi aur ko ticket dete toh hum bhi vote dene ka sochte*

...par Arif bhai ne humien iss baar Panje ka samarthan karne ko kaha hai!' (It is picking up, but Sadhvi Pragya has an edge because of Modi. If BJP would have given the ticket to someone else, then even we would have thought of voting for the BJP. But Arif Aqueel has asked us to support the Congress this time.)

The response reflected the general sentiment in the constituency. Bhopal, being the capital of Madhya Pradesh, hosts government servants at large. Unlike other places where government servants generally tend to incline towards the Congress, in Bhopal they recalled Chief Minister Digvijay Singh's tenure—he was reluctant to increase their pay. Singh's record as chief minister also drove many pro-development voters away from the Congress. In their testimonies they recalled repeated power cuts in the state. Some also said that it was a political tactic by Chief Minister Kamal Nath to nudge Congress Chief Sonia Gandhi to give Digvijay Singh the ticket from Bhopal. A loss suffered by Singh in the state would increase Kamal Nath's hold on the state Congress unit. The state Congress has historically been known for three factions—Scindia, Kamal Nath and Digvijay camps. Nevertheless, the youth was not conscious of these factors and was majorly supporting Modi beyond caste lines.

Chhindwara

Chhindwara was one of the most high-profile seats. Kamal Nath, the current chief minister of Madhya Pradesh, had retained this seat since 1980, except once when Sundar Lal Patwa of the BJP managed to win it in the 1997 bypolls. This is one of the two seats (other than Guna) which the Congress had won in 2014, despite a huge Modi wave.

It was a prestige seat for Kamal Nath as his son Nakul Kamal Nath was contesting from here. Contesting against him was BJP's Nathan Shah who wasn't a popular face. In fact, independent candidate Manmohan Shah Batti was more famous, but the BJP did not give him a ticket as he once had set the Ramayan ablaze.

Among all the seats which the BJP was possibly losing, Chhindwara was the most likely and Guna was second in line. Results, however, saw the BJP winning in Guna while the Congress won Chhindwara.

Ratlam

Formerly known as Jhabua constituency, this is one constituency where the Congress lost due to its own internal tussle, upsetting their ground cadre to the point where they did not campaign or work at all.

This constituency has two main assemblies, namely Ratlam (Rural and City) and Jhabua. Jhabua is an assembly that tends to go with the Congress and the Congress managed an easy lead here, whereas the BJP has an edge in Ratlam. Since 1980, the Jhabua seat was won by the Congress, except in 2014, when the BJP managed to win it owing to the huge Modi wave. More specifically, this seat had always been won by a member of the Bhuria family. This time too, the Congress gave a ticket to the Bhurias, upsetting its cadre all the more. The Bhuria family assumed that it would be an easy win, but they had not accounted for the tribal voters who were in majority here and had witnessed rapid development under Prime Minister Modi. Schemes like the Pradhan Mantri Aawas Yojana and Ujjwala Yojana were doing wonders for the BJP here. However, it wasn't the Congress that was defeated here, but it was a defeat of the Bhurias, as voters were voting against them and not the Congress. Many Congress cadres in private complained: *'Agar ek hi pariwar ko ticket milte rahega toh hum kis liye raajneeti mein hai?'* (If one family keeps getting the ticket, then why are we in politics?)

Indore

My birthplace Indore, which is also the cleanest city in India, came to the limelight after the BJP did not give a ticket to former Lok Sabha Speaker Sumitra Mahajan. There were reports that Maharastrian voters, who were sizeable in number in Indore, might go against the BJP. BJP's Shankar Lalwani was given a ticket to contest against Congress' Pankaj Sanghvi. The upper castes were with Modi. The youth and women too were supporting the BJP. The only concern for the saffron party were the Maharastrian voters, who were later pacified after Sumitra Mahajan appealed to them in public and in private group meetings. The BJP won this seat with a record margin of over five lakh votes.

JHARKHAND

With over 32 per cent tribal voters, Jharkhand is a state of silent voters. I had to converse with a lot of people to get an idea about the direction of the political wind. Voters here largely move according to the region to which they belong. Jharkhand can be broadly divided into five regions: North Chhota Nagpur, South Chhota Nagpur, Palamu, Santhal Pargana division and Kolhar division.

North Chhota Nagpur

The area is dominated by tribals. It includes three constituencies: Kodarma, Dhanbad and Giridih. The Dhanbad and Giridih constituencies were BJP's strong seats, with the party winning these seats since 2009. In the Kodarma constituency, Jharkhand Vikas Morcha (JVM) and Jharkhand Mukti Morcha (JMM) had a stronghold.

For the 2019 Lok Sabha elections, the BJP fielded Annapurna Devi Yadav, an ex-RJD leader, against Babulal Marandi of JVM. Annapurna Devi could beat Babulal Marandi in popularity any day. Similar to Madhya Pradesh, here too development work and Modi's government schemes had a bigger role to play than the nationalism wave.

Santhal Pargana Divison

It is the northernmost region of Jharkhand. It has more than 93 per cent rural voters and 46 per cent tribal voters, and it includes Rajmahal, Godda and Dumka constituencies. In all these constituencies JMM and JVM had a more solid grip than the BJP. However, in 2009, the BJP managed to win the Rajmahal constituency; in 2014, though, JMM took this seat away from them. In 2019, the BJP fielded Hemlal Murmu, who wasn't a very strong leader against JMM's Vijay Kumar Hansdak.

From the Dumka seat, JMM's Shibu Soren was contesting against

BJP's Sunil Soren. Sunil, a disciple of Shibu Soren, had contested elections earlier too but had not managed to win. However, this time he appealed to voters to vote for him as it was his last election. But the sympathy factor could not overcome the developmental work undertaken by the BJP under Chief Minister Raghubar Das.

Raghubar Das had been preparing for the elections for quite some time. He took various initiatives to defeat JVM and JMM in their own ground. One such initiative was starting announcements in Santhali language at the railway stations in these regions. Santhali was also taught to students at school. All this led to an increase in tribal vote base of the BJP.

Shibu Soren was contesting elections with *Jal, Jungle, Zameen* (water, forests, land) campaign. However, the tribal voters who voted for the JMM or JVM earlier had now witnessed development in the last five years of the Modi government, and so for them *Jal, Jungle, Zameen* was not the main political plank in the Lok Sabha. While Sunil Soren contested keeping Hindutva and 'his last election' as the main issue, what the tribal voters wanted was tangible development.

Palamu Division

The Palamu Division has two constituencies—Palamu and Chatra. In 2009, the BJP had almost no existence in these two constituencies, but this was changing fast and the party started gaining considerable grounds here after Modi took over at the centre.

I was talking to a local person of Chatra, who explained how they wanted the BJP to win, but if the ticket was given to Sunil Kumar Singh, they would oppose him. Sunil Kumar Singh was a sitting MP and was infamous for staying aloof from the ground realities and never engaging with the local people. On the polling day, I spoke to a person who had come to vote. He was angry that Sunil Kumar Singh had been given a ticket, but still went with the BJP because they could not let Modi lose. Yet again it was evident that people were not electing an MP, but electing a prime minister.

South Chhota Nagpur

The region comprises of Lohardaga, Ranchi, Hazaribagh and Khunti. Ranchi had been a Congress forte until 2014, when the BJP managed to win the seat riding the Modi wave. Sahu voters are the biggest factor in this region owing to their considerable numbers. There was pro-incumbency wave for BJP on ground.

The Khunti constituency has been a BJP stronghold and BJP's Karia Munda had consistently won this seat since 1991, except losing once in 2004. In this constituency there were soft Hindus and converted Christians. While soft Hindus were the fixed vote base of the BJP, converted Christians had an inclination towards the JMM, JVM and Congress. This polarized the elections. There were some sentiments against Karia Munda, which the BJP realized, and fielded Arjun Munda from this seat. Arjun Munda won the seat by a narrow margin.

CHHATTISGARH

Of the states where elections were held in 2018, Chhattisgarh was one that gave a lot of confidence to the Congress. The BJP suffered a major loss of 34 seats in the state and the Congress swept the election, winning 68 out of 90 seats. While conducting a survey before the assembly elections, we found that there was some anti-incumbency against the Raman Singh government; we hadn't anticipated it to be of the quantum which the result reflected. It also meant that the voters were silent. Unlike in Madhya Pradesh and Rajasthan, the Congress here formed the government on its own and hence it was widely expected that it would do well in the Lok Sabha elections as well. However, it was difficult to say anything with certainty, since assembly elections and general elections are fought on different factors.

While the Congress was feeling rejuvenated a few months ahead of the Lok Sabha elections, the BJP was spending time mulling over what went wrong.

Chhattisgarh is broadly divided into five regions: Durg, Raipur, Bastar, Kanker and Sarguja. Bastar is one such region where the BJP has always been weak in assembly elections, the reason for it being the proclivity of the tribal voters to go with the Congress. A popular tribal leader, Kawasi Lakhma, has a stronghold in this region and the people are familiar with him. He won the assembly elections from Konta constituency. Similarly, Sarguja region has Sitapur seat, which is a tribal seat, and tribal voters here have historically been inclined towards the Congress.

However, in some areas of Sarguja, such as Bharatpur–Sonhat, which shares a border with Madhya Pradesh, the BJP was organizationally strong, but the anti-incumbency against the sitting MLA led to BJP's defeat in this assembly.

The major factors that helped the Congress defeat the BJP in the assembly elections were Congress' promises such as loan waiver to farmers, minimum support price of ₹2,500/quintal for paddy, two-year bonus to farmers, reducing electricity rate to half and unemployment allowance to the youth. Apart from this, there was very strong anti-incumbency against the ministers in the Raman Singh government. On interacting with the party workers, I could sense a lack of enthusiasm among them to mobilize voters for the candidates. The BJP tried to make the election about Raman Singh, but it ended up becoming about the candidates. Generally, the BJP performs well in an election which has a broad narrative; the more local and micro an election gets, the BJP ends up facing more electoral struggle.

Demographically, Chhattisgarh has over 16 per cent population belonging to the Sahu caste, a core voter group of the BJP, who play a decisive role in the political narrative of the state. BJP fielded 14 candidates belonging to the Sahu caste, out of which only one of them won. This indicated resentment against the BJP. One of the prominent reasons for the Sahu caste to not rally with the BJP was the insensitive remark by the then sports minister, Bhaiya Lal, who abused some of the Sahu voters when they approached him for work. A video of the same had gone viral ahead of the assembly elections. The BJP tried to placate the Sahu voters, but they were not convinced and catalysed the silent wave against the BJP.

There were five seats (Navagarh, Bilaspur, Baikunthpur, Raipur and Mahendragarh) where the BJP always had a stronghold, but silent voters led to the BJP losing even these five seats.

If we talk about the 2019 elections, the main factors deciding the narrative in Chhattisgarh were not local issues, but national development and the Hindutva ideology. Since the issues were national and the BJP managed to successfully weave a broad narrative, the mandate was for Modi, as the BJP started on a strong electoral wicket. However, since the Congress was coming out of a massive electoral victory in the assembly elections in the state, it was a serious contender for all 11 seats. The BJP did not repeat its mistakes committed in the assembly elections, and changed the tickets in most of the seats. New MP candidates were fielded to restrict any possible anti-incumbency. This also gave a positive signal to the voters and party workers.

Our survey on the ground also suggested that the Pulwama attack also played an important role in swaying the middle- and upper-class voters in the state. Add to this the Modi factor in the state, and the BJP had a winning combination in the Lok Sabha elections. Further, the voters had vented their anger a few months back in the assembly elections. There was no remaining motive to punish the BJP.

The youth, who were first lured by the Congress when it promised unemployment allowance, went with the BJP when the Congress failed to fulfil its promise ahead of the Lok Sabha elections. It is difficult for any government to fulfil expectations in such a short period of time, but the inability to move in the direction of the promises made at the time of the assembly elections made voters question the 'neeyat (intention)' of the Congress in the state. The BJP capitalized on this sentiment.

Apart from these broad factors, there were some constituencies where some more local factors also played a role in deciding the electoral verdict. In Korba, there was a very strong anti-incumbency against the sitting MP Dr Banshilal Mahto. The new BJP candidate, Jyotinand Dubey, was popular among the masses but the Congress' candidate, Jyotsna Charan Das Mahant, wife of Charan Das Mahant, was preferred by most because of her past association to the constituency. Bastar was the only region where the Congress could deliver some of its promises made during the assembly elections before the Lok Sabha elections. With aggressive campaigning by the state leaders, the Congress was successful in building a narrative which did not circle around Prime Minister Modi. Despite the disbursement of central government welfare schemes in the region, the tribal preferred the Congress over the BJP.

Apart from these two seats, the BJP ended up victorious in the remaining nine seats.

◆

In short, the surge and dominance of the BJP in Madhya Pradesh, Rajasthan, and Chhattisgarh months after the loss in the assembly elections demonstrated the maturity of Indian voters. When it came to state elections, the voters gave preference to state issues, and in the national elections, they looked at the credibility of the prime ministerial candidates. This also proved how even a day is a long time in Indian politics, and outcomes are dynamic and not static. It also brought to light the successful welfare schemes which acted as the catalyst in all the three states. Election management is secondary; giving a reason to the voter is primary. The elections in these three states and the 2019 general elections were fought more by the people compared to the party workers. The outcome also busted the mistake committed by many analysts when they extrapolate state election result and the vote shares therein on national elections.

5

STRATEGIC WINS: MAHARASHTRA AND GUJARAT

Maharashtra went into election in a zone of unpredictability. Since 2015, the Shiv Sena, one of the oldest alliance partners of the BJP, had been acting as its opponent inside the government. Every second edition of the Shiv Sena mouthpiece *Saamna* carried a critique of the BJP. In parallel, the BJP was emerging stronger in Maharashtra by gaining in the bypolls and Brihanmumbai Municipal Corporation (BMC) polls as compared to its past tally. The era of 2014–19 witnessed the Shiv Sena relegated to being a junior and less relevant partner in its alliance with the BJP. There were reports that the two might part ways; however, after continuous consultations between BJP President Amit Shah and Shiv Sena Chief Uddhav Thackeray, the two were able to seal a deal of 25–23 seats for BJP–Shiv Sena in February. This chapter explores the factors which went into the alliance registering a 41/48 seat victory in the Lok Sabha elections, and the evident fault lines which sowed the seeds for a possible divorce post the Maharashtra assembly elections.

MAHARASHTRA

Maharashtra, India's second-most populous state and the third-largest state by area, constitutes 48 Lok Sabha seats, the highest after UP which has 80 Lok Sabha seats. With the Congress, BJP, Nationalist Congress Party (NCP) and Shiv Sena as the main parties in the state and no signs of any alliance to begin with, the 2019 elections were going to be a contest to watch out for. However, alliances did culminate. The BJP and Shiv Sena came together, and the Congress and NCP too worked out an alliance.

Devendra Fadnavis was going to be the first non-Maratha chief minister to complete a full five-year term. He had his own vote base by now and was acting as a catalyst to the already swelling Modi wave. The Maharashtra government under Fadanavis proposed a 16 per cent reservation in government jobs and education for Marathas under the socially and educationally backward category, thus fulfilling the long-standing reservation demands of the Maratha community. The Maratha community constitutes over 30 per cent of the state's population, and this reservation proposal which was upheld by the Bombay High Court gave the BJP a good headstart ahead of the elections. Although the High Court upheld reservation for Marathas, it cut down the percentage from 16 per cent to 12–13 per cent. Nevertheless, it was enough to communicate the intent of the Fadanavis government, which was appreciated by the Maratha community and translated into their support.

It was speculated that the BJP would not be able to perform well in the Vidarbha areas in eastern Maharashtra due to several agriculture-related issues. However, upon travelling to these areas and talking to the local people, I realized that it was a myth waiting to be busted.

If we talk about the sentiments of the people on the ground, the BJP with around 60 per cent vote base, better than the Shiv Sena, which stood at around 40 per cent. Additionally, people were not too happy with the Shiv Sena as many of its MPs had not performed their duties. This can be further established by the fact that Aurangabad, which had traditionally been a Shiv Sena stronghold, went to AIMIM, although the vote margin was small.

Despite being one of the major critics of the BJP, the Shiv Sena entered into an alliance with the party in Maharashtra with the seat-sharing ratio in BJP's favour. Maharashtra's politics has always seen the Shiv Sena as a senior partner in any alliance, but the scenario had changed after the BJP managed to receive a huge mandate in the 2014 general elections, and then again in the 2015 assembly elections. The Shiv Sena was now a junior partner in the state which had traditionally been its stronghold.

Some questions, however, still remained unanswered: After criticizing the BJP throughout its five-year term, why did the Shiv Sena choose to partner with it? Why did the BJP look for an ally in Shiv Sena despite getting a good mandate on its own in the 2014 and 2015 elections?

Shiv Sena Chief Uddhav Thackeray could not swallow the loss pill served to him in the 2014 elections and then again in the 2015 assembly elections, which effectively reduced the party's relevance in Maharashtra's politics. To regain its lost relevance, the Shiv Sena had to outperform the BJP in Maharashtra and there were two ways to do this: one, ensure that the Shiv Sena secured the maximum seats or two, ensure that the BJP fell short of majority and was unable to form a government without Shiv Sena's support.

Unconfirmed voices in the Shiv Sena pointed towards a strong influence of Rashmi Thackeray, Uddhav Thackeray's wife, in the party. According to Shiv Sena supporters, Rashmi wanted Uddhav to be the chief minister of Maharasthra and that was possible only if the BJP fell short of majority and the Shiv Sena held the bargaining chip. In the recent elections—be it assembly, local civic body or the panchayat—the BJP had performed better, making things all the more difficult for Uddhav Thackeray. Even in the BMC elections, the BJP had improved its tally. In the preceding year and a half, Shiv Sena's posturing damaged the BJP, but Modi's leadership was driving the party in an upward direction. In addition to the Modi factor, national security and various flagship schemes for women made the BJP strong. Shiv Sena had no option but to ally with the BJP and at the same time the BJP did not want to lose even a marginal percentage of its 2014 voters. If Shiv Sena contested alone it would mean dividing some core right wing voters. The BJP also realized that if a pre-poll alliance was not worked out and, in the possibility that it fell short of a majority by a few seats, the Shiv Sena would have an upper hand.

One question that still remained unanswered was: 'Why not a post-poll alliance?'

Ahead of the Lok Sabha elections, Shiv Sena conducted a survey to know how it would fare in the elections and the result was rather disappointing for the party. In case of contending alone, the party's tally was likely be even lower than in 2014. An alliance was inevitable. One thing that was different for the BJP in comparison to 2014 was how a gathbandhan was shaping in UP where the BJP had secured 71 seats five years ago. If BJP lost big in UP, then it would have to compensate with other states. In such a scenario it could not afford losing seats elsewhere in the country, which made an alliance in Maharashtra imperative for it too.

The two key agendas in Maharashtra for the 2019 elections were Maratha reservation and farmers' distress. Although the BJP got the Maratha community rallying behind it after the passage of the Maratha Reservation Bill, the issue of farmers' distress had not yet been addressed effectively.

In March 2018, a farmers' agitation led by the CPI originated in Nasik and turned into a huge movement. Around 40,000–50,000 farmers marched a distance of 180 km from Nashik to Mumbai to convene a gherao outside the Maharashtra Vidhan Sabha. Their main demands were complete implementation of the farm loan waiver scheme announced the previous year, the effectuation of the Forest Rights Act, 2006, and extending compensation to the farmers whose cotton crop had been destroyed due to bollworm infestation and unseasonal rains or hailstorm. The peaceful march concluded on 12 March 2018, after the Government of Maharashtra assured the said demands would be fulfilled. However, these assurances were not executed in full, which sparked a Kisan march again on 27 February 2019. This was, however, suspended soon after.

While Devendra Fadanavis' irrigation schemes and welfare initiatives for farmers were widely appreciated, the farmers' distress was not close to over and was likely to impact the election results. While the farmers were protesting against the incumbent BJP government, at the same time they were aware that even though the CPI could make their voices heard, it was incapable of resolving their issues. The farmers were naturally inclined towards the BJP who had worked and launched schemes worth ₹20,000 crore to reduce their distress. A weak opposition further strengthened their choice.

During the last 20–25 years, farmers had been in a distressed state, primarily because they and their needs had largely remained ignored. Farmers suffer when there is less produce and they even suffer when there is surplus production. In times of high produce, they get the desirable value for their crops and when production is low, they have to face an inevitable loss anyway. However, many believe that agriculture was now being viewed with the perspective of increasing farmers' income. The target was to double the farmers' income instead of augmenting agricultural production. This surely instilled a hope in the Modi-led BJP government. The payment of ₹6,000 to the farmers was also received positively.

The BJP had resolved these issues well before the elections and Fadnavis was working as a catalyst over and above Modi's popularity. All this was ensuring a comfortable mandate from Maharashtra. However, in order to ensure maximum seats in the state, BJP President Amit Shah decided to enter into an alliance with the Shiv Sena.

A few key constituencies such as Baramati and Nanded, which had been NCP's and Congress' stronghold respectively, proved that the Opposition had minimal relevance in the state in the 2019 elections. NCP's Supriya Sule won the Baramati seat with a narrow margin and Congress' Ashok Chavan lost the Nanded seat. Since the first general elections of independent India in 1951, the Congress had lost this seat only thrice.

Before reading and analysing constituency-wise election outcomes it is important to know that Maharashtra, despite having a rich history, lacked basic infrastructure. Apart from the golden triangle, Mumbai–Pune–Nasik, Maharashtra is yet to witness a lot of infrastructural development. Hence, the BJP, which not only kept development as its top agenda, but also brought infrastructural transformation such as better roads, a greater number of airports and increase in the number of colleges and universities was likely to find favour with voters—and it did.

Let us now analyse the key constituencies, the outliers in these elections and their possible future implications.

Baramati

One of the high-profile seats of Maharashtra, Baramati is the hometown of NCP President Sharad Pawar, and the party's stronghold. Pawar is a big name in Indian politics and Baramati derives most of its popularity because of him. However, it was Pawar's daughter, Supriya Sule, who had been contesting from the seat since 2009. While she had retained the seat, the margin of win had narrowed down over subsequent elections. This gave the BJP–Shiv Sena alliance a ray of hope. If they were to win the seat, it would become the biggest news of the election.

In 2009, Sule had defeated the BJP candidate Kanta Nalawade by a margin of over 3.3 lakh votes. However, in 2014, the contest was between her and Mahadev Jagannath Jankar of the Rashtriya Samaj Paksha (RSPS). While Sule won again, this time she did so by less than 70,000 votes—a cause of worry for NCP leaders.

The Rashtriya Samaj Paksha (National Social Party) was founded by Mahadev Jagannath Jankar in 2003. Jankar led the agitation launched by the Dhangar (shepherd) community to press for their demand for reservation under the ST category. Before the 2014 elections, RSPS joined the NDA for contesting elections.

During the election campaign it was misrepresented that Sharad Pawar and his party was against the demand for reservation of the Dhangar community, which in turn became the main reason for a reduction in the vote margin for Supriya Sule. However, soon after the election results, Pawar clarified his stand: 'The demand of the Dhangar community is justified and we support it but without compromising on existing reservation quota meant for the adivasis,'[20] he had said. In 2019, NCP leaders were confident of Supriya Sule's victory. Contesting against her was BJP's Kanchan Rahul Kul who was quite confident of

---

[20]https://www.business-standard.com/article/current-affairs/ncp-backs-reservation-for-dhangar-community-under-st-category-114081600649_1.html, last accessed 27 December 2019.

a win owing to the Modi wave. The BJP was expecting to draw the support of Dhangar voters as Kanchan Kul's husband was associated with the RSPS, but things didn't pan out as expected. The Dhangar community, who unanimously voted for Mahadev Jankar, could not make him win as they realized that their votes could not be wasted again. They went back to voting for the NCP again.

The key issues of the constituency were water crisis and the villagers' protest against displacement because of the Purandar airport. Local people of the constituency believed that Supriya Sule would work towards resolving the water crisis and that it would be resolved soon. The proposed Purandar airport received a strong backlash from farmers who protested against the project claiming it would take a toll on their livelihoods and affect future generations.

At a popular tea and vadapav stall in Baramati, I spoke to several people and almost all of them supported Supriya Sule. However, when asked whom they wanted as the prime minister, all of them favoured Modi.

Then I went to a paan shop. I asked a man about his choice and he instantly replied, 'Desh mein Rajiv Gandhi... lekin yahan par Supriya Sule.' I immediately understood that he was not talking about Rajiv Gandhi but the then Congress President Rahul Gandhi. Rahul Gandhi was yet to do something significant so as to leave a mark on people's memory.

Later the same day, I held *Lalkar* show's segment *'Target Par Neta Ji.'* It was the same day when Rahul Gandhi had addressed the famous terrorist Azhar Masood in a rally as 'Azhar Masoodji', sparking a debate and inviting a lot of criticism.

With me were the local leaders of the parties, NCP's Sadhubala, Shiv Sena's Raju Kale and Vishnu from Vanchit Bahujan Aghadi (VBA).

Raju Kale raised the issue of water crisis and reminded the NCP leader how once even a leader like Indira Gandhi was defeated and how history was going to repeat itself this time. The NCP leaders brought up the subject of the Dhangar community's reservation and how Shiv Sena and VBA had fooled the people of the community. The

NCP leaders were confident of winning the seat and their confidence reflected on their faces as well as in their body language.

The micromanagement in Baramati helped Supriya Sule edge out a victory with a lead margin of less than 20,000 votes. The election here was not a referendum on Sharad Pawar, and Prime Minister Modi also did not make the election in Maharashtra about Sharad Pawar. This helped the BJP, as it did not allow Pawar to rouse any emotive sentiment. However, the party's state leadership made this mistake in the assembly elections, where it went with the motive of relegating the NCP supremo Sharad Pawar to political irrelevance. It even imported NCP strongman Udyan Raje Bhosle in order to turn tides in Satara. Pawar's rally in Satara, which he continued despite being drenched in the rain, was the turning point for an NCP revival in the Pune Satara region. From losing an MLA before the assembly elections to emerging as the kingmaker in Maharastra assembly elections, the NCP was the biggest gainer politically in the 2019 Maharashtra assembly elections.

Solapur

In Solapur constituency, the Koregaon Bhima violence that took place in January 2018 was likely to influence local politics. The caste riots which were expected to shape the Dalit narrative did not resonate well among voters, except in some parts of Solapur where VBA's Dalit leader Prakash Ambedkar was contesting.

In 2018, during an annual affair to celebrate the two-hundredth year of victory of the Battle of Koregaon Bhima, stone-pelters attacked the gathering, causing a riot. The gathering which largely consisted of Mahars saw stone-pelting by anti-social elements, which eventually ended up taking the life of 28-year-old Rahul Patangale. In the various protests held across the country in the aftermath of the Koregaon Bhima violence, one death was reported. In addition, 30 policemen were injured and 300 protestors were detained.

The Battle of Koregaon Bhima was fought in 1818 between high-caste Brahmins, the Peshwas and the British East India Company. Arabs, Gosains and Marathas were Peshwa soldiers and the Dalit

Mahars were included in the Company's troops. The battle caused losses to the Maratha Empire which was then under the Peshwas. The control over most parts of southern, central and northern India was lost to the East India Company. Of the 49 East India Company soldiers killed in the battle, 22 belonged to the Mahar caste. Some people even go as far as to portray the Battle of Koregaon Bhima as the Mahars' battle against caste oppression under Peshwa rule and even today the Dalits gather around this pillar to celebrate their unity.

Although the Congress and the NCP accused right-wing Hindutva elements for orchestrating the riots, none of them took a clear political stand on the issue as they could not afford upsetting the Marathas, by raking up the Koregaon Bhima episode during elections. With politicians maintaining a radio silence over it, voters too weren't talking about the issue.

While the BJP won the Solapur seat with over 1.6 lakh votes, the Congress came second and Prakash Ambedkar's VBA was a distant third.

Nashik

Nashik is the very constituency from where the farmers' agitation led by the CPI was prompted. The 'long march' had been called by the All India Kisan Sabha (AIKS),[21] which is affiliated to the CPI (M). In a silent protest, farmers demanded loan waivers, minimum support price and land rights. The government was ready to address their concerns and wanted the protesters to call off the march. After the government accepted their demands and assured that the water flowing in Maharashtra's rivers like the Nar, Par, Damanganga and Pinjal shall be transferred to the Godavari basin through lift irrigation and will be used in drought-hit areas of the state, the AIKS called off the protest.

As we go up towards Nashik, water crisis becomes a more intense problem and the issue has remained unresolved for decades. Villages

---

[21] Also known as the Akhil Bharatiya Kisan Sabha.

far from the Godavari dam faced water crisis every year. The Nashik region had onion and grapes as a major produce for which the rainfall period was rather more important than the mere amount of rainfall. As the crop of grapes is taken during the dry period, it needs assured supply of water through irrigation, which made water crisis the main issue in the region. The Fadnavis government had been appreciated for its various irrigation and water conservation initiatives, but the results were yet to be witnessed. Prime Minister Modi's Pradhan Mantri Kisan Samman Nidhi scheme, which promised to transfer a sum of ₹6,000 in three installments to around one crore beneficiary farmers, gave farmers a further boost and their agitation was suppressed to a large extent. Farmers, therefore, reposed their faith in the BJP government, which has arguably been more sensitive towards their needs than previous governments.

On my way to Nashik, I spent some time in Jaategaon and Mulegaon, among other villages, and spoke to many farmers. I assumed the farmers would be distressed and I would have to hear a lot of resentment against the government, but the reality was far away from my presumptions. Although the farmers did complain about money not reaching them, a majority of them—around 60–70 per cent—acknowledged the government's work towards improving agriculture and the lives of farmers. Many of these farmers were happy that the current government at least thought about the farmers. People also acknowledged and appreciated Modi's stand on national security.

Like several other constituencies, women here were unanimously supporting the Modi government. The overall trend suggested that the Shiv Sena would comfortably retain the seat with a higher vote margin than in previous elections. In 2009, Hemant Godse of the Shiv Sena had defeated NCP's Sameer Bhujbal, the nephew of former Maharashtra Chief Minister Chhagan Bhujbal. In 2014, Chhagan Bhujbal had contested against Hemant Godse and was defeated with an even bigger margin. In 2019, the contest was again between Hemant Godse and Sameer Bhujbal.

Shirdi

A seat reserved for the SC category, the Shirdi constituency was created in 2008 and since then the Shiv Sena had consistently emerged victorious from here. This time too the on-ground situation reflected similar sentiments. A majority of people were happy with the BJP–Shiv Sena government and were acknowledging what the government was doing for farmers. While visiting a village in the Kopargaon assembly, I met a Muslim woman who seemed unhappy with the Modi government. She said: *'Modi kaise aayega...kuch nahi kiya...gas cylinder mehenga ho gaya hai...'* (How will Modi come [to power]... [He] hasn't done anything...the gas cylinder has become more expensive...)

Even before I could say anything, a man corrected her, saying: *'Subsidy aati to hai magar,'* (But we receive subsidy) to which she hesitatingly replied, *'Hafte bhar baad aati hai...'* (It comes a week later...) The man then explained how things had changed in the last five years and how electricity was available 24x7 in the entire village.

An interesting thing to note here was how almost in every political debate or conversation throughout my election journey, I found people were not only defending the Modi government but were also campaigning for him voluntarily.

The Shiv Sena candidate Sadashiv Lokhande was riding on the Modi wave. Congress' Bhausaheb Kamble was fighting a lost battle. People here did not even know who Rahul Gandhi was—which was a worrisome sign for the party.

Aurangabad

With over 35 per cent Muslims as part of its demography, the only seat which the AIMIM could win in all likelihood was Aurangabad. Although the Congress was contesting, they had almost no role to play here. What would have, in effect, been a contest between the AIMIM and the Shiv Sena got an interesting twist with the coming of the independent candidate, Harshvardhan Jadhav.

The sitting Shiv Sena MP Chandrakant Khaire was given a ticket again despite the anti-incumbency factor against him. The Modi wave was expected to help Shiv Sena sail through. However, Jadhav's entry had made it into a triangular contest, with the votes getting divided. Muslims and a portion of Dalits were going the AIMIM way, giving it an edge over others. Even though AIMIM was not part of the alliance, it had suggested to the Congress–NCP gathbandhan to field a strong candidate who could defeat the BJP, while it would field a strong candidate in another constituency, so that between them they could defeat the BJP on two seats.

Harshvardhan represented the Kannad assembly constituency and had been elected to the Maharashtra Legislative Assembly twice—once in 2009 with Maharashtra Navnirman Sena (MNS) ticket and then again in 2014 with a Shiv Sena ticket. He had a strong hold over Kannad votes and hence was expected to take a sizeable number of votes to his side, thus impacting Khaire's vote share.

At a local tea shop I spoke to a middle-aged man who believed Khaire was set to win, despite what people said. His statement made me think whether he was a Shiv Sena worker because he was promoting him without any substantial data to back his claim.

On speaking to many local people and party workers, I learnt that Khaire had some understanding with the Congress, due to which the Congress had not fielded a strong leader against him in the last 15–20 years, making it an easy win for the Shiv Sena.

Khaire was popular among urban voters and Harshvardhan Jadhav was famous among rural voters which, though it made the contest interesting, made things difficult for Khaire. Although the Modi wave was evident, anti-incumbency against Khaire was negating it.

The Nirmal Gram Puraskra (NGP) put Aurangabad's Patoda on the map. This award by the government of India was envisaged to recognize and incentivize efforts towards sanitation coverage. Patoda had set the ball rolling for nearby villages to follow suit. In Patoda, I spoke to many people to understand what inspired them and what had changed. A middle-aged man said something which I still remember quite clearly: *'Upar swarg hai ya nahi ye toh pata nahi, par iss dharti ko zaroor swarg bana sakte hain.'* (Nobody knows if there's a heaven up there, but we can make this earth a heaven for sure.)

Another man who must be in his sixties and was speaking on behalf of a group of people who ensured cleanliness, revealed how the medical expenses of nearly every family in the village had reduced. He also pointed out how toilets in villages were just the beginning of cleanliness, and dustbins and washbasins were going to take these efforts to the next level. Throughout the village, people were not just aware of this cleanliness drive but were also following it religiously for a larger benefit.

Parbhani

Parbhani was yet another constituency with an anti-incumbency wave against the sitting Shiv Sena MP Sanjay Haribhau Jadhav. In the 2014 elections, riding on the huge Modi wave, Jadhav had defeated Vijay Manikrao Bhamble by over one lakh votes. However, this time the vote margin was bound to fall. The anti-incumbency against Jadhav was at such a peak that even Shiv Sena workers admitted that the NCP was going to win Parbhani. I visited this constituency after the poll and spoke to more than a hundred people, 70 per cent of whom claimed they had voted for the Shiv Sena but it was the NCP who would win.

This is one of the seats where voters were expected to choose the MP keeping Modi in their minds and that was the only thing that could save the seat for the Shiv Sena. The alliance between Prakash Ambedkar-led VBA and the AIMIM was giving tough competition to the Congress–NCP alliance. Alamgir Mohammed Khan, the VBA candidate, was dividing the Muslims and some part of Dalit voters too who would have otherwise gone with the Congress–NCP alliance.

Shiv Sena won the seat by a margin of around 42,000 votes over NCP, and VBA ended up in the third spot with around 1.5 lakh votes. It clearly proved that the Congress, despite being a national-level party, failed miserably at binding small regional parties together, resulting in its own loss.

Osmanabad

The population of Osmanabad has over 25 per cent Muslims and a sizeable number of Dalits. Owing to the Congress–NCP's poor image, the Dalit votes shifted to VBA, thereby directly benefitting the Shiv Sena. Maratha votes were swinging fully in the direction of the BJP–Shiv Sena alliance. Dalit and Muslims, who once used to be the core voters of the NCP and the Congress, were now moving towards the VBA–AIMIM alliance.

I preferred early morning runs from my hotel to the bus stand for two reasons—one, to have the vadapav and chai breakfast, and two, to be able to converse with people. At the bus stand one day, I saw an old man who must have been in his seventies. I got to know that he belonged to Palaswadi, a village in the Osmanabad district. He was a bit apprehensive about having a conversation with me as I am not a Marathi, but after explaining that my questions were for a survey and his opinion would benefit people, he opened up.

'*Modi accha aadmi hai...kaam to shuru kiya hai...aur fir Modi nahi to kaun?*' (Modi is a good man. He has started work. And if not Modi, then who?) he said in his Marathi accent, a few Marathi words effortlessly spilling into his sentences. He also revealed how there was a serious water crisis in Marathwada areas like Latur but now these problems were being addressed and corrective measures being taken.

The Tuljapur assembly of Osmanabad constituency was once considered an NCP stronghold, but now the NCP was weak even here. Throughout the elections, the Maharashtra opposition was struggling to make its mark.

The Shiv Sena did not hand out a ticket to the sitting MP Ravindra Gaikwad, owing to a huge anti-incumbency wave against him and instead gave a ticket to Omraje Pawanraje Nimbalkar. Nimbalkar was very popular among locals and the rural public. NCP fielded Ranajagjitsinha Padmasinha Patil who was more of a dynast leader and did not have a good understanding of ground realities. It was difficult for the BJP–Shiv Sena alliance to repeat its 2014 performance, but they still managed a comfortable win.

Maval

The Maval constituency covers the assemblies of Panvel, Karjat, Uran, Maval, Chinchwad and Pimpri. As we move towards the ghats of

Maharashtra, the Shiv Sena grows stronger and in this constituency the contest was especially easier for the Shiv Sena because of the work done by its sitting MP Shrirang Barne. Barne had not only worked a lot but had been awarded with the Sansad Ratna Award too. He was among the top performers of the Indian Parliament every year from 2015 to 2019, and every second voter knew his name—a rarity for an Indian MP. In contrast, NCP's candidate Parth Ajit Pawar, son of Ajit Pawar, was popular only among Muslims. Local people believed that the only way Parth Pawar could win was by throwing money and Ajit Pawar was ready to go to any extent for ensuring his son's win.

The BJP–Shiv Sena alliance was working quite well, with the two parties complementing each other in this constituency. While the BJP under Modi was the first choice among the people of Pimpri and Chinchwad, which had maximum number of working people in the adjacent city of Pune, the Shiv Sena was the first choice among the people of Panvel and Karjat due to religious ideology. Together, these regions had a sizeable number of Maharastrians, giving the BJP–Shiv Sena alliance an upper hand here.

I spoke to many autowallahs and almost all had a common opinion of bringing back Modi. Outside a bank in Chinchwad, I spoke to a middle-aged man who was accompanied by his wife. I asked who, according to him, would win.

'Modi sahi hai desh ke liye...aur log bhi yahi chahte hain,' (Modi is right for the country. And people too want this) he said.

'Modiji se accha pradhan mantri iss desh ko nahi mil sakta!' (This country can't get a prime minister better than Modi!) his wife added.

This pro-Modi wave was trending in almost all the urban areas of Maharashtra.

Bhiwandi

Bhiwandi constituency comprises Bhiwandi Rural, Bhiwandi East, Bhiwandi West, Kalyan West, Shahapur and Murbad. Bhiwandi had often been in the news owing to Rahul Gandhi's rallies which were actually quite frequent due to court appearances for a defamation suit filed by the RSS. In an election rally, Rahul Gandhi had alleged that the RSS was behind Mahatma Gandhi's assassination. He had also claimed that the Hindutva organization opposed Sardar Patel (freedom fighter and India's first deputy prime minister).

The Congress Party did not have a good image in Bhiwandi but was banking on a huge Muslim vote base. It was a direct contest between two MPs—BJP's Kapil Patil, who had been the MP from 2014 to 2019, and the Congress' Suresh Taware, who had been the MP from 2009 to 2014. Both Patil and Taware had worked well during their respective tenures and it made the contest even more interesting.

The Shiv Sena had a stronghold in this constituency and when the BJP–Shiv Sena alliance had broken down earlier, Kapil Patil had vehemently targeted the Shiv Sena workers, resulting in local Shiv Sena workers turning against him. Upon speaking to people here I gathered that although there was a huge Modi wave and the BJP had a fair chance to sail through, the agitation of Shiv Sena workers against Kapil Patil could damage his chances. On the other hand, Suresh Taware was carrying the burden of the Congress Party's poor image and of its being arguably the weakest opposition ever.

I spoke to a fruit-seller about the chances of Kapil Patil and Suresh Taware. He explained how the Shiv Sena was a huge factor in the area and whichever party got their support would win. Then I spoke to the people of the Agri community, who comes under OBC, and observed a clear Modi undercurrent, with almost all of them supporting him. I then spoke to a cobbler, a Dalit, who got a bit emotional and revealed that it was for the first time that their basti had a sauchalaya (toilet) and no one had to defecate in the open. Modi, with his various schemes and development initiatives, had been able to make people rise above the caste lines to support him.

Talking to people belonging to all castes, religions and classes, I understood that the BJP was about to win this seat, however small the margin might be. The party ended up winning with over 1.5 lakh votes.

Konkan

The Konkan division of Maharashtra comprises seven districts: Mumbai City, Mumbai Suburban, Thane, Palghar, Raigad, Ratnagiri and Sindhudurg. All these seven districts are coastal districts of Maharashtra, and are rich in natural resources. People living here don't have high expectations from the government. Wanting to preserve natural resources, people here did not want infrastructural development at the cost of nature. With agriculture being the main source of livelihood here, people were happy with basic infrastructure of railways, buses and electric supply.

Two constituencies that came under the Konkan region were Raigad and Ratnagiri–Sindhudurg. Both the constituencies had similar demography and ecology but vastly distinctive politics.

Ratnagiri–Sindhudurg

In Ratnagiri–Sindhudurg, one of the major points of discussion with regard to politics was the proposed Nanar oil refinery, which was facing stiff resistance from the local populace and the Shiv Sena due to its location in the ecologically sensitive Konkan area. It was, in fact, one of the conditions put forward by the Shiv Sena while working out an alliance with the BJP. Entailing an investment to the tune of ₹3 lakh crore, the project was announced after Saudi Arabia's His Royal Highness Crown Prince Mohammed bin Salman Andulaziz Al Saud's visit to India earlier in the year. Chief Minister Devendra Fadnavis ceded to the Shiv Sena's demand of shifting the proposed mega oil refinery from Nanar.

It was imperative for the BJP to ally with the Shiv Sena as the latter was strong here and was set for a comfortable win. However, the reason behind the Shiv Sena being strong here is the constant pocket vote of Narayan Rane, a very popular leader with his own core voter base, who was expelled from the Shiv Sena by Bal Thackeray in 2005 for revolting against Uddhav Thackeray's authority. Rane had then joined the Congress, but later founded his own party— the Maharashtra Swabhiman Party (MSP)—a few months before the 2019 Lok Sabha elections. It was now to be a triangular contest between Shiv Sena's sitting MP Vinayak Raut, Congress' Navinchandra Bandivadekar and MSP's Nilesh Narayan Rane, son of Narayan Rane. Although the real contest was between the Shiv Sena and MSP, the fact that Bandivadekar was from the Bhandari community, which had a strong presence in the constituency, made the contest triangular.

In the 2014 general elections, Nilesh Rane had contested on a Congress ticket against Vinayak Raut and lost by over 1.5 lakh votes. Even this time the Shiv Sena had an upper hand owing to its grassroots-level presence and its latest 'victory' in shifting the mega oil refinery project from Ratnagiri's Nanar.

Raigad

It was proving to be difficult for the Shiv Sena to retain Raigad, the main reason for it being anti-incumbency against the sitting MP Anant Geete. In 2014, Geete won owing to the huge Modi wave but with a very narrow margin of 2,110 votes. The major difference between Raigad and Ratnagiri–Sindhudurg constituencies was the presence of the Kunbi community, a non-elite farmers' community, in sizeable numbers.

The Kunbi community played the most important role in Raigad constituency and whichever party received their support was sure to win comfortably. Since the sitting MP did not work significantly for them, the Kunbi community unanimously decided to vote for the NCP, and the party emerged victorious with a margin of over 23,000 votes against its closest competitor, the Shiv Sena.

Thane

Next to Mumbai, Thane had witnessed a lot of development lately, but increasing population in the city overshadowed it. The city still needed a lot more infrastructural development. Owing to cheaper rent and better accessibility compared to Mumbai, Thane accommodated a lot of people working in different parts of Mumbai. Local trains of Mumbai are often called the backbone of the city and who can vouch better for it than the people living in Thane constituency, which comprises Mira–Bhayander, Kopri–Pachpakhadi, Ovala–Majiwada, Thane, Belapur and Airoli.

An interesting yet a little concerning thing about the people living in Thane was their blind support for the Shiv Sena and how the mere thought of Shiv Sena's loss made them uncomfortable. With almost 90 per cent of the population here rooting for the Shiv Sena, the party was set to win. While the BJP was riding the Modi tide, Shiv Sena was still enjoying Balasaheb's legacy, with some ardent supporters believing that it was the only party that could make their lives better.

In urban areas like Mumbai and Pune, the Congress–NCP alliance did not have a significant chance. The presence of RSS ensured that even though the Shiv Sena and BJP remained each other's opponent, their alliance did not confuse the voters and vote transferability reached its peak.

Pune

Pune used to be a Congress stronghold, but it was now all for the BJP. Suresh Kalmadi of the Congress represented this constituency from 2004 to 2014. However, Kalmadi's involvement in corrupt practices during his tenure as the president of the Indian Olympic Association and chairman of the Commonwealth Games 2010 had brought the party to disrepute, losing its chances of winning in the near future.

The BJP under the Modi–Shah duo had been sweeping all the elections in Pune, making the Congress and NCP irrelevant in what had once been their stronghold. In the Pune Lok Sabha constituency, the contest was not that difficult since the BJP candidate, Girish Bapat, one of the top BJP leaders in the Vidhan Sabha, was a very popular face against the lesser known Mohan Joshi of the Congress Party.

With several software companies having a base in Pune, the city has a strong presence of the working class. As a result, metro and road construction was one of the biggest factors that would determine the voters' choice. The working class being significant contributors to the income tax kitty, they were interested in seeing their tax money utilized for developing the city.

The intensity of the Modi wave could be judged by an incident that happened with me when I was in Pune. I was travelling in an auto and was chatting with the driver. The driver, likely in his sixties, was a Marathi but was fluent in Hindi as he had been living in Pune for quite some time. When I asked him about his views on who had undertaken more work and who he thought should win from there, he did not give a direct answer, but I still remember his reply verbatim.

'Pehle logon ko Rashtrapati aur pradhan mantri mein antar nahi pata tha aur Modi ke aane ke baad baccha baccha raajneeti ki baat karta hai!' (Earlier people did not know the difference between a president and a prime minister. But with Modi taking over, even young people discuss politics and take keen interest in it!)

He made sense. Political literacy, if I can call it so, had certainly gone up nationwide and a good sign of a healthy democracy is when the youth talks about political issues.

Mumbai South

With Congress' Milind Deora contesting against the sitting Shiv Sena MP, Arvind Ganpat Sawant, Mumbai South was one of the most high-profile seats. According to media houses, it was going to be a close contest. However, after traveling on-ground I realized that public reports were perpetually inconsistent with their analysis.

Arvind Ganpat Sawant hailed from a modest family and had risen from the lowest rank of the party hierarchy. He not only understood ground realities but had also worked towards solving local issues. In the Maharashtra assembly he raised issues pertaining to slum development and demanded prominence for Marathi language, which increased his popularity among the Marathis and the poor class.

Milind Deora is a Marwari and many political analysts believed that Marwaris, who are in sizeable numbers in south Mumbai, were going with Deora. But that was not the case. Upon talking to people in Colaba, I found that a majority of Marwaris were supporting Modi. I spoke to one such Marwari businessman who dealt in steel utensils. He revealed how he was happy with Modi and how he welcomed the GST but was at the same time unhappy with demonetization as it had impacted his business. The impact was not the cardinal vote-determining factor. It was unique to watch businesses rally behind Modi even after their complaints. The 'neeyat' factor—many businessmen believed Modi had the right intention behind the introduction of GST—surpassed other grievances. For the Muslims in Bhindi Bazaar, it was a one-way traffic against the BJP. There was minor division among Muslim women and some Muslim youth, but apart from these exceptions most Muslim voters did not trust the BJP. They still preferred a non-BJP party over the BJP.

After speaking to many people, I realized that voters were not limited to voting for their caste and Milind Deora might face a jolt if he was banking solely on Marwari votes. The Colaba area had a considerable number of Gujaratis too, who were unanimously supporting Modi.

In Bhindi Bazaar, I spoke to Muslims, who were voting for the Congress at large. Marathis were, however, supporting the Shiv Sena.

GUJARAT

A state with 26 Lok Sabha constituencies, Gujarat was going to witness a prestige war. After winning all 26 seats in Gujarat in 2014, anything less than that would mean the BJP was losing its ground in its own fort. Amit Shah was contesting a Lok Sabha election for the first time. He was contesting from Gandhinagar, which had long been BJP's stronghold, having seen tall leaders such as Atal Bihari Vajpayee, Shanker Singh Vaghela and L.K. Advani contesting and winning from there in the past. In the 2009 Lok Sabha elections, L.K. Advani had won the seat with a margin of over 4.8 lakh votes, which was one of the highest victory margins. Amit Shah was now looking to secure an even bigger victory.

Even though Amit Shah was contesting a Lok Sabha election for the first time, he was not new to election campaigns. During Advani's campaign in 1991, Amit Shah was the key architect of his day-to-day electoral campaign. In 1997, he won his first MLA election from Sarkhej. Being a local he added his personal vote to the BJP's vote base. In 2019, even though he did not campaign much in Gandhinagar, his limited precise campaign was strategic. In his standalone road show he covered all the vote-mobilizing spots. Finally, Amit Shah won the seat with a margin of more than 5 lakh votes—greater than what had been L.K. Advani's winning margin in 2009.

The 2017 assembly elections, where the BJP witnessed a drop in its vote share and the Congress outperformed itself, was rendering poll analysis tougher this time. If we observe previous elections, the BJP managed to increase its vote share from 47.4 per cent in 2009 to 59.1 per cent in 2014. In contrast, the Congress' vote share had fallen from 43.9 per cent in 2009 to 33 per cent in 2014. However, in the 2017 assembly elections the vote share witnessed a shift, with the BJP getting only 49 per cent and the Congress securing 43 per cent. It was a positive sign for the Congress Party as it had managed to reduce the vote share differential in a state where the BJP had been practically unbeatable for more than two decades. Although the BJP managed a comfortable victory in the 2017 assembly elections, the vote share situation gave the Congress hope for the 2019 elections.

Several factors were responsible for the Congress' improved performance in the assembly elections, with the biggest factor being the Patidar movement. Seeking OBC status, the Patidar community had held demonstrations across the state. There are two communities within the Patidars: Leuva and Kadva. The main agitation was led by the Kadva community and it was launched from Mehsana in July 2015 by the Sardar Patel Group (SPG) which was led by Lalji Patel. Hardik Patel was an active member of the group then. However, later in the same year, Hardik Patel and his supporters broke away to form the Patidar Anamat Andolan Samiti (PAAS). In August 2015, the largest demonstration of Patidars was held in Ahmedabad, after which the movement turned violent in many places, resulting in curfew in several cities and towns. The agitation lingered on for two more years and became the biggest influencing factor for the Gujarat assembly elections.

In the 2017 Gujarat assembly elections, the PAAS supported the the Congress which had agreed to its demands. However, several Patidar leaders also aligned with the BJP. The BJP received a majority in the elections, but performed below par in comparison to the results of the previous election in 2012.

In January 2019, the BJP-led NDA government proposed 10 per cent reservation for the economically weaker sections (EWS) of the society. The Bill was passed by both the houses of Parliament. The government of Gujarat announced the implementation of the Bill on the same date, pushing the Patidar movement to oblivion and rendering it as no longer being a decisive factor in the 2019 elections. While Hardik Patel joined hands with the Congress Party, other Patidar leaders showed an inclination towards joining the BJP. At a press conference right after joining the Congress, Hardik Patel, in response to a question, said: 'Now I have joined Congress, so party comes first and the government has given 10 per cent reservation to EBC that included Patidars too.'[22]

Although it was said that demonetization followed by the GST disturbed the trader community and that they were likely to go against the BJP, the same was proved wrong during the assembly elections itself, with the BJP winning 14 out of 16 seats in the city of Surat, the centre of trading and business.

The Balakot air strikes and farmers' distress were two key factors that were set to influence the 2019 elections. While nationalism and the Modi factor were giving a big edge to the BJP, the Congress was trying to capitalize on farmers' distress and water crisis issues. After a detailed ground analysis, I placed the BJP's tally at a comfortable 22 seats, with 4 seats—Junagarh, Surendra Nagar, Amreli and Anand—being quite difficult to predict. Before we analyse the key constituencies of Gujarat, let us understand the geography and demography of the state. Gujarat can be broadly divided into five parts: north Gujarat, south Gujarat, madhya Gujarat, Saurashtra and Kutch.

For a better analysis we can divide the issues in Gujarat into micro issues and macro issues, according to the extent of their impact on ground. Farmers' distress, which was seen in three constituencies of Saurashtra, was limited to rural voters and hence was a micro issue whereas the Hardik Patel–Jignesh Mevani–Alpesh Thakor trio

---

[22]https://youtu.be/PaMENtsLrQ0, last accessed 27 December 2019.

was a macro issue as they had an effect on over 10 constituencies of north, madhya and south Gujarat. Amit Shah resolved both the micro and macro issues, which enabled the BJP to win all the 26 constituencies.

Micro Issues

Saurashtra, a peninsular region of Gujarat, is located on the Arabian Sea coast. The region is characterized by low rainfall and high political opportunity. Here, farmers' distress was the main factor which was likely to impact the election outcome; however, urban voters were with the BJP, giving it an overall edge. Ahead of the Lok Sabha elections, Chief Minister Vijay Rupani ensured more water in Aji-I dam to meet the drinking water requirements during summer.

The Modi government announced the Pradhan Mantri Kisan Samman Nidhi (PM-KISAN) Yojana, a minimum income support scheme, under which more than 20 million additional farmers were to get two installments of ₹2,000 each ahead of the forthcoming general elections. Sixty per cent of the beneficiaries were from the BJP-ruled states. Gujarat took the lead in identifying farmers who were eligible under the scheme and thus was able to pacify the farmers to a large extent.

Three constituencies where farmers' distress needed to be addressed were Junagadh, Surendranagar and Amreli. The election results for these three seats were difficult to predict.

Junagadh

In Junagadh the sitting MP of the BJP, Rajeshbhai Naranbhai Chudasama, was contesting against Vansh Punjabhai Bhimabhai of the Congress Party, who had lost to Rajeshbhai in 2014. However, unlike 2014, this time Junagadh had major farmers' distress, owing to crop insurance and other government schemes not reaching the farmers and other beneficiaries. In this constituency, rural voters, who constituted approximately 34 per cent of the population, were largely against the sitting MP and the BJP. I spoke to hundreds of farmers in this constituency and most of them were distressed and had made up their mind to go against the BJP this time. The urban voters, who constituted the remaining 66 per cent, were largely with the BJP due to the Modi factor and the prevailing nationalism wave after India conducted the Balakot air strikes to avenge the Pulwama attack by Pakistan-based terror outfit Jaish-e-Mohammad. In urban areas near Somnath, the Koli community had a sizeable number to influence the election and had been sway voters; however, this time they unanimously supported the BJP after Kunvarji Bavaliya, who represented the All India Koli community, quit the Congress and joined the BJP in July 2018, citing dissent with the Congress. The Koli community was a deciding factor in the two constituencies of Junagadh and Surendranagar.

Surendranagar

After Kunvarji Bavaliya joined the BJP, a candidate of his choice, Mahendra Munjapara, was given a ticket from Surendranagar. Munjapara, a doctor and social worker, had a good rapport with the local people. While the Modi wave was working as a catalyst to ensure BJP's victory, there were discussions of the Congress' grand scheme NYAY—the ₹72,000 income support to five crore poor families. The Congress, however, had serious credibility issues and even a scheme as large as the NYAY was not enough to motivate the people to vote for it. The Congress could not convert farmers' distress into votes.

It was difficult to defeat the BJP in Gujarat, which had been its bastion for over two decades. Simply placing a strong Congress candidate was not going to be enough. It was imperative that the BJP fielded a relatively weak candidate, but that was not the case. With issues like farmers' distress and water crisis posing a threat, the BJP not only pitted a strong candidate but also tried pacifying the afflicted farmers.

The Kisan Samman Nidhi Yojana seemed to placate the distressed farmers to some extent. In December 2018, a few months before the elections, Chief Minister Vijay Rupani announced an input assistance of ₹2,285.59 crore to 23.25 lakh farmers in the state who were reeling under a severe financial crunch due to crop failure caused by low rainfalls.

Amreli

Another constituency of Saurashtra with farmers' distress as the main issue was Amreli, but the Congress failed here too despite having a strong candidate. During the 2017 assembly elections, the Congress managed to win 4 out of 7 assembly seats from Amreli. However, when it came to the Lok Sabha elections, Modi's popularity was overshadowing the local candidates across the nation, and the same happened in Amreli too.

Contesting from Amreli was Paresh Danani, who had acted as the catalyst for the Congress in the assembly elections. For the Congress to repeat its performance in Amreli, they had to bank on his personal appeal as the Patidar effect had faded away in the region. After Hardik Patel joined the Congress, his ability to pull Patidar votes diminished and it became difficult for the Congress to attract the Patidars like they had done during the assembly elections. In a situation when most of the state was tilting towards the BJP, the Patidars in Amreli did not want to be singled out by siding with the Congress.

Macro Issues

The Hardik–Jignesh–Alpesh trio had given the BJP a tough time during the assembly elections, giving the Congress a hope of ending up with a better tally in the 2019 general elections as compared to 2014. However, the trio was no longer effective and the BJP seemed to have totally overcome the caste composition. Hardik Patel had influence over Patidar votes, Jignesh Mevani over Dalit votes and Alpesh Thakor over Thakur OBC votes. Unhappy with the party's leadership, Alpesh Thakor quit the Congress a few days before the elections, giving a big jolt to the party. He had influence over three constituencies of north Gujarat, namely Patan, Mehsana and Banas Kantha, and his turning against the Congress indirectly benefitted the BJP, which now had the unanimous support of Thakor voters. It was also speculated that Alpesh would join the BJP and it turned out to be true—he indeed joined the BJP soon after the elections.

Dalit leader Jignesh Mevani too became irrelevant as the Lok Sabha constituency was bigger in size as compared to assembly seats, and hence Dalit votes, which were not in considerable numbers in Gujarat, lost their significance. Mevani's campaign for the CPI candidate Kanhaiya Kumar, who had been associated with the infamous *tukde-tukde* controversy, worked against him. At a time when the entire nation was overwhelmed with the idea of nationalism and patriotism, Mevani and Kanhaiya Kumar were obviously set to lose. Further, Mevani's victory in the assembly elections was largely derived from the Congress' support to him as an independent in their traditional stronghold Vadgam. There was no 'Jignesh Mevani Effect' that contributed to his victory.

Hardik Patel, who was leading the Patidar agitation during the 2017 assembly elections, was now officially a Congress member, but Modi government's 10 per cent reservation to EBC faded away the Patidar movement. By now many senior Patidar leaders had either joined the BJP or had extended their support to the saffron party.

◆

In short, if Maharashtra was about a compulsive alliance of BJP–Shiv Sena, one (BJP) fighting for NDA dominance on the national front, the other utilizing the Modi popularity to stay relevant in Maharashtra (Shiv Sena), Gujarat was about BJP working to repeat its 2014 performance of winning all 26 seats. We live in times where voters do not like wasting their vote. In Gujarat, there was a one-way narrative to vote for Prime Minister Modi in all except for three or four seats. Modi's personal connect with the state, which moved beyond just political connect, and micromanagement by the party helped him swing the undecided voters on the voting day. There was no opportunity for some unhappy undecided voters to pick a political pole, as it was clear that in Gujarat the BJP will be convincingly winning more than 22 seats.

The voters had also seen the trio of Hardik Patel, Jignesh Mevani and Alpesh Thakor during the time of the assembly elections where what started as a social movement eventually turned out to be yet another political launchpad for new youngsters to enter opposition (barring Thakor who joined the BJP, but he too lost the recent by-election in Radhanpur by 3,814 votes). This also reduced the Opposition's ability to swing any neutral voter in their favour, as their credibility quotient compared to Prime Minister Modi was significantly lower. Voters' mission to re-elect their erstwhile chief minister as the prime minister in 2019 was a bigger reason, than give single-digit victory seats to the Opposition in Gujarat. Gujarat did not hate but love the prime minister. This messaging also got some fence voters on the BJP's side. Lastly, Amit Shah contesting in Gandhinagar was the icing on the cake for the BJP. With all these factors, BJP repeating its 2014 clean sweep in 2019 was an imminent foregone conclusion.

6

AAP OR NOT: DELHI

With the 2019 Lok Sabha elections, India's largest people's revolution—India against Corruption (IAC) which was led by Anna Hazare—finally kicked the bucket. Since its commencement in 2011 and through the years that followed, Hazare had maintained that it would be better for the movement to not be politically aligned. Arvind Kejriwal, however, felt that the agitation route was not enough to make a loud noise. By 2013, the movement had reached a critical juncture where it demanded a direct political involvement to make political ripples. The movement that had originated with a demand for a Jan Lokpal Bill ended up paving the way for a stunning debut for the Aam Aadmi Party in the 2013 Delhi assembly elections. The party emerged as the second-largest party in its very debut, winning 28 out of the 70 seats.

The dramatic irony to AAP's story was when it teamed up with the Congress Party, which was inimical to its core foundational bases in all aspects. With no party attaining an overall majority, the minority government of AAP was formed with conditional support from the Congress. The entire IAC movement, recognized as the genesis of AAP, was solely based on the corrupt practices of the Congress government. AAP joined hands with what it had sought to fight against.

As soon as it came to power, a significant part of the AAP's agenda involved introduction of the Jan Lokpal Bill in Delhi. It did not take very long for AAP to realize that no other major party would lend support to the Bill. The AAP government thus resigned after being in power for only 49 days. It later returned with a historic mandate, winning 67 out of 70 seats in the 2015 assembly elections.

The IAC movement and then the AAP traded the anti-corruption narration all this while, and left no stone unturned to make people believe that the Congress was synonymous with corruption. UPA-II was a disaster with scams worth thousands of crores tainting its tenure. The Congress had lost all its credibility and people were just waiting to root it out of power. This was a window of opportunity that the AAP capitalized on very well.

Delhi, which ended up being a three-cornered contest between the BJP, AAP and the Congress in the 2019 elections, could have seen a battle between two forces had AAP and the Congress entered into an alliance. With the Congress' continuous dismal performance and AAP looking for an aggressive expansion after facing crushing defeat in the MCD polls right after the Punjab and Goa debacle, the only way to stop BJP's victory march in these elections was to fight together. Vote share data also suggested the same, if one assumed AAP and Congress, which had been rivals, would be able to transfer their votes to each other entirely. In the 2014 Lok Sabha elections, the BJP had a vote share of 46.4 per cent, AAP 32.9 per cent and the Congress a distant third with a vote share of 15.1 per cent. From winning 67 out of 70 seats in 2015, AAP had been reduced to 48 out of 270 seats in the civic body polls merely within two years.

It wasn't that the possibility of an alliance was not explored by these two parties. In November 2018, AAP Chief Arvind Kejriwal and Congress President Rahul Gandhi shared the stage at a Kisan Mukti Morcha rally. It was then that the talk of the possibility of the two parties coming together had started doing the rounds. However, the alliance did not come through: AAP was looking at an alliance with the Congress for 18 seats, including seven in Delhi, 10 in Haryana and one in Chandigarh; the Congress, however, insisted on restricting the tie-up to the national capital and Rahul Gandhi was willing to give out only 4 of the 7 seats to the AAP.

Almost four months later, the AAP announced its candidates for six seats of Delhi and re-approached the Congress for an alliance, this time coming up with two equations: one, which left only one seat for the Congress in Delhi and the second, with the option to contest for more than one seat in Delhi but on the condition of allying with the AAP in Punjab and Haryana too. Rahul Gandhi did call a meeting of senior Congress leaders to discuss a possible alliance with the AAP, but there was vehement opposition from the Congress Party's Delhi unit.

The former chief minister of Delhi, Late Sheila Dixit was never in favour of allying with the AAP. In fact, she even wrote a letter to Sonia Gandhi and Rahul Gandhi advising them against forging an alliance with the party for the upcoming Lok Sabha polls in Delhi. She was of the opinion that an alliance with the AAP would harm the Congress' image in the long run. She also made the case about how there was unanimity within the Congress Party against an alliance with the AAP.

The Balakot air strikes conducted to avenge the Pulwama attack gave BJP an upper hand in the Lok Sabha elections, and the Congress realized that it had become essential to enter into an alliance to take on the BJP. In April 2019, when the elections were just around the corner, the Congress approached the AAP for a liaison which was rejected by the latter. The Congress had demanded three seats in Delhi, where the AAP was in power. The Congress had also rejected the offer for alliances in Haryana and Punjab; it wanted to ally, but on its own terms. AAP MP Sanjay Singh, who was mediating the alliance, attacked the Congress of not being ready for an alliance in Haryana where they had only one MP. Sanjay Singh even went on to accuse the Congress of helping the BJP win the elections.

In a press conference, Chief Minister Arvind Kejriwal displayed what was termed as helplessness to form an alliance with the Congress, saying *'Unhone lagbhag mana kar diya hai.'* (They [Congress] have more or less refused.) This became an oft-quoted statement.

Despite all attempts, with an alliance not working out, the real worry for the AAP and Congress now was the division of Muslim votes. Arvind Kejriwal, in turn, was reduced to a level of such desperateness that in several of his rallies he consciously began using the words 'Hindu' and 'Muslim'. Speaking at the launch of AAP's manifesto for the Lok Sabha elections he went on to claim that the

Congress was not getting even a single Hindu vote, thus inviting a lot of criticism.

Whilst the AAP and Congress were in a dilemma about tying up, the BJP was riding a NaMo popularity wave, saddling which almost any candidate projected by the party seemed likely to gain acceptance among the Indian populace. This became evident when the sitting MP Udit Raj, denied a ticket from the North West Delhi Constituency which is an SC seat, joined the Congress, but failed to take along his core voters with him. BJP's new candidate, Hans Raj Hans, won the seat with a vote margin of over 5 lakh.

Before a seat-wise analysis, it is imperative to understand that Delhi being the capital, continuously witnesses or at least remains aware of all the political happenings across the country. Also, it is home to people from various states, which gives it a dynamic demography and a very dynamic form of politics.

SOUTH DELHI

In a three-cornered contest, the sitting MP Ramesh Bidhuri contested against AAP's Raghav Chadha and Congress' Vijender Singh. South Delhi constituency has considerable numbers of Gujars, who are the core voters of Bidhuri and a small percentage of Punjabis who were likely to go with Raghav Chadha. Chadha was a popular name only among the Punjabis and Vijender Singh, despite being a known face for many due to his boxing career, did not have any specific take-off vote. Bidhuri's take-off Gujar votes helped him in Badarpur and Tughlaqabad. Moreover, Bidhuri, apart from having taken off the Gujar votes, was riding on NaMo's popularity which had only gone up after 2014.

South Delhi is home to the most affluent class of Delhi residents that consists of builders, realtors and so on. I got an opportunity to interact with a few of them. One day, at around 11:30 in the morning, while outside a Starbucks outlet, I decided to speak to a woman who had just stepped out. I approached her and spoke about the prevailing political scenarios and asked her what she thought about it. I was shocked at her response.

'*Bas Modi jaana chahiye...Modi bekaar hai...Sab ka dhanda chaupat kar diya...pehle almirah mein hamesha paise hote the... ab kuch nahi...briefcase se bhar ke paise laate the husband, ab sab bandh ho gaya!*' (Anyhow, Modi should go. His government has got our business down. Earlier our cupboards used to be always full of money. Now, nothing. Earlier, my husband would come home with a briefcase full of money. Now all that has stopped!)

This is just one of the many examples of resentment against Modi for his demonetization decision that I observed among well-to-do families in Delhi. However, what the stance also revealed was rampant corruption—a briefcase filled with cash suggests hoards of black money, and it had indeed been a common sight in the past. After demonetization, unless there was a big occasion like a wedding in the family, there weren't too many dealings in hard cash. Modi's push for digital transactions after demonetization made the lives of the corrupt difficult, which was a possible cause for this resentment.

In contrast to Delhi was Mumbai. I was in Bandra doing my regular show, *Lalkar*, where people are an active part of the debate. There were some Congress workers who were chanting anti-Modi slogans when a woman, who must be in her forties, said in a loud voice:

'*Ye aap log kyon Modi ke khilaaf naare laga rahe hain?*' (Why are you chanting against Modi?)

There was pin drop silence.

'*Kya galat kiya hai Modi ne? Jo bhi decisions liye hain usne wahi pareshaan hain jo chor hain aur corrupt hain!*' (What wrong did Modi commit? His decisions have caused problems only for the corrupt!)

The woman seemed quite well-off herself. And she was not the only person I met in Mumbai who had a pro-Modi stance. The affluent class in Mumbai not only supported Modi, but was actively campaigning for him. Moreover, while the affluent families of south Delhi were angry with Modi, they did not go on to play a significant role in the elections, as they represented only a microsegment of the constituency.

In Delhi, I visited Okhla Mandi, a famous Muslim-dominated area, to understand the direction in which the wind was blowing. Travelling through the area I spoke to more than a hundred people of different classes, both men and women. The answer was the same: 'No BJP'. There was, however, a clear divide between the Congress and AAP, and the more interesting thing to note was that many of those who said they would vote against the BJP knew that Modi would come back to power. The same was evident on the voting day when it seemed the Muslims had resigned to the fact that Modi and the BJP were going to win anyway, and considering their vote did not hold much impact value as it did in the assembly elections and the bypolls, they were relatively reluctant to vote.

Priyanka Gandhi's back-to-back road show didn't make any difference and the Congress' attempt to project her akin to Indira Gandhi didn't work with the people. Wearing a maroon saree and perched atop a white SUV, Priyanka Gandhi canvassed for Vijender Singh and Sheila Dixit. Although Congress workers chanted slogans like *'Priyanka nahin ye aandhi hai, doosri Indira Gandhi hai'* (This isn't Priyanka but a political storm; she is the next Indira Gandhi) during the road show, there was a big disconnect with the voters which was evident with the quick conclusion of the road show— much earlier than it should have been. Several videos of empty roads where Priyanka Gandhi's road show was convening started doing the rounds on social media and influenced the voters. No one wanted to board a sinking ship and that's probably one of the reasons why even some core Congress voters were not going with the grand old party this time.

NORTH EAST DELHI

This constituency saw three popular figures contesting against one another: Bhojpuri actor and sitting MP Manoj Tiwari was contesting on a BJP ticket; pitted against him were one of the longest-serving chief ministers of Delhi, Sheila Dixit, and the AAP leader Dilip Pandey.

While Sheila Dixit had her previous work in Delhi to boast about,

Manoj Tiwari had Bihari voters in considerable numbers on his side and he was also backed by Modi's popularity. AAP's Dilip Pandey was not really in the contest and the best outcome for him could be to finish second.

A big section of migrant workers which comprised a significant population in this constituency played an important role. Also, the Purvanchalis, a sizeable number of whom live in this constituency, were expected to support Manoj Tiwari, owing to similar ethnicity and his background as a Bhojpuri movie star.

According to opinion polls, the BJP was expected to win a maximum of 4 out of the 7 seats in Delhi. The ground reality, however, seemed quite different.

I have spent a significant portion of my working life in Delhi. As I travel a lot, I tend to ask cab drivers for their opinions as a matter of habit. I was in a cab in Karol Bagh and the driver was a Punjabi. Humming to the tune of the soothing Punjabi song playing in the cab, he asked me: *'Raajneeti mein hain kya, sir?'* (Are you in politics, Sir?)

He must have heard me discussing politics with my team member over the phone.

'Raajneeti to nahi kahenge magar usse milta-julta samajh lijiye,' (I won't call it politics, but somewhat similar) I said smiling.

Before he could pose another question, I asked him: *'Aap ko kya lagta hai waise kaun jeetna chahiye iss baar?'* (Who do you think should win this time?)

'Sir, sahi bataun to raajneeti kam samajh mein aati hai magar kuch achcha hona hai to Modiji ko aana chahiye, baaki sab waahe guru ki kripa,' (Sir, I don't understand politics too well, but if something good has to happen, Modi should return to power. The rest is God's will) he replied.

It was one of my first conversations as a part of the groundwork in North East Delhi.

I disembarked from the cab near a small nimbu-soda stall, and asked the vendor for a glass of nimbu paani (lemonade), which was majorly my cue to strike a conversation with him. I found out that he was from Bihar and could provide me a taste of how migrants from Bihar would vote in Delhi.

He told me that he wanted Modi to win and that 100–150 people who stayed in the same neighbourhood as him were going to vote for Manoj Tiwari as he was one of them. In his words, he called Manoj Tiwari as 'apna aadmi' (our man).

However, this feeling was not consistent across all migrants from Bihar. Even those who weren't too happy with Tiwari were supporting him only because they were looking at the bigger picture—Modi. Manoj Tiwari had more than 80 per cent of his core vote base intact, which worked as a catalyst, and Modi's popularity was already gaining votes across caste lines. That took the BJP to a comfortable victory.

North East Delhi has a sizeable Muslim population. Although Muslim votes were expected to be divided between the Congress and the AAP, Tiwari managed to build a good image for himself among the Muslims. His candid approach towards canvassing worked for him. During the election campaign he arranged multiple small meetings with the Muslims of his constituency while being quite upfront with them in seeking votes.

He said: *'Main jhooth nahi bolunga; main vote maangne hi aaya hun...aur uske liye apna kaam bataunga...kya humari constituency mein ek bhi dange fasad hue hain? Ek bhi badi maar-peet ki ghatna nahi hui hai?'* (I won't lie; I have come to ask for votes. And for that I would tell you the work has been done. Has there been any riot in our constituency? Has there been even one incident of a major fight?) The Muslims present in the meeting applauded. Muslims may not have voted for him in large numbers, but he certainly managed to sway a small number of them in his direction.

There was a time when it was said that BJP workers themselves weren't too sure about Manoj Tiwari winning the elections. If a local BJP worker was to be believed, due to internal politics, a few BJP workers made Tiwari look incompetent. Thus, several assumed that he was set to lose, despite the fact that he had the highest take-off votes to begin with.

Sheila Dixit, who wanted to contest from the Chandni Chowk

constituency, was made to contest from North East Delhi. Staying away from power for a long time worked against her. Moreover, the Modi wave which had swept the capital in the 2014 elections was even stronger now.

The BJP was strong in Burari, Rohtas Nagar and Karawal Nagar areas whereas the AAP had some influence in Timarpur. The Congress and AAP were locking horns in Babarpur.

AAP's Dilip Pandey wasn't really in the picture despite working on local issues such as provision of free water supply and free electricity to low-end consumers. Under all circumstances the Modi tide was going to sweep over others. Manoj Tiwari was all set to win the seat.

WEST DELHI

In the West Delhi constituency, a pro-incumbency wave in favour of BJP's Parvesh Sahib Singh Verma, a nationalistic sentiment among voters and a favourable voter demography worked in BJP's favour. Contesting against Verma were Congress heavyweight Mahabal Mishra and the AAP's Balbir Singh Jhakar. In the last elections, Verma had defeated AAP's candidate Jarnail Singh by a 20 per cent vote differential. West Delhi had a considerable number of Punjabis (roughly over 40 per cent), a majority of whom supported the BJP and its candidate. Apart from the Punjabi votes, the migrants in Purvanchal staying in Paschim Puri added to the BJP's tally. There were migrant women from Gujarat who voted in BJP's favour. The BJP was strong in Dwarka, Janakpuri and Mahavirnagar. Most of the first-time voters and women only rallied behind the party because of Modi. These factors further strengthened an already strong candidate, Parvesh Verma, who won the seat with more than five lakh votes. This turned out to be the constituency with the maximum lead margin for the BJP in Delhi.

NEW DELHI

In a triangular contest between the sitting BJP MP Meenakshi Lekhi, Congress' Ajay Maken and AAP's Brijesh Goyal, it was earlier assumed that Maken had an upper hand. However, as the campaign progressed, Lekhi got into the lead position.

One of the key reasons behind this sudden surge in Lekhi's popularity was the defamation case she filed against Congress President Rahul Gandhi with respect to the Rafale issue, forcing a court-ordered apology from him. This gave Lekhi the BJP's blessings, silenced errant factions inside the party and gave her a good headstart.

Rahul Gandhi, whose entire 2019 election campaign centred on Rafale, had falsely annotated the Supreme Court's verdict on Rafale in one of his rallies, suggesting that the Supreme Court itself had accepted that *'Chowkidar chor hai'* (the watchman himself is the robber—a reference to Modi). Following this, the BJP MP candidate from New Delhi, Meenakshi Lekhi filed a criminal contempt plea against the Gandhi scion for his defamatory remarks and for twisting the Supreme Court's quote. Later, the Supreme Court gave a categorical clarification that in its Rafale verdict there was no occasion wherein the Honourable Court had mentioned the contemptuous observation *'Chowkidar Narendra Modi chor hain'* as had been attributed to it by Rahul Gandhi. Rahul Gandhi then expressed 'regret' in the Supreme Court over his remarks, tendered an apology and cited 'heat of political campaigning' as the reason behind it.

The entire episode not only exposed Rahul Gandhi's string of lies but also acted as a speed breaker to the Congress' political narrative in the election. The episode didn't limit itself to New Delhi but also made it to primetime debates and almost the entire country got to know about it. Rahul Gandhi, through his actions, handed out a certificate of honesty to Modi.

There was pro-incumbency sentiment in favour of Meenakshi Lekhi in most parts of New Delhi constituency, except in Sarojini Nagar and New Delhi–South Delhi intersection where the sealing drive was the main talking point.

When New Delhi was selected for the smart city proposal, the BJP-ruled municipal corporations started a sealing drive to remove all illegal shops at the centre of the action, thus pushing traders' bodies to take a stand against the BJP. However, owners of large shops, most of whose establishments were legal, were quite happy with the sealing drive as it was reducing competition for them. The sealing drive did not swing the voting outcome in the Lok Sabha elections but could be a talking point in the upcoming political calendar.

Despite all these odds, Meenakshi Lekhi was confident that her report card would pave the way for her return to the Lok Sabha. New Delhi has a sizeable number of Punjabis and they were Lekhi's core voters. Small traders who were mostly from UP and Bihar wanted Modi back, thus giving the BJP an overall edge over its competitors.

The AAP had fielded Brijesh Goyal, the head of the party's traders' wing, and the party was hoping to benefit from the anger in the community over the 'unjust' sealing of commercial establishments.

Voters, however, were smart enough to differentiate between local issues and national issues. Keeping in mind Modi's stand and his work on national security and international relations, the voters saw the BJP as a better option.

Ajay Maken, who represented the Congress from the New Delhi seat twice, from 2004 to 2014, was trying to encash the sentiment against the 'draconian' provisions of the Seventh Central Pay Commission among government employees. However, government employees in reality had diverse opinion on the same. With the Congress Party already lacking political credibility despite being a victor in the assembly elections in 2018, Rahul Gandhi's apology to the Supreme Court on his remark against Modi regarding Rafale impacted Maken's chances further.

NORTH WEST

One of the most talked-about constituencies of Delhi, North West was in the limelight mostly after the BJP picked singer Hans Raj Hans as its candidate, snubbing Udit Raj who had threatened to leave the party if dropped. North West was also the only reserved seat in Delhi.

Hans Raj Hans, a popular Punjabi folk and Sufi singer, joined the BJP in 2016 after quitting the Congress. He was also formerly a member of the Akali Dal. Udit Raj, on the other hand, had merged his Indian Justice Party with the BJP in February 2014 and later won the election from North West Delhi. The BJP had won all seven seats in Delhi in the 2014 election.

Hans Raj Hans was considered an outsider in Delhi, and the BJP's decision to not give a ticket to Udit Raj was expected to put off a section of the Dalits, resulting in definite repercussions for the party in the remaining four phases of voting. Udit Raj, belonging to the Khatik community (a sub-caste of Dalits), shared considerable popularity among the voters from the community. There were two narratives playing on the ground. First, that the shift of Udit Raj to the Congress would take a sizeable number of Khatik voters to the Congress and second, that electing Hans Raj Hans would make it difficult for the voters to get day-to-day work done from the MP as he resides in Jalandhar.

'Hum Jalandhar toh nahi jaenge na sign karane!' (We can't go to Jalandhar to get something signed!) grumbled one of the voters in the Badli area.

However, in the triangular fight, AAP's Guggan Singh also attracted some of the cluster votes which would have otherwise gone to the Congress. Many localities in Bawana and Narela saw voters drifting to the AAP. This was also reflected in the Bawana bypoll which AAP had won in 2017. These were traditional voters of the Congress. In 2009, the Congress had won this seat with a vote share of 56.8 per cent. The division of anti-BJP votes made the contest one-way for the BJP, which was successful in consolidating more than 50 per cent voters in the name of Prime Minister Modi. Group meetings were held close to the the polling date to convince unhappy local party workers and prevent last-minute defections. Third-party campaigns to convince voters that a vote for Hans Raj Hans was actually a vote for Modi and that they were electing the prime minister and not an MP helped in keeping the ideological voters together. High voter turnout on the polling day benefitted the BJP and, irrespective of the popular perception, the BJP swept the seat with one of the highest vote margins.

EAST DELHI

The AAP focused on negative campaigning in the 2019 elections despite having positive policy touchpoints to talk about, such as improvement of education in government schools. East Delhi was one such constituency where AAP's negative campaigning worked against the party.

East Delhi was about to witness the most-awaited contest, a competition between BJP's Gautam Gambhir, AAP's Atishi Marlena and Congress' Arvinder Singh Lovely. The constituency has a significant Muslim population, most of whom are migrants from UP. Muslims have been core voters of the Congress Party, but the AAP swayed a major portion of them in its direction, thus robbing the Congress of a significant vote base. However, in the Lok Sabha elections, Muslims were likely to go with the Congress as AAP could not possibly make any difference even after winning and only a national party like the Congress could counter the BJP. Out of seven seats, AAP managed to come second only on two seats (South Delhi and North West Delhi).

Gambhir replaced the sitting MP Mahesh Giri who had lost touch with voters, as he had not made many public appearances in his stint as an MP. Gautam Gambhir, besides his batting prowess, was famous for his statements on national interest and humanitarian issues. Gambhir had expressed his anger over the Pulwama terror attack in which over 40 CRPF jawans were killed, and also openly supported the idea of a full-scale military response following the dastardly attack.

Gambhir was chosen by senior BJP leader Late Arun Jaitley who was born and brought up in Delhi. Jaitley had mentioned how Gambhir would prove to be an asset for the BJP and how the party could utilize his abilities in the best way possible for the betterment of the people of Delhi.

In a shocking turn of events, a few days before voting day, AAP candidate Atishi Marlena alleged that Gambhir and his team had distributed pamphlets containing extremely obscene and derogatory content against her. The pamphlet also targeted Chief Minister

Arvind Kejriwal and Deputy Chief Minister Manish Sisodia. The charge evoked a strong reaction from Gambhir, who not only hurled a counter-allegation at Kejriwal but also announced that he would withdraw from the contest if it was proved this was his handiwork.

'Never imagined Gautam Gambhir to stoop so low. How can women expect safety if people with such mentality are voted in?' Kejriwal had tweeted.

In a tweet, Gambhir too challenged: 'I declare that if it's proven that I did it, I will withdraw my candidature right now. If not, will you (Kejriwal) quit politics?'

Gambhir's clean image and his stand of withdrawing from the contest if found guilty gave him an upper hand in the contest. The entire episode backfired on the AAP and things got worse for Atishi who was earlier seen as the lead contender.

The pamphlet was in English, which logically meant that it was not meant for wider public distribution but was an electoral attempt to galvanize votes. Speaking to locals of the constituency, I realized that this attempt had totally gone against the AAP.

Voters were not convinced—they saw it as a story 'manufactured' by the AAP and the incident did not change their mood. Gautam Gambhir, who is not only known for his good image but also for promoting women empowerment on several occasions, was further supported by Modi's clean image and was all set to win the contest. Marlena, on the other hand, was struggling to finish second.

Another jolt to the AAP was given by the Congress candidate Arvinder Singh Lovely. Lovely, who had been affiliated with the Congress for over 30 years, han briefly joined the BJP owing to certain differences within the Delhi State Congress, but returned to the Congress in less than a year claiming to be an 'ideological misfit' in the BJP. Lovely was a popular candidate and the 24 per cent vote share that he pulled was entirely in his personal capacity.

The Modi wave reduced the contest to a bipolar one, with Modi and anti-Modi being the only two options. The anti-Modi votes got divided between the AAP and the Congress while pro-Modi votes were united in support of Gambhir, who won with a margin of over

3.9 lakh votes. With no alliances in place, the AAP enabled its vote base to shift either to the Congress or to the BJP, as it could have won only three or four seats in Delhi at the maximum. Marlena, despite a huge media buzz, ended up third in the race.

CHANDNI CHOWK

Popular as one of the oldest and busiest markets of India, Chandni Chowk has a substantial number of voters from the underprivileged sections of society. Government welfare schemes and their implementation played a huge role in deciding the fate of the candidates here. In a three-cornered contest, BJP's Dr Harsh Vardhan, the sitting MP, was contesting against Congress' Jai Prakash Agarwal and AAP's Pankaj Kumar Gupta.

Chandni Chowk has a considerable number of Muslim voters too, and I happened to interact with some of them. While Muslim men were unanimously against the BJP, Muslim women were sway voters and could go with the BJP. I spoke to a burqa-clad Muslim woman.

'*Kya lag raha hai, didi...yahan kaun jeetega?*' (What does it seem, sister...who will win from here?) I asked.

She didn't say anything but held up a victory sign with her fingers. I was a little confused until I saw a big poster of Modi on a wall behind me where Modi too was pictured showing the same victory sign. The Bill against Triple Talaq had made some Muslim women support Modi and the BJP. There was evident and unexplainable admiration for Modi among women of different castes and religions—Modi had become the hope for them and his various schemes and initiatives had culminated in a pro-women and pro-poor image of him.

Muslims were largely divided between the Congress and the AAP. While the AAP had a stronghold in Delhi, voters were unable to see the bigger picture with the AAP and were likely to go with the Congress, which had very little ground in Delhi.

Dr Harsh Vardhan carried a clean and soft image. His popularity helped him gauge more votes from areas adjoining the Chandni Chowk assembly. In the Chandni Chowk assembly, Congress' Jai

Prakash Agarwal could also pull some votes. The AAP was not really in the contest in this constituency and mainly ended up dividing the votes of the Congress Party.

Looking back at the question of whether an AAP and Congress alliance would have had a drastic impact on the electoral outcome in Delhi, a minute analysis reveals that even an alliance would have attracted the same voter demography, and may not have dented the Modi wave in Delhi. At best it would have reduced the vote margin and increased the voting in slums and minority-dominated areas. Voters in Delhi were conscious that they were voting for the prime minister and not the chief minister.

With respect to the chief minister, people disapproved Kejriwal attacking the prime minster. The more he attacked the prime minster, the greater was his loss of goodwill in Delhi. He realized this mistake after being wiped out in Delhi, and focused his political narrative about his public policy work in Delhi—schools and free electricity. Not attacking the prime minister even once in 2019 helped him regain lost political ground in Delhi.

7

THE OUTLIERS: THE NORTHEAST AND ODISHA

The Northeast and Odisha, which were once ridiculed as not being Indian enough, were ready to observe a different brand of politics this time—the politics of development. In the 2014 elections, the BJP had won over 90 per cent seats out of the 60 per cent demography and more than 60 per cent of seats had come from the Hindi heartland. However, with the SP–BSP gathbandhan in UP and setbacks in Madhya Pradesh, Rajasthan and Chhattisgarh assembly elections, the Northeast and Odisha became all the more important for BJP.

NORTHEAST

The Shahrukh Khan starrer *Chak De India* portrayed 70 years of ignorance about the Northeast with great precision. In a scene where hockey players from various states arrive for the national team training camp, the hockey players from Mizoram and Manipur were welcomed with *'Desh ke bahar se bhi log aaye hain?'* (People from outside of India have also come [for the camp]?)

The Northeast had been deliberately kept separated from the rest of India—and its politics.

Since 2014, the north-eastern states of Assam, Tripura, Arunachal Pradesh, Manipur, Mizoram, Meghalaya, Nagaland and Sikkim, along with the eastern state of Odisha, witnessed a lot of infrastructural developments, which led to these states becoming part of the country's mainstream.

Speaking to several people in the Northeast, I grasped that development was going to be one of the biggest political agendas here. Railways and roadways had seen multifold development in a short span of five years. Cleanliness at railway stations was also a common feedback throughout the north-eastern states.

A general trend which I observed during my journey through the Northeast and after speaking to people belonging to various castes, communities and religions was that the Hindi-speaking local people were invariably with the BJP whereas Muslims were largely with the Congress. Bangladeshi Muslims, who were called illegal immigrants, had the All India United Democratic Party (AIUDF) and the Congress as their first and second preference, respectively.

In the 2014 Lok Sabha elections, the BJP had won 7 out of 14 seats in Assam and the NDA had secured 10 of the 25 parliamentary seats across the eight states of the Northeast. This prompted the saffron party to further increase its tally. Assam, among all the north-eastern states, had the highest number of seats at 14.

Assam

Along the Brahmaputra River, which flows through Arunachal Pradesh and Assam, is an industrial area which houses people from various communities such as Marwaris, Gujaratis, Rajasthanis and Biharis. These communities had a considerable influence in Guwahati, Silchar and Lakhimpur constituencies of Assam. Before we do a seat-wise analysis of Assam and other north-eastern states, let us understand the region's demography and the political parties contesting from the state.

The Congress is the oldest political party in the Northeast and had dominated the elections since Independence. However, regional parties had started altering the political discourse since the early 1980s. The Asom Gana Parishad (AGP), a regional party, was formed in 1985 in response to the six-year-long Assam Agitation (1979–85) against illegal infiltration of foreigners from Bangladesh into Assam. The Assam Agitation stemmed from the fear of illegal immigrants altering the demographic, social and economic make-up of the state.

Being a regional party, the AGP always fought to protect Assamese culture and had formed the government twice, once from 1985 to 1989 and then from 1996 to 2001. It was only in May 2016 that the BJP-led NDA which included parties such as AGP and Bodoland People's Front (BPF) formed its first government in Assam. The new alliance with Himanta Biswa Sarma as its convener was called the North-East Democratic Alliance (NEDA).

While the AGP pulled out of its alliance with the BJP in the backdrop of the NRC, the seat-sharing formula made them come together. The BJP gave AGP all the three seats (Dhubri, Barpeta and Kaliabor) where the BJP had less chances and where AGP had performed well in the previous elections. The BJP soon realized after the assembly elections in the Hindi heartland that it may make some losses there, which needed to be recovered in the Northeast. So, it ensured an alliance with the AGP, as it was not ready to take even the tiniest risk. This is clearly evident with the example of the Mangaldoi seat which the BJP won in 2014 with a small margin of around 22,000 votes and 1.9 per cent vote share. Without AGP's support they would have lost Mangaldoi, which made the alliance extremely important for the BJP.

Another strategic regional alliance that the BJP made in Assam was with BPF. A tribal party formed in 2005 having a historic demand of Bodoland territorial area, BPF was given one seat—Kokrajhar—by the BJP. Allying with the BPF gave the BJP a base tribal voter in Mangaldoi district, the autonomous districts and the Barpeta Lok Sabha seats. Using this strategy, it also neutralized BPF's demand for a separate land.

An interesting incident which changed the politics of the Northeast was when Himanta Biswa Sharma, popularly known as the Amit Shah of the Northeast, switched from the Congress to BJP. It was a huge loss for the Congress and political experts went as far as claiming that 'Congress lost its Kohinoor.'

Reportedly, in 2015, Himanta Biswa Sharma went to meet Congress President Rahul Gandhi to discuss urgent issues in Assam. However, nothing could be discussed as Rahul Gandhi did not pay enough attention; he saw feeding biscuits to his pet dog, Pidi, as something which demanded his immediate attention, while the issues in Assam could wait. Disgruntled with Rahul Gandhi's behaviour, Himanta Biswa Sharma quit the party only to join the BJP later. The incident came to the limelight when Rahul Gandhi tweeted a video of Pidi eating a biscuit. Himanta Biswa Sharma quoted the tweet saying 'Sir Rahul Gandhi, who knows him (Pidi) better than me. Still remember you busy feeding biscuits to him while we wanted to discuss urgent issues of my state Assam.'

Himanta Biswa Sharma, with his political acumen and popularity in the Northeast, ensured that the BJP form the government in Assam, Manipur, Tripura and Arunachal Pradesh. Alliances with the National People's Party (NPP) and the National Democratic Progressive Party (NDPP) in Meghalaya and Nagaland respectively ensured that the BJP was a part of the government in these states. The BJP was not a part of the ruling governments in Mizoram and Sikkim, but the ruling parties were a part of the NEDA, which supported the NDA.

AIUDF also played a decisive role in a few seats of Assam. In the 2014 Lok Sabha elections, the AIUDF, which was founded by Maulana Badruddin Ajmal on 3 October 2005, took the Congress Party by surprise when it managed to win 3 out of the 8 seats it contested in Assam. AIUDF had Indian Muslims and illegal immigrants of Bangladesh as its core voter base. If an alliance did not culminate between the Congress and the AIUDF, then one would become a vote-cutter for the other.

AIUDF begged the Congress for an alliance but Congress' Assam unit was too confident of winning alone after a political expert predicted the NRC was going to backfire on the BJP. AIUDF was demanding the 5–6 seats it had won in 2014, but the Congress believed that the dynamics had changed since then and was in favour of going alone.

In some constituencies in North Bank of Brahmaputra, adivasis and Rohingya Muslims are in a sizeable number and hence can easily influence the elections. On the other hand, in Tezpur, the Gorkha community is in considerable number. In constituencies like

Mangaldoi, Kaliabor, Kokrajhar and Autonomous District Council (ADC), the adivasis were in sizeable numbers.

The BJP marked its entry in the Northeast in the 2014 Lok Sabha elections when it won 10 out of 25 seats. However, there was not even one BJP-led government in the Northeast till 2016. And now the BJP was leading the government in 6 out of 8 states, of which four had chief ministers from the BJP. This time the saffron party was eyeing 21 out of 25 seats which looked possible till the NRC issue made things interesting on paper.

In its 2019 manifesto, the BJP vowed to introduce the NRC across the country in a phased manner, if it retained power at the centre. As of then, Assam was the only state to have such a document. Many political experts believed that the promise to introduce NRC to control the fast-changing demography of the states would backfire for the BJP. Documentary evidence, which was necessary to produce in order to get listed in the NRC, was also a factor that was going against the BJP, further slimming its chances of winning a majority in the 25 Lok Sabha seats from the Northeast. However, the voting pattern was largely supposed to remain the same as in 2014. Hindus would majorly go with the BJP; Assamese Muslims had Congress, BJP and AIUDF as their first, second and third preferences respectively; the BJP did not feature at all in the preference list of the Bangladeshi Muslims, whose first preference was the Congress and second, the AIUDF.

Kaliabor

The Kaliabor constituency had always been a Congress Gogoi dynasty seat, except on two occasions—in 1984 and again in 1996 when the AGP won this seat. The sitting MP, Gaurav Gogoi, was contesting against AGP's Moni Madhab Mahanta.

AIUDF, which had received a little over 2.3 lakh votes in the 2014 Lok Sabha elections, was not contesting this time. This consolidated the Muslim votes in favour of the Congress. This area is also known for tea garden farmers who are roughly 40,000 in numbers. Disgruntled with the BJP for not delivering welfare schemes effectively, most of them moved towards the Congress this time. Both AIUDF and the Congress had a tacit arrangement with each other to not field strong candidates in Kaliabor and Dhubri. In Kaliabor, even though the AIUDF had a strong candidate, it did not field anyone in order to help Gaurav Gogoi, who was also the son of former chief minister of Assam (Congress Party), Tarun Gogoi. In Dhubri, the Congress fielded a weak candidate, Abu Taher, and this ended up benefitting the AIUDF.

Dhubri

Three-fourths of Dhubri constituency's population comprises Muslims. Considerable numbers of these Muslims are Rohingya Muslims. The BJP had almost no chance of winning here and after the Congress fielded a weak leader, AIUDF leader Badruddin Ajmal became the obvious choice for voters. Ajmal was worried that the perception of anti-incumbency could translate into fewer votes. His strategy of a tacit alliance with Tarun Gogoi was born from this fear. There was a young Muslim from a moderate background named Sukur Ali who had challenged Ajmal. The fight between him and Ajmal was called 'Fifty-thousand rupees vs seventy-five crore', indicating the comparison of wealth declared in the affidavits of Sukur Ali and Badruddin Ajmal. Ali was an agitated local Muslim who complained that Ajmal had not done any progressive development in Dhubri except arousing sentiments based on religion. Locals used to narrate their experiences while interacting with Ajmal. One of the locals, Safaruddin from Alomganj, said, 'Our relatives in Mecca tell us that Badruddin takes funds from the people there in the name of developing our community here, but the reality is that he has not done anything monumental for us!' However, these voices of dissent were few and Ajmal comfortably won the constituency by a margin higher than that in 2014, and with a resoundingly high voting percentage of 90.6 per cent.

Karimganj and Barpeta

There were two seats—Barpeta and Karimganj—where the Congress and the AIUDF were seen acting as mutual vote cutters.

The population of Karimganj had over 55 per cent Muslims. Even as AIUDF had fielded a Hindu—Radheshyam Biswas—in the 2014 Lok Sabha elections, as it is an SC seat, the party had won, as the illegal Bangladeshi immigrants in the constituency that borders Bangladesh have a natural inclination towards the party.

In the 2019 Lok Sabha elections, Assamese Muslims wanted to vote for the Congress due to its stature as a national party. They felt a national party could raise their issues in the Parliament. In the 2014 elections, Muslims had believed that only the AIUDF could stand for Muslim rights and help the Rohingya Muslims; hence they sided with the party. On the voting day, reports from the ground suggested a lead for the Congress till mid-day. However, post-noon many maulavis, through their network, nudged Muslims towards the AIUDF. The BJP capitalized on this divide and won the seat in spite of the majority population being Muslims. BJP's core vote base was urban and rural Hindus.[23]

Barpeta too witnessed a similar politics owing to high number of Muslims in the constituency. However, here the Congress candidate was much stronger than the AIUDF candidate, due to which Muslim votes did not get equally divided between the two parties and the Congress emerged victorious with over 1.4 lakh votes more than the runner-up AGP.

Guwahati

One of the most developed constituencies of Assam, Guwahati has a different politics altogether. It has over 19 lakh voters, with around 10–11 lakh urban voters. The constituency has an international airport and an AIIMS too. It is also the unofficial financial centre of the Northeast. Himanta Biswa Sarma has a huge influence in the constituency and voters wanted him to contest from there, but with bigger responsibilities of being the chairman of NEDA and the development of the entire Northeast region on his mind, Sarma chose

---

[23]https://economictimes.indiatimes.com/news/et-explains/how-indias-cities-vote-why-the-urban-vote-matters/articleshow/68161241.cms?from=mdr, last accessed 27 December 2019.

not to contest the elections. This was the only constituency in the Northeast where both the BJP and the Congress fielded a woman candidate.

However, Himanta Biswa Sarma was in a full campaign mood and singlehandedly managed NDA's victory in the Northeast despite replacing Bijoya Chakravarty, who had won the 2014 elections with a big margin, with Queen Oja. Sarma organized three to four meetings every day in order to address public issues and campaigned in his very own style with music and folk dance.

Guwahati also witnessed a wave of nationalism after the Pulwama attack and the Balakot air strikes that followed. Being a developed city, Guwahati has a lot of people from states like Bihar and Jharkhand who had a natural inclination towards the BJP. Many of these people from other states work at railway stations which have seen a dramatic improvement in the last five years. One more factor that ensured the BJP's victory in Guwahati was a dedicated BJP cadre and booth-level outreach by top leaders. As for the candidates, both Queen Oja of the BJP and Bobeeta Sharma of the Congress Party were equally strong.

Lakhimpur and Dibrugarh

Both these constituencies have relatively fewer Muslim voters at around 10–15 per cent. As a result, the BJP had a favourable chance of winning the elections. The party had won both seats in the 2014 elections as well. There are two main things that we need to know in order to understand the outcome here.

First, there were two divisions of Hindus and Muslims each. The two sets of Hindus were the Assamese Hindus and those who had migrated from Bangladesh after 1972. The division among Hindus, however, did not play a game-changing role in the elections, as both sets were supporting the BJP. When it came to Muslims, one of the two divisions was the Assamese Muslims who largely supported the BJP in 2014, but were expected to support either the Congress or the AIUDF this time due to extreme polarization. The second set comprised the Rohingyas who had illegally migrated from Bangladesh and were facing the threat of being deported, and hence were supporting the

AIUDF or the Congress Party, but not the BJP in any scenario.

Speaking to one of the Rohingya Muslims, I got to know that they have more faith in AIUDF than in the Congress, for the former had helped them get ration cards, Aadhaar cards, access to electricity and so on, and had also helped expedite law and order cases against them.

The second important thing to note is that the BJP here worked on 3C strategy—candidate, caste and cadre. National issues did not resonate much with the local people of these constituencies. However, RSS and BJP cadres had been working here actively since 2012, thereby making strong grounds for the BJP to emerge in 2014 and become even stronger in 2019. The BJP and RSS cadres had made it a point that various government schemes reached the beneficiaries. Ujjwala Yojana, Awas Yojana, rural electrification, trains and highways pushed up the BJP as the voters' first preference. All this hard work resulted in the BJP's victory for a consecutive term in both the constituencies.

Tezpur

The BJP had won the Tezpur constituency in 2014 with a margin of around 86,000 votes. However, the sitting MP, Ram Prasad Sharma, was denied a ticket for the 2019 elections after his daughter, an Assam Police Service officer, was arrested in connection with the Assam Public Service Commission (APSC) job scam. Ram Prasad Sharma quit the party alleging 'neglect by the new intruders'. It was assumed that his exit would hurt the BJP's chances as Sharma was the president of Assam Gorkha Sammelan and Tezpur had a sizeable number of Gorkhas who played a decisive role in electing an MP.

The BJP announced Pallab Lochan Das as its candidate from Tezpur. The Congress had fielded a retired IAS bureaucrat, M.G.V.K. Bhanu as its candidate. Bhanu hailed from Andhra Pradesh but was posted in Assam for 30 years and a very popular face among the youth.

A BJP minister had made the contest tough for the party by claiming that the party did not need the Gorkhas to win. However, the Modi factor, rail and road development and fund allocated to Assam overshadowed all these negative factors that were expected to work against the BJP. The saffron party managed a comfortable victory, winning by around 3.4 lakh votes—a margin even greater than the 2014 elections.

En route Mangaldoi from Tezpur, I spoke to a truck driver who had been in the business for quite some time. The driver revealed that due to better roads the time per trip had reduced and as a result he was now able to take more trips per week, which had led to increased earnings for him. This was one of many such narratives of development reverberating on the ground. Even the Gorkhas' initial disassociation after a series of conspiracies was superseded by the development narrative. Changing the candidate also helped the BJP galvanize more votes. The BJP was able to win this constituency by a differential of more than 20 per cent votes.

Mangaldoi

The BJP had won the constituency in the past four consecutive terms. The current MP, Ramen Deka, was unpopular and had managed to barely squeeze a victory by a margin of around 22,000 votes in the previous election. This time the BJP gave the ticket to Dilip Saikia, which helped the party contain the public's ire to an extent. The base vote provided by the AGP–BDF alliance was more than 1.5 lakh. Most of the 3.5 lakh Muslims chose the Congress as their first preference. In fact, the Congress was in the position to get more Muslim votes than it had in 2014, as AIUDF which had pulled away 74,000 Muslim votes last time, was not contesting on this seat this time. This made it imperative for the BJP to address Ramen Deka's non-performance. The victory margin for the BJP had reduced over the past two elections because of the candidate. Proper allocation of finances for the tribal after the victory in the assembly elections added the tribal votes in this constituency which borders Bhutan. Since Deka's non-performance on the development front was not completely forgotten, the BJP could manage victory by only around 1.3 lakh votes, which was much smaller in comparison to Guwahati where the BJP won by more than 3.4 lakh votes.

Silchar

In 2014, the then president of Mahila Congress, Sushmita Dev, won the constituency by a small margin of around 35,000 votes. She defeated Kabindra Purkayastha who had defeated Dev's father, Sontosh Mohan Dev, in 2009. In the 2019 elections, the BJP fielded Rajdeep Roy, whose father had defeated Congress' Kamlendu Bhattacharya by just 1,500 votes. This constituency has more than 35 per cent Muslim voters, and Sushmita Dev had to at least get 15 per cent of the non-Muslim votes in order to win. She had built a strong personal cadre which rallied behind her despite the state of the Congress Party. In this election, Himanta divided her personal cadre nearing the counting day. Some of them supported the BJP internally. Sushmita Dev personally could not counter the Modi factor which drove a majority of the urban voters towards the BJP. In rural areas, the BJP candidates provided few additional votes to the party. Nearly complete support from upper Silchar for the BJP and a small division of votes in lower Silchar helped the BJP win the constituency with around 80,000 votes.

Overall in Assam, a higher voting turnout was a constant phenomenon, and unlike popular perception the NRC and the Citizenship Bill did not have unanimous anti-BJP votes. I remember speaking to an old man who was rushing to catch a bus at the Silchar bus stand with his grandson. I asked *'Kahan jaa rahe ho?'* (Where are you going?)

He replied: *'Main apne pote ke NRC documents lekar 400 km door Naogaon jaa raha hun!'* (I am taking my grandson's NRC documents to Naogaon, which is 400 km away!)

I provoked him: *'Aap toh rehne wale idhar ke ho na?'* (Don't you belong to this area?)

'Haan, par officer ne document mein galti ki hai...' (Yes, but the officer has made a mistake in the document...) he replied in an irritated tone.

I finally asked: *'Toh fir iss baar NRC ke vajah se BJP chunao haar jayegi!'* (So, this time the BJP will lose the elections due to NRC!)

His tone changed and he said assertively: '*Vote Modi ko denge... aakhir mein sab thik hojaega...desh ke liye Modi achhe hai!*' (My vote will go to Modi only. In the end, everything will fall into place. Modi is good for the country!)

Tripura, Meghalaya, Arunachal Pradesh, Nagaland and Manipur

Tripura

In Tripura, the 2019 elections were viewed as a ray of hope and development. The win in Tripura can be seen in continuation with the recently held assembly elections where the BJP swept the state reducing the CPI (M) to a state of existential crisis. From 1 per cent in 2014 to close to 50 per cent in 2019, Tripura has been the state where the BJP saw the largest increase in vote share.

Despite CPI (M)'s former Chief Minister Manik Sarkar's huge popularity, the BJP was set to win both the Lok Sabha seats. The report from the ground further cemented my claims. While tall leaders from the BJP like Sunil Deodhar, Himanta Biswa Sarma and Ram Madhav had strengthened the BJP cadre, the Congress left the responsibility of drawing up an election strategy and campaigning to the National Students' Union of India (NSUI) members, who stood no chance against top BJP leaders. The BJP also had an alliance with the Indigenous Peoples Front of Tripura (IPFT) in Tripura, which had won 8 out of 9 seats contested in the 2018 legislative assembly elections.

Another reason behind the public choosing the BJP collectively was the anti-incumbency wave against CPI (M), which had failed miserably at providing even the most basic facilities to the public. Besides anti-incumbency, the CPI (M) goons had apparently also created an environment of fear,[24] and with people now seeking a change, Modi was their only hope.

While the CPI (M) and the Congress had come together in

---

[24]https://www.youtube.com/watch?v=fb_P-IchKa0&t=37s, last accessed 27 December 2019.

West Bengal, they were totally against each other in Tripura. West Bengal's politics, however, had its own impact: it led to the dilution of CPI (M) vote base in Tripura. A major chunk of CPI (M)'s vote base shifted to the BJP.

Manik Sarkar had always maintained a low profile and was considered as an honest leader. But Modi seemed to outshine Sarkar's image. Although people weren't against Sarkar, they sought fast-track development which the CPI (M) had failed to provide.

In Tripura, social media, especially Facebook, is vastly popular. Out of the average 28,000 voters in a constituency, roughly 22,000 were on Facebook. As a result, parties using the social media platform could directly communicate with the voters effectively. This was unique, because unlike in other places, the youth in even rural parts of Tripura had active social media accounts, and had a cogent political opinion. Young women were unanimously in support of Modi. The BJP quite smartly politicized the adivasis' demand for a separate land and kept the issue alive and relevant until only after winning the assembly elections. The Lok Sabha elections then became an extended part of the assembly elections.

There were some key issues which were at the base of the election battle. First, when Prime Minister Modi had inaugurated the Garje–Bilonia railway line at a public rally in Agartala earlier in the year, he had introduced the HIRA (H for highway, I for Internet way, R for roadways and A for Airways) model to the public. Development activities were touching new heights under the BJP-led government in the state. People in Tripura were, for the first time, witnessing development activities in the state. This further motivated them to vote for Modi once again. Second, in January 2018, the Modi-led BJP government de-notified bamboo as a type of tree—remedial action towards its erroneous categorization as a tree under the Indian Forest Act, 1927. After the interim order by the Supreme Court in 1996, cutting trees and timber was entirely banned in the Northeast. With bamboo falling under the category, it could not be commercially exported outside the Northeast, which adversely impacted the livelihoods of several bamboo farmers.

The Modi government had taken steps to amend the Indian Forest Act, which helped circumvent the 1996 order by the Supreme Court. Commercialization of bamboo trade was going to spike the income levels of local farmers and create greater opportunities for employment in the region. This played a significant role in the elections. Third, Tripura is one of the first few states in the Northeast to have commercially adopted the cultivation of rubber. In the past four decades, Tripura's rubber production did not see any large-scale changes and had almost come to a standstill. Majority of these rubber plants were illegally owned by CPI (M) workers. The only party in which the public saw hope of expanding the production of rubber plants was the BJP, which gave the people of Tripura yet another reason to wipe out CPI (M) from the state. Last but not the least, during the Tripura assembly elections, state government employees were drawing salaries on the basis of the Fourth Pay Commission. This was in contrast to the central government employees who were receiving salaries on the basis of the Seventh Pay Commission recommendations. The BJP promised the implementation of the Seventh Pay Commission in Tripura. Tripura, which has nearly 2.5 lakh state government employees, voted in favour of the BJP.

Meghalaya

Renowned for its tourism, Meghalaya has two Lok Sabha constituencies—Tura and Shillong. In the 2018 assembly elections, the Congress, with 21 seats, emerged as the party with the highest number of seats. However, the NPP, which had won 19 seats, announced that it would form a government with the support of the United Democratic Party (UDP), the BJP and other regional parties. Conrad Sangma, leader of the NPP, was sworn in as the chief minister, along with 11 other ministers.

If we look at Meghalaya's demography, there are two major communities—the Khasis and the Garos. The Khasi community comprising of urban voters majorly dominates east Meghalaya's Shillong constituency and forms a core vote base of the Congress.

They are essentially legacy voters who have been voting for the party for long. The reason for doing so is often given as 'because our forefathers voted for the Congress too'. The Garo community is mostly in west Meghalaya's Tura constituency and mainly vote for the NPP.

In Meghalaya and other states of the Northeast, it was rumoured that a victory for the BJP–NPP alliance would lead to implementation of the NRC, which would result in the adivasi areas being occupied by Hindus. In Meghalaya, the two parties did not get into an alliance. The BJP had urban voters on its side but had almost no support in the proportionately larger tribal vote bank. It can be safely said that the decision to contest separately along with the negative promotion around the NRC hurt the BJP's cause. The party lost the Shillong seat. With Tura being a bastion of current Chief Minister Conrad Sangma, NPP had an initial edge. His sister, Agatha Sangma, was contesting from this seat. The fight became interesting when former Chief Minister Mukul Sangma decided to contest on a Congress ticket. The Congress got a major support in the hilly areas, but the NPP swept certain areas of Tura. The sentiment attached with the passing away of Conrad and Agatha's father, P.A. Sangma, still prevailed. This further added votes to the tally of Agatha Sangma, who won with 3.04 lakh votes in her favour. Mukul Sangma got 2.4 lakh votes. The BJP got a little over 30,000 votes. Had the BJP and NPP not fought separately, the NPP's lead margin would have been bigger. Interestingly, Agatha Sangma had won Tura on an NCP ticket in 2009.

Arunachal Pradesh

Arunachal Pradesh has two Lok Sabha seats, namely Arunachal West and Arunachal East. In 2014, the BJP had won Arunachal West, the region from where popular BJP leader Kiren Rijiju hails. The Congress won the Arunachal East seat, but only with a narrow margin of around 12,000 votes. Towards the 2019 elections, the BJP was emerging as the strongest party in the state and was gaining ground at a rapid pace. Despite ruling for 30–35 years (elections here started after 1965), the Congress had lost ground.

Bigger fund allocation, roadways, highways, railways, airport and the like came under the all-round infrastructural development which the BJP had managed within a short span of five years. Frequent visits by top BJP leaders such as Prime Minister Narendra Modi, party President Amit Shah and Home Minister Rajnath Singh also contributed to increasing public support for the BJP. Arunachal Pradesh had witnessed slow infrastructure development—particularly road development—in the past. The rationale as per the locals was that the previous governments felt bad roads would deter the Chinese troops from entering Arunachal. Contrast this to the current strategy, which focuses to build more roads to enable the Indian troops with a faster response time in the case of a conflict. This development activity along with micro planning by Kiren Rijiju and Chief Minister Pema Khandu gave the BJP an edge in the state. Pema Khandu is the son of Dorjee Khandu, the popular chief minister of Arunachal Pradesh who died in a helicopter crash in 2011. Pema Khandu felt neglected in the Congress government of 2014, when he was given charge of the Ministry of Water Resources. Differences with the Congress chief minister aggravated his disillusionment. He broke away from the Congress and formed his own party—the People's Party of Arunachal (PPA)—along with 33 MLAs. PPA, along with the BJP, formed the government in 2016. Close to the 2019 Lok Sabha elections, most of the remaining Congress cadre either joined the BJP or supported it, thus making it an easy victory in both seats. The level of Congress dissolution can be understood from the fact that in the West Arunachal seat, the BJP got 2.2 lakh votes while the Congress got 50,000 votes. This same seat was won by the Congress in 2009 with a margin of less than 2,000 votes and lost by just 30,000 votes in 2014. From 2014 to 2019, the BJP became the most prominent party in the Northeast, a position that was historically occupied by the Congress.

Nagaland

The state of Nagaland has only one Lok Sabha constituency. The NDPP founded by Neiphiu Rio along with the BJP had formed the government after the 2018 assembly elections, where they had won 17 and 12 seats, respectively. When Rio fought the Lok Sabha elections in 2014, he had won this seat with a margin of 4 around lakh votes. This time Tokheho Yepthomi was contesting from the NDPP against Congress' K.L. Chishi who was supported by NPF.

Even though many strong leaders of NPF had joined NDPP, NPF still had the ability to poll votes irrespective of the switch by its cadres. Their support to the Congress added a minimum catalyst vote in the election. Unconfirmed reports from the ground also indicated the existence of an ambivalent political stand by NDPP. One prominent opinion that emerged from NDPP suggested a minority government to be formed at the centre. In this scenario, NDPP tried to avoid an expressive anti-Congress stand. In fact, Rio's letter to Rahul Gandhi which was leaked to the media on 22 April 2018 made things between the BJP and NDPP infructuous. Rio no longer enjoyed the same popularity as in 2014 when he was in the NPF. In the 2019 Lok Sabha elections, the NDPP candidate trailed behind the Congress in most of the assemblies that NDPP had won. NDPP's candidates had a better strike rate in assemblies which were won by the BJP. Being in a position of power (chief minister), Rio still managed to save this seat for the party by a margin of only 16,000 votes. Maybe he had planned for a low victory margin?

Manipur

Manipur is the only state which implemented an all-women polling booth for the first time. An erstwhile Congress bastion, Manipur had seen the Congress emerging victorious on both seats—Outer Manipur and Inner Manipur—in 2009 and 2014. However, with the emergence of the BJP in the Northeast, Manipur had become a new battleground. The BJP had fielded Dr Rajkumar Singh against Congress' Oinam Nabakishore Singh in Inner Manipur. In Outer Manipur, BJP fielded Houlim Shokhopao Mate and NPF fielded Lorho S. Pfoze. Additionally, an independent candidate, Kaiku Rajkumar Singh, also contested from the Inner Manipur constiuency.

Consolidation of the Nagas towards NPF in Outer Manipur along with some Muslim votes and support from several Naga underground groups made NPF get most of the 3 lakh Naga votes. Internal party divide and disunity among Kuki voters who were roughly 2 lakh in number had put the BJP in a position of disadvantage.

The Modi factor was prevalent in Inner Manipur, which also hosts a substantial Hindu population and a lesser Muslim population. This gave the BJP an initial edge, but consolidation of Kuki votes was important for winning the seat. The division in Kuki votes which was seen in Outer Manipur area was managed by a united BJP party in Inner Manipur. Moreover, development work in the form of railways and roadways construction was also seen here. Neutralization of anti-militant activity by the centre also helped get positive votes. The BJP won Inner Manipur by a margin of roughly 18,000 votes. The margin was low because the independent candidate (Kaiku Rajkumar) from the Kaiku community had cut more than 80,000 votes. On the other hand, the BJP lost Outer Manipur, as expected, by a margin of around 74,000 votes.

ODISHA

Odisha is one state where the Modi wave was restricted by the Naveen Patnaik-led Biju Janta Dal (BJD). The votes that the BJD got in Odisha were solely because of personal connect that Patnaik had with a cross-section of voters. In the state that ranks among the top three in terms of poverty level, his political strategy—soft socialism—was to create a population dependent on the government's social welfare schemes.[25] The continuous dependence created a bond between Patnaik and the voters which was difficult to break. In 2014,

---

[25]Soft socialism refers to a mechanism where significant population is dependent on welfare scheme of the government for survival, and the executive head(chief minister) does not have an aggressive messaging of this delivery. https://www.livemint.com/news/india/rural-poverty-has-shot-up-nso-data-shows-11575352445478.html, last accessed 27 December 2019.

BJD got a vote share of 44.8 per cent, while BJP's vote share was 21.9 per cent. In 2019, the BJP saw an exponential jump in its vote share, which climbed to 38.4 per cent, whereas the BJD's vote share dipped to 42.8 per cent. Even on the seat count, the BJP increased its tally from one to eight, while the BJD's reduced from 20 to 12. The Congress, which was a dominant player in the 2014 elections, ended up transferring most of its vote share to the BJP and some of it to BJD. The battle of 2019 thus became one between the BJD and the BJP. Post the panchayat polls, the BJP had started to rise in western Odisha, which has a sizeable tribal population. Since the time of Biju Patnaik, the BJD has a strong vote base in the coastal districts of Odisha, which had been consolidated by Naveen Patnaik in his tenure.

Despite overwhelming support of women for Prime Minister Modi in the rest of India, in Odisha, Patnaik—and not Modi—was the first preference. Each Self Help Group (SHG) in Odisha, with roughly 10 women comprising an SHG, was given ₹15,000 by the Patnaik government. Around 70 lakh women were associated with SHGs in Odisha. Apart from this, the Peoples Empowerment Enabling Transparency Accountability (PEETHA) scheme was launched, wherein between 15 and 20 of every month, women were organized at the panchayat level to disburse benefits from Mission Shakti and Madhubabu Pension Yojana. This created awareness among the women about Naveen babu's (as Naveen Patnaik is popularly called in Odisha) social work for them. These schemes played a very important role in preventing women voters to drift towards the BJP. Ujjwala Yojana was successful in Odisha and covered at least 33 lakh female beneficiaries. Also, every month, each family below the poverty line (BPL) received 25 kg of rice at a subsidized rate of ₹1 per kg from the state government. When BJP claimed that most of the money for the scheme was allocated by the centre, BJD announced addition of more beneficiaries to the subsidized rice scheme. This helped the BJD in claiming credit, and consecutively the votes from the scheme.

The BJP had a weaker party cadre compared to the BJD.

BJD's posters were visible across the state, whereas the BJP was largely limited to its stronghold of western Odisha, and some areas surrounding Bhubaneswar. Even BJD's campaign was more widespread. Strategically, the BJD curtailed the anti-incumbency factor by changing tickets of many contesting candidates. In case of any controversy or non-performance, Naveen Patnaik suspended the party representative immediately. Through this, Patnaik gave an impression to the voters that he is listening and is concerned about them. Moreover, he did not believe in delegation of political power to the MLAs and was rather comfortable in working through the bureaucracy. The bureaucracy was not limited to administrative responsibilities, but also executed political work unofficially. Most of the regional TV channels adopted a balanced editorial line, and avoided questioning Patnaik on the effectiveness of the welfare schemes. Development, for Patnaik, was not about growth rates or wealth creation; his governance model focused on modern socialism. Modern socialism brought voters' loyalty. Apart from Dharmendra Pradhan, who was the first leader from Odisha after Biju Patnaik to represent the state in an influential ministry at the centre, the BJP did not have any vote-mobilizing leaders in the state unit.

These factors in totality gave the BJD an edge in the electoral battle with the BJP, and contributed in restricting the impact of the 'Modi Wave' in the state. Odisha was witnessing simultaneous elections similar to 2014. Simultaneous elections have always been advantageous for Naveen Patnaik. Over time voters had cultivated a mindset of 'MLA first MP later'. In the past, no other party could project a face which could take on Patnaik. This made the Lok Sabha elections less relevant for voters, and they ended up voting for Patnaik in both the assembly and Lok Sabha elections. Modi was a new phenomenon in 2014, and could not reach voters in Odisha. However, post the panchayat polls, the BJP had worked hard on projecting Modi as the alternate face in Odisha, helping the party improve its 2014 tally. However, Patnaik's dominance as the most prominent face in Odisha restricted any possible gains for the BJP in the assembly elections. Like 2014, the BJD swept the assembly polls in 2019 winning 112 of the 146 seats. The BJP improved its tally marginally by 13 seats. The rational for simultaneous polls which has been a talking point and floated by the prime minister deserves a good debate. I think simultaneous polls will give way to 'One Year One Election' in which all the elections happening in different states can be conducted together. Elections are an important part of democracy. It is an opportunity given to voters to reward or punish public representatives. Having travelled on the ground, I have also realized it is the most legitimate means of expression of happiness and frustration by the voters. In the absence of this legitimate valve, democracy needs to search for other avenues to channelize voters' expression.

It was just not the macro factors which played a role in Odisha. There were many seats in Odisha where the national media had focused its attention. Let us discuss some of them.

Puri

This seat came under media glare after the popular national spokesperson of the BJP, Sambit Patra, was given a ticket from Puri. Earlier there were rumours that Prime Minister Narendra Modi might be contesting from Puri. In 2013, Modi had addressed his first rally in the state from Puri. I remember being in the city for *Lalkar*. Visiting the Puri temple was first on my list on reaching the city. I had to park my car some distance away from the majestic temple and started interacting with the people. I stopped a man on a motorcycle who was wearing a red helmet and must have been in his mid-fifties.

'*Kya lag raha hai iss baar?*' (What do you think would happen this time?) I asked.

'*Modi ka lag raha hai.*' (It seems Modi will win.)

'*Aur Naveen?*' (And what about Naveen?) I further enquired.

His response was puzzling :'*Naveen bhi aaiga aur Modi bhi aaiga*' (Both Naveen and Modi would come to power.)

While elections in Odisha had always been about MLA first MP later, this time even the MP elections were gaining importance because of Modi. I further stopped at a puja shop on the way to the temple. Seeing my mic, the owner was a bit reluctant to talk, but after requesting her, she agreed.

'*Aur kya Modiji jeet rahe hain Odisha?*' (So, is Modi going to win in Odisha?) I purposefully asked a leading question.

'*Modiji acche hain par Naveenji bhi hamare liye kaafi kiye hain*' (Modi is good, but Naveen is enough for us.)

The division of women voters between Modi and Patnaik was clearly visible. This was unlike other places where women were going largely with the BJP because of Modi.

Sambit Patra's entry in Puri happened a bit late. This gave him less time at his disposal. However, he utilized the time effectively by touring maximum number of villages. Puri has been a stronghold of the BJD since 1997. Pinaki Misra from the BJD was not a weak candidate, and was supported by coastal voters who were rallying behind the BJD because of Patnaik. The Brahmin-dominated constituency has seven assembly seats. Patra was seen as Modi's representative and was pulling substantial crowds at his public engagements. Out of seven assemblies, Patra managed to get a lead in three—Satyavadi, Brahmagur and Puri. However, in order to win the seat, the BJP had to curtail the loss from Nayagarh assembly. Nayagarh gave the BJD a decisive lead where both the Naveen Patnaik and Pinaki Misra factors worked in BJD's favour. Apart from this the BJP could not prevent the minor division of SC and fishermen votes to the BSP and Akhil Bharatiya Hindu Mahasabha (ABHM), which captured 6,283 and 5,000 votes respectively. BJD's cadre also supported those who voted 'None of the above' (NOTA) behind the scene and there was a strategic 7,000 vote polled for NOTA. In total, there were roughly 17,000 non-BJP votes which made the strategic difference between the BJP and BJD. The BJD managed to win in the constituency by a narrow margin of 11,714 votes. Minute planning in the last 48 hours and tacit support to the NOTA and BSP voters were the swing factors.

The mistake in Puri was not repeated in the high-profile seat of Bhubaneshwar.

Bhubaneshwar

Like Puri, Bhubaneshwar also has seven seats in the assembly. The BJP fielded former IAS officer Aparajita Sarangi against BJD's Arup Patnaik. Arup Patnaik is a former IPS officer and has been the police commissioner of Mumbai earlier. When I spoke to people, majority of them were appreciative of the work done by Aparajita Sarangi during her tenure as an IAS officer. After knowing that the party will be fielding her from Bhubaneshwar, she began her campaign the very next day. This gave her time to reach different assemblies of Bhubaneswar. On the other hand, Arup Patnaik began late and had lesser acceptance among the voters. Many called him an 'outsider' privately. There was also an internal defection, and many local BJD workers did not actively campaign for Arup Patnaik. Most urban voters swung the BJP way after Prime Minister Narendra Modi's massive road show and public meeting close to the election. Sarangi also had a good hold on slum-dwellers' votes because of her work during her tenure. There were roughly more than 400 slums which voted completely for Sarangi. Out of the seven MLA seats, a lead in Jaydev and Ekamra constituencies helped the BJP sail through with a margin of more than 20,000 votes.

Kendrapara

This coastal constituency saw a battle between Naveen Patnaik and Baijayant Panda. Though Patnaik was not contesting from this seat, he had converted the fight from BJD vs BJP to Naveen vs Baijayant. Panda was with Patnaik since the initial days of the BJD. Closer to the 2019 elections, he decided to join the BJP, as his influence in the party had reduced, and his differences with Patnaik had widened. Moreover, the IAS officer Mr V. Karthikeyan Pandiyan—and not Panda—had Patnaik's ears now and Panda was left with no option but to leave the party. He was given the post of national vice president and spokesperson in the BJP. The fight was popularly called as *Swabhiman* vs *Baiman* (prestige vs betrayal) by the BJD. The BJD applied its entire resource base and party machinery on this seat. It had fielded cinestar and former Rajya Sabha MP from the BJD,

Anubhav Mohanty, against Panda. Anubhav Mohanty is one of the most popular cinestars in Odisha. Patnaik actively campaigned in Kendrapara for two days. The BJD had marked every booth and SHG in the constituency. It became difficult for Baijayant Panda to counter Patnaik's election machinery. Panda enjoyed the support of the youth in his constituency, but that was not enough. The BJD won in the constituency by a margin of more than one lakh votes. People attributed this victory to Naveen Patnaik.

Apart from these constituencies which were in national media glare, some other constituencies also deserve mention.

Other Constituencies

In Koraput, the BJP candidate Jayram Pangi was not accepted by the people. The Congress had fielded Saptagiri Ulaka, the son of former minister and Odisha Pradesh Congress Committee (OPCC) president Ramchandra Ulaka. Ramchandra Ulaka provided some base vote. The vote-defining factor in this constituency was local, not national and the Congress became the preferred choice. The Congress here had also actively fought against the state government in the Kundali gangrape case. (The incident happened on 10 October 2017 when the victim, a class 9 student of Government Welfare School Sorisapadar, while returning from Kundali market was allegedly gangraped by four 'uniformed personnel' in Lanjiguda forest. The girl later committed suicide at her village, Masguda, in January 2018). The BJP local unit did not actively revolt against the BJD government on this sensitive issue, and the Congress made the voice of opposition in Koraput. Further, being in the southern region, the BJP also did not have any base voter like it did in the western part of Odisha. The Congress won the seat by a narrow margin of only around 3,000 votes.

Cuttack was BJD's stronghold, and the party had won all seven assembly seats. Infact, its candidate, Bhartuhari Mohabbat, has been an MP five times in the past. Yet again, the BJP declared its candidate late. The candidate, former DGP Prakash Mishra, got less time to break into the BJD's citadel. Moreover, the BJP cadre was relatively weak, and the BJD could manage yet another victory.

In western Odisha, BJP had a relatively stronger base, and had consolidated its position post the surge in the panchayat polls. Most of the seats the BJP won came from western Odisha—Sambalpur, Bolangir, Kalahandi, Sundargarh and Bargarh. In Sundargarh, BJP received the support of its veteran leader Jual Oram, and former MLA Dilip Roy who consolidated the silent tribal voters in favour of the BJP.

The BJP could make only marginal—and not exponential—gain in Odisha because of the Naveen Patnaik factor, which made him win with a landslide in the assembly elections, but at the same time also impacted the Lok Sabha elections. This is why in some of his rallies, Prime Minister Modi avoided attacking Naveen Patnaik personally. The gains in the western region were consolidated, but lack of strength in the coastal areas did not make Odisha a 'Bengal result' for the BJP. However, going forward, the BJD will face the 'great successor' dilemma after Naveen Patnaik, and BJP is emerging as a preferred option. Like Bengal, the Congress or the Left is no longer a dominant force. If Odisha shows a bright long-term future for the BJP, the party has to be cautious of the Northeast. Having emerged as a political option in the Northeast, the BJP needs to have a state-specific strategy to prevent coming down from its current peak political performance. Of course, development in the Northeast is its X factor, but at the same time, ability to communicate perception on sensitive issues will also be critical.

8

MODI'S MAGICAL CAPTAINCY: THE HILLY STATES OF UTTARAKHAND, HIMACHAL PRADESH, HARYANA, PUNJAB AND JAMMU & KASHMIR

In 2014, the BJP won 21 out of 38 seats in the hilly states of Punjab and Jammu & Kashmir (now a Union Teritory) combined. Many believed that the BJP had already peaked in these areas, and 2019 would see them slide down in seat count. Haryana had come out of the Jat agitation, and witnessed a strong Jat–Non-Jat consolidation. Uttarakhand and Himachal Pradesh had been swept by the BJP last time, and were displaying similar signs post a wave of expressive nationalism near the elections. Respect for the army and emotional attachment with the soldier are part of the society in these states. In fact, many regiments in the Indian Army have countless soldiers from these states apart from Haryana.

Even though Punjab echoed similar sentiments, the charisma of Captain Amarinder Singh outplayed the anti-Congress sentiment in the neighbouring states of Himachal Pradesh and Haryana. The BJP in Punjab was a tag-along party of the Shiromani Akali Dal (SAD). Whenever the Akali Dal gains strength in Punjab, the NDA gains, and vice versa. The BJP since long did not expand its organization pan Punjab. Amarinder Singh's anti-Pakistan line did not give the NDA any chance to attack him. Further, in the entire campaign rally, there were rare instances where Prime Minister Modi attacked Amarinder Singh personally. The job to counter Amarinder Singh was with the Badal-led Akali Dal. Badal's party was also occupied in its electoral battles of Firozpur and Bhatinda. Also, the entire campaign of the Congress in Punjab was spearheaded by Amarinder Singh and not by the then Congress President Rahul Gandhi. This averted what could have been a Modi vs Rahul battle in Punjab.

Jammu & Kashmir had all the focal attention. BJP experimented with an alliance with its ideological opponent, the Peoples Democratic Party (PDP). After Mufti Sayeed's demise, the fissures were visible and the BJP decided to pull out of the alliance. It has been my view that a political union between ideological opponents is a short-lived marriage. We have seen this with SP–BSP in UP, and Congress–JD(S) in Karnataka. It only ends up weakening either of the two parties. The BJP had a traditional stronghold in Jammu division, which had three seats; the Kashmir division had PDP and the National Conference (NC) competing for the remaining three seats. While PDP's core constituency was unhappy with the party over its decision to ally with the BJP to form a government, the BJP had unwavering support in Jammu and Ladakh over their stance on national issues and the promise of revoking Article 370.

Let us look at the key constituencies of Haryana, Uttarakhand, Himachal Pradesh, Punjab and Jammu & Kashmir for analysing micro factors that shaped the verdict.

HARYANA

Haryana has Yadavs, Brahmins and Punjabis among significant caste groups, but the Jats are the dominant caste. In the 2014 elections, the BJP had won 7 out of 10 seats due to the huge Modi wave, but this time it was said that due to Jat vs non-Jat and anti-incumbency against the Modi government, the BJP would win fewer seats. And yet again I could not find this reasoning resonating with the people of Haryana.

Caste-based politics was clearly getting overshadowed by the Modi factor and a nationalism wave which had soared after the Pulwama attack and further ascended after the Balakot air strikes. Modi's schemes were popular among the women in Haryana too.

Women and youngsters who felt proud of India's global image were becoming the core vote base for the BJP.

To understand Haryana's demography and politics better, we need to analyse the state as divided into three regions according to the national highways: (a) the region around NH-1 is populated mostly by non-Jat communities and boasts primarily of a wealthy population. One of the constituencies of this region is Yamuna Nagar, which is an SC seat. This region also includes Sonipat, Ambala and Kurukshetra. (b) NH-8 is an OBC-dominated region and includes Revadi and the Gurguram areas. (c) NH-9 is a Jat-dominated region and an industrial belt which includes Sirsa, Hissar and Rohtak.

Jat-dominated regions were going to be tricky for the BJP as these had traditionally been the Congress' bastions. Non-Jat-dominated regions like Yamuna Nagar, Ambala, Kurukshetra, Kaithal and Panipat, on the other hand, were safe zones for the BJP. The demography of Haryana is: Jats constitute around 24 per cent; OBC, 24 per cent; SC, 21 per cent; Brahmins, 18 per cent; Punjabis around 8–9 per cent and Baniyas around 3–4 per cent.

Before the BJP rose to power, regional parties had a stronghold in Haryana's politics. Devi Lal, Bansi Lal and Bhajan Lal and their families were key players in Haryana's politics. While Devi Lal was from the Janta Dal, Bansi Lal and Bhajan Lal were from the Congress.

There was a high probability of the Jat agitation—a demand to include Jats from Delhi, Haryana, Madhya Pradesh, Rajasthan and UP in the Central OBC list—turning the tide against the BJP, which would have made it difficult for the party to match its 2014 tally, let alone exceed it. However, a well-known fact about Jats is that they never compromise with two things—their land and patriotism. After the Pulwama attack, there was a widespread current of nationalism which was supposedly engulfing the Jats too. The BJP now stood a better chance of winning all 10 seats.

The Hissar seat was going to witness a match between families and was also called the contest of young leadership. BJP's Brijendra Singh, son of Virendra Singh, was contesting against Jannayak Janata Party's (JJP) Dushyant Chautala, grandson of Choudhary Devi Lal, and Congress' Bhavya Bishnoi, grandson of Bhajan Lal.

Just ahead of the 2019 elections, Dushyant Chautala left the Indian National Lok Dal (INLD) to start his own party, JJP, named after the ideology of his grandfather Choudhary Devi Lal.

The three-cornered contest between BJP, Congress and JJP turned out to be a direct fight between Modi and anti-Modi narratives. While the media was busy projecting the Haryana election as Jat vs non-Jat, people on the ground had already moulded it into a fight between nationalism and anti-nationalism. The Congress' statement on the Indian Army and the subsequent demands for proof of the Balakot air strikes was likely to hurt the party badly.

Under the previous governments, Haryana had been a victim of skewed administration: the Congress-led government had developed only those regions of the state where they had received votes. The Rohtak region was better developed in comparison to the rest of Haryana. However, under Manohar Lal Khattar, the state had witnessed development across geography.

A majority of Haryana's population is into agriculture and the Modi government's schemes for farmers ensured higher minimum support price (MSP), sufficient water and access to electricity, for which the Khattar government had some credits to share too.

The wave of nationalism and a consolidation of non-Jats had made the BJP a favourable choice in most of the constituencies. However, there were three seats where micro factors had the potential to significantly affect the voting outcome and if the BJP were to get a perfect score of 10 or to increase its tally from 2014, these seats were critical.

Rohtak

Rohtak had traditionally been the bastion of Deepender Singh Hooda. There are nine assembly seats in Rohtak Lok Sabha constituency, and the Jats dominate the narrative in all assembly constituencies except Kosli, Rohtak city, Beri and Bahadurgarh. In these, other castes also play an important role. Kosli assembly is one such assembly constituency in Rohtak where Hooda used to traditionally lag behind with a margin of around 40,000 votes. However, he used to cover the lead from Kalanor, Bahadurgarh, Rohtak and Beri assembly constituencies. This time the Kosli assembly turned out to be a swinger constituency, expecting to give the BJP a lead of around 80,000 votes. This Yadav-dominated assembly constituency polled one-way in favour of the BJP as a result of Modi's nationalism wave and strong leadership. Apart from Kosli, the BJP unexpectedly was poised to lead from Rohtak, Kalanor and Bahadurgarh. When I asked the Jats in these constituencies, they explained in an animated tone:

'Hamaare muddon ko hum Vidhan Sabha mein nipat lenge... abhi desh ke naam vote daalenge! (We will tackle our issues in the Vidhan Sabha...right now we will vote for the nation!)

They clearly expressed their unhappiness for Manohar Lal Khattar, but were rallying behind Modi. The 20–30 per cent Jat division in favour of the BJP dented Deepender Hooda's core base vote and could swing the constituency in BJP's favour. The magnitude of the Modi wave could be seen from the fact that in Hooda's own assembly constituency Kanohi Sapla, he could not prevent as high as 20 per cent Jats moving away from the Congress to the BJP. The BJP won the Lok Sabha elections by a margin of a little over 7,500 votes.

Hisar

Hisar, a seat which the BJP had lost in 2014, was witnessing a triangular fight this time after the split of INLD into JJP and INLD factions. Dushyant Chautala, the founder of JJP, was contesting from Hisar. Out of 15 lakh voters, Jats constituted at least 7 lakh and SC around 2.5 lakh. Hisar is an agrarian constituency. To make the fight interesting, the Congress had fielded Kuldeep Bishnoi's son. His selection had angered some of the local Congress workers who were hoping to get a ticket for years of loyal service or would have campaigned in the name of Kuldeep Bishnoi. Family-driven politics did not have active takers even in local Congress units. In this situation, the OBCs who used to rally behind Bishnoi in the past saw the BJP as a stronger option. In this third-generation family fight between JJP and INLD, some Jat voters drifted away to the BJP, giving it a clear edge in the constituency.

Sirsa

'Jisko Devi Lal ne ungli pakda di vo raajneetik roop se aage badh gaya.' (Whoever's hand Devi Lal holds, he moves ahead in politics.) This popular saying sums up the sentiment Devi Lal used to echo in Sirsa. However, post his demise, this SC seat was in the news for political 'gutbaazi'. The then Congress State President Ashok Pawar was fighting from this constituency. He faced an internal rebellion from Bhupinder Hooda's faction. A divided Congress Party confused the voters. Even though it was an SC seat, the Jats and Jat Sikhs played an important role in deciding the electoral fate. None of them wanted to waste their votes. In a situation where the Congress was divided, and INLD and JJP were busy diluting each other's votes, the Jats and Jat Sikhs drifted away from the Congress and INLD to the BJP. The BJP fielded a female SC face who divided the female SC voters. This division of SC votes and the drift of Jat Sikh votes made it possible for the BJP to edge out a victory.

Overall, if one has to rank the states based on Modi's personal image and nationalism, Haryana would rank at the top apart from Karnataka, Bihar and the hilly states.

UTTARAKHAND

One of the hilly states in the northern part of India, Uttarakhand—also known as Devbhoomi—had witnessed the BJP emerging victorious in all five seats in the 2014 elections. In Uttarakhand it had always been a linear contest between the BJP and the Congress. Gorkhas and Garhwalis are the two most dominant communities in the region, together constituting over 60 per cent of the total population.

A strong Modi wave and upsurge in nationalism were clearly evident here, but the unemployment issue on the other end of the spectrum was also glaring at the face of electoral onlookers.

Haridwar

In the Haridwar constituency, former Uttarakhand Chief Minister Harish Rawat was expected to contest. However, seeing the sitting MP Ramesh Pokhriyal's popularity due to the public work undertaken by him, Rawat did not contest. While the Congress was relying on Muslims who constituted around 20 per cent of the population in the Haridwar constituency, the BJP was relying on its performance and a favourable wave. Muslims and SCs together constituted around 30–35 per cent of the population, which meant it was not going to be a straightforward contest for the BJP.

At this stage, the Congress fielded Ambrish Kumar, the former MLA from Haridwar, who lacked substantial political influence. This made the situation more conducive for a BJP win.

Tehri Garhwal

An out and out hilly constituency, Tehri Garhwal had Garhwalis and Gorkhas as factors shaping the ballot outcome. The sitting MP and the current queen of the Tehri Garhwal community, Mala Rajya Laxmi Shah, was contesting against Congress' Pritam Singh.

There is a popular story among the Tehri Garhwal community. At the time when Jawaharlal Nehru became the prime minister, he offered a cabinet post to the king of Tehri Garhwal, which was met with a refusal. Nehru was told that a king could not accept anything less than the prime ministerial post.

The constituency had witnessed remarkable development in the last five years under the Modi government. Hilly areas were usually left less developed owing to the difficult terrain, but the Modi government had ensured that railways and roadways were developed, which made the party an easy choice for the voters. In addition, the surgical strikes and Balakot air strikes were acting as vote pullers in all the constituencies of Uttarakhand.

I spoke to a chaiwala about the possible outcome of the elections and he pointed out how nobody could deny Modi was set to make a comeback. Modi had carried off his duties well and he deserved to come back.

Another person I spoke to belonged to the SC community. He worked in a small cobbler shop. He revealed how in the past he had never voted for the BJP, but after looking at the party's work he was going to vote for it this time.

Modi government's 'chaar-dhaam' connectivity was viewed as an enormous employment opportunity by the people of Uttarakhand, as enhanced connectivity would mean increase in pilgrimage and tourism on which a large part of Uttarakhand and Himachal are dependent.

Nainital–Udhamsingh Nagar

This constituency was set for a close contest, as a tall Congress leader and former Chief Minister Harish Rawat was up against BJP's Ajay Bhatt. Between the two candidates, Rawat enjoyed greater popularity and was referred to as 'dada' (older brother) by many. In fact, Ajay Bhatt had even lost an election from his own constituency of Ranikhet.

The Congress' internal politics was likely to hurt Rawat. Indira Hridayesh, a very popular Congress leader, had silently revolted against Harish Rawat, as she feared that Rawat's win would escalate him to the position of a much bigger leader than her and it would result in her political career coming to a standstill. If Rawat was to lose, Hridayesh stood a chance of winning the ticket in the next Lok Sabha elections.

Hridayesh had been elected from the Haldwani constituency in the 2012 Uttarakhand Legislative Assembly elections and had a stronghold in the Haldwani assembly. However, she didn't campaign for the Congress and as a result the Congress cadre did not work on the ground. Around 30–35 per cent Muslims and Bengalis did not turn up to vote and there was less enthusiasm among core voters of the Congress, which in turn made BJP's victory obvious.

Almora

In the Almora constituency, palayan (migration) was the most important issue, as many people were leaving the place citing lack of job opportunities and earnings. However, in a direct contest between BJP's Ajay Tamta and Congress' Pradeep Tamta, both from the same family, Ajay Tamta, despite his underperformance, had an upper hand because of Modi. Another reason that was giving BJP an upper hand was the Congress' internal politics.

HIMACHAL PRADESH

Himachal Pradesh has four constituencies: Kangra, Hamirpur, Mandi and Shimla. In 2014, the BJP had won all four and this time the swelling nationalism tide was making the win even more certain for the party. In Himachal Pradesh almost every third family has at least one member serving in the armed forces and the Congress' statement questioning the Balakot air strikes had turned voters against them.

Kangra

Kangra, the biggest district of Himachal, had handed over the victory crown to the BJP in the 2014 election when the two-time Chief Minister Shanta Kumar contested with a BJP ticket. Shanta Kumar was popular for the slogan *'Har ghar mein nal, har ghar mein hal'* (Water in every home, plough in every home). However, by 2019, Shanta Kumar had crossed the 75-year age limit set by the BJP for candidates and the party was forced to give a ticket to someone else. Although the candidate did not matter much in these elections, the BJP still continued to play safe by giving the ticket to Kishan Kapoor who belonged to the Gaddhi community of Charwahe, which come under the ST category.

The ST and OBC communities here constitute over 40 per cent of the mass who were now fast-shifting to the BJP due to its politics of development and Prime Minister Modi's clear vision. Development done by the BJP had improved tourism, the main source of livelihood for most of the people here, much to the voters' delight.

The BJP had paved the road to its victory in 2017 itself when the party chose Jai Ram Thakur as the chief minister after winning the elections, giving out a statement that the saffron party chose a chief ministerial candidate based on merit and not caste.

I was at a timber shop near Gaggal airport (Dharamshala airport) and was talking to the shopkeeper. About 5–6 people were circled around us. I asked the shopkeeper about the current political situation and the possible outcome. I can still recall his statement which stung through me. He claimed that even if a dog contested from the BJP, it would win. The scenario was crystal clear here.

I then spoke to a police officer to gather information about the changes there. He requested me to keep his name anonymous and then bared how Modi was everywhere. He also explained that after handing out schemes like the Ujjwala Yojana and constructing roadways and railways, Modi had become synonymous with development and nobody could defeat him.

Himachal Pradesh was one place where people were happy with the introduction of GST, as now they were getting pucca bills, thus eliminating the ills of bribery. The revision of GST's limit for goods business from 20 to 40 lakh made them even happier, as most of the traders here were small-sized traders with revenue of around 25–30 lakh.

The Congress had all the Chaudhary voters on its side after distributing canal (khet strips) for free, but the surging nationalism wave swept them away from the Congress to the BJP. They had voted enough number of times for the Congress and this time their vote was going for the nation and for Modi.

Shimla

In Shimla, the Kashyap community was the most dominant community and in 2014, Virender Kashyap had won the seat for the BJP. However, he faced multiple corruption charges during his five-year tenure and voters now demanded a change. The BJP played smartly and gave a ticket to his brother-in-law Suresh Kumar Kashyap. By doing so the party ensured a change while containing its Kashyap voters at the same time.

Apart from this, development work, especially the four-lane highway work which extended to the China border, gave the BJP a big boost and the party's performance itself campaigned for them.

A part of Thakur voters who used to go with the Congress shifted to the BJP after the party gave a Thakur the post of chief minister.

This completely altered the equation, with almost 90 per cent Thakur and Sharma voters going with the BJP.

Hamirpur

In Hamirpur, Anurag Thakur had been contesting and winning this seat since 2008. Hamirpur witnessed a lot of infrastructural development and now there were roadways and railways even in the remotest of mountains, thereby boosting tourism.

This constituency had a considerable number of Paswan voters who voted for the Congress and considered BJP as a party of the upper caste. However, the scenario was changing fast. I spoke to a local who accepted that people received a roof on top of their heads under Modi's Awas Yojana and this is why many were now contemplating voting for the party, breaking the decades-old rule of voting for the Congress.

The Congress knew that defeating Anurag Thakur was impossible and hence it fielded Ram Lal Thakur, an ex-Kabaddi player and a former cabinet minister from Himachal Pradesh, as the scapegoat. The Congress workers also did not display any enthusiasm in campaigning.

Mandi

Of all the constituencies of Himachal Pradesh, Mandi had the most interesting politics. Aashray Sharma of the Congress was contesting against the sitting BJP MP, Ram Swaroop Sharma. In 2014, the BJP had won this seat with a tiny margin of less than 40,000 votes. Aashray Sharma is the son of Anil Sharma who belongs to the BJP. Anil Sharma refused to campaign for the BJP, as it would mean campaigning against his own son.

Despite such huge advantage, the Congress failed to capitalize on it owing to internal party politics. In Mandi, the Congress was divided in two camps. Former Chief Minister Virbhadra Singh wanted his wife to get a ticket from Mandi. Sukhram, Aashray Sharma's grandfather and a tall leader of the Congress, wanted his grandson to get a ticket. Once the party got divided, the ground cadre of the Congress also got divided and the BJP received the full benefit of the same, with the party's victory sealed with an even larger margin than in the 2014 elections.[26]

There is a general understanding among people to choose the party at the centre which is ruling in the state as it would mean development at a faster pace. This was an added advantage for the BJP.

PUNJAB

In Punjab the MP candidates mattered more than the prime ministerial candidate. In 2014 Punjab witnessed a triangular contest, as AAP had managed to make big inroads into the state and won four seats. However, it was no longer going to be a three-cornered contest in the 2019 election, as leaders of AAP's Punjab Unit had rebelled and quit the party to float a new political outfit, the Punjab Ekta Party (PEP).

Leaving aside Sangrur where AAP's Bhagwant Mann was in prominence, nearly all other regions of Punjab had disregarded AAP's 'alternative' politics owing to the party's descending graph and erratic political behaviour. AAP, which was a strong contender in 2014, was now serving just as a vote-cutter party. In 2014, a part of the Congress' votes shifted to the AAP as the latter had managed to provide people a hope to put an end to the drug menace. When the SAD was in power, the Congress did not talk much about the drug issue. The SAD was losing, but the bigger question was who to vote for. A considerable number of people who had till now considered the Congress as the only option was now seeing the AAP as an alternative. Thus, division of voters helped the SAD which managed to get four seats despite a huge anti-incumbency welling up. In 2019, when the AAP dissolved, the votes that had shifted to its kitty once again went back to the Congress, which then managed to get more seats. The AAP was reduced to just one seat. It was being said in Punjab that the BJP's local unit helped the Congress in order to prevent the AAP from sweeping the assembly elections.

---

[26] In 2014, the margin was around 40,000 votes whereas in 2019 the vote margin was more than 4 lakh.

The Congress looked confident under Captain Amarinder Singh whereas BJP was trying its best to get a few seats. Cricketer turned politician Navjot Singh Sidhu remained the point of discussion throughout the elections, though not for all good reasons. Sidhu's high political ambitions rendered him irrelevant. When he was in the SAD–BJP alliance, Sidhu had tried to surpass Sukhbir Singh Badal and when he joined the Congress he tried surpassing Captain Amarinder Singh by projecting himself as the future chief minister of Punjab. Sidhu played the politics of opportunism without realizing that politics isn't a one-day affair but a marriage which needs a lifelong 24x7 commitment. Sidhu, a performer, could manage to get crowds but not voters.

Let us now analyse a few key constituencies.

Ferozpur

In 2014, Sher Singh Ghubaya of SAD defeated Congress' Sunil Kumar Jhakar with a small margin of around 30,000 votes, despite the huge Modi tide back then. However, this time too, the SAD had a good chance of winning the seat as it had worked in the constituency and managed to get more funds for the assembly. In 2019, Sher Singh Ghubaya's son joined the Congress to contest against SAD. Sukhbir Singh Badal was contesting from Ferozpur and this made the contest not only interesting but also a high-profile one.

Ferozpur had over 60 per cent (that is, 5 lakh voters) Rai Sikhs, a Sikh community mainly associated with agriculture. Businesses were majorly owned by SAD supporters and they extended their full support to Sukhbir Badal who was one of them and was contesting from the constituency. Voters aged more than 60 years identified with the SAD based on historical linkage.

However, the youth from this constituency were seen siding with the Congress and some locals alleged that the drug menace continued under the SAD government. Ferozpur shares its border with Pakistan, which was where drug smuggling originated and the general perception was that if the SAD wins, the drug menace in the state would not be solved.

Older Sikhs who were ingrained in deeper politics understood that if the BJP wins, then the SAD–BJP alliance in Punjab would have more say and Sukhbir Badal could get a cabinet post which will then help their voices to be heard. In rural areas, the SAD was already strong, giving it an edge in the constituency. Sukhbir Singh Badal was an MLA from the Jalalabad assembly, which voted for him unanimously in the Lok Sabha elections.

Bhatinda

Another high-profile seat retained by the SAD was Bhatinda. It was, however, not retained on the basis of performance but allegedly only due to the power of money. The sitting MP and a cabinet minister, Harsimrat Kaur Badal was contesting against Congress' Amarinder Singh Raja Warring.

In 2014, Harsimrat Kaur Badal had contested against her brother-in-law, Manpreet Singh Badal (member of the Congress' manifesto committee), son of Prakash Singh Badal's brother. Both Manpreet Singh Badal and Harsimrat Kaur had corruption allegations against them. Harsimrat won with a vote margin of less than one per cent.

The on-ground perception was not in favour of Harsimrat Kaur Badal. Local people pointed out how money was an important factor in the elections. Another novel piece of local trivia for me was that many Volvo buses plying between Punjab and Delhi were managed by sympathizers close to the Akali Dal.

Prakash Singh Badal headed the SAD committee, which received funds from the Sikh community from different parts of the world, and here too Prakash Singh Badal was facing corruption allegations. As per locals, money was an important factor in deciding the course of the seat.

Drug menace under the SAD government was not solved, and even some influential people started parting ways from the party. Many IPS officers had started getting frustrated with the party when their own sons slid into drug addiction and drug abuse. This marked the downfall of the SAD in Punjab. The Congress opened up many rehabilitation centres for drug addicts, giving the people of Punjab a ray of hope that the drug menace would end soon.

Amidst so many factors working against Harsimrat Kaur, the nationalism wave after the Pulwama attack and Balakot air strikes was working in her favour. Nationalism had engulfed the entire country and Punjab was no different. Under Modi's leadership, constituencies of Punjab which were under UPA also witnessed growth. Harsimrat Kaur Badal reiterated in her election campaign that she had worked a lot and if she won again she would not only finish the work that was left incomplete but would also double up the work she had undertaken so far.

Both the AAP and PEP were going to impact the elections, though with a comparatively diminished effect than earlier, as the AAP had lost its charm in Punjab after its leader rebelled to form the PEP. Sukhpal Singh Khaira, the leader of the PEP (former senior leader of AAP), popular for anti-drug campaign, was likely to cut the votes of the Congress, ultimately benefitting the SAD.

Anandpur Sahib

One of the most interesting seats owing to the brand of politics it witnessed was Anandpur Sahib which was won by the SAD in 2014, when Prem Singh Chandumajra defeated Congress' Ambika Soni with a small vote margin of two per cent.

This time Manish Tewari was fielded against Prem Singh Chandumajra who was facing huge anti-incumbency. Chandumajra had never visited the constituency in these five years, and while under Prime Minister Modi's leadership he had adopted a village, he did not go there even once, let alone carry out any work there.

The AAP had managed 28 per cent votes in this constituency in 2014 and after its depletion by 2019; a majority of its voters were now shifting to the Congress Party, reducing the chances of the SAD of retaining this seat to nearly zero.

A few SAD leaders who had accused Sukhbir Singh Badal and Bikram Singh Majithia of destroying the party's reputation were subsequently expelled from the party. As a result, the expelled leaders:

Sewa Singh Ekhwan, Ranjit Singh Brahmpura and Rattan Singh Ajnala formed the Shiromani Akali Dal Taksali, which was nothing but a party that was floated to cut the votes of the SAD, thus making it difficult for the SAD to retain the seat.

Sangrur

Sangrur was one of the four constituencies that the AAP had won in the 2014 elections, bringing the party to the mainstream political arena. This result also helped the AAP gain ground in assembly elections where it became the second-largest party, shifting the SAD to the third position.

In 2014, AAP managed to snatch rural voters from the Congress' kitty and its anti-drug narrative worked wonders. Voters were also looking for a new party and by targeting the SAD, the AAP gave voters what they were looking for. Bhagwant Mann defeated the SAD candidate Sukhdev Singh Dhindsa by over two lakh votes.

By 2019, Bhagwant Mann became infamous as he was often caught drunk. However, he was still popular among the local people of his constituency as he resolved their issues and ensured their voices were heard in the Parliament.

While 2014 was AAP vs SAD, 2019 was AAP vs Congress. In 2019, the sitting MP, Bhagwant Mann, was contesting against Congress' Kewal Singh Dhillon and SAD's Parminder Singh Dhindsa, son of Sukhdev Singh Dhindsa. Kewal Singh Dhillon was famous only among urban voters and therefore had influence over only a few assemblies, unlike Bhagwant Mann who was popular in all the assemblies of his constituencies. The SAD did not repeat its MP candidate and the new candidate was not on good terms with the previous candidate, which meant that the party could not even keep its core voters intact. The caste equation didn't look conducive for the SAD either, and there was internal fighting within the Congress after ticket distribution. All these factors gave an overall edge to the AAP.

Amritsar

One of the most talked-about constituencies nationwide, Amritsar had witnessed a very interesting contest in 2014, when Congress' Captain Amarinder Singh and BJP's Arun Jaitley came face to face. In this high-profile contest, Singh defeated Jaitley by over one lakh votes. In 2014, the BSP too contested from this constituency as it had a considerable number of SC votes. The SC here were from the Valmiki community who preferred to side with the Congress while they had sided with the BJP in the rest of the country. Punjab in many ways was a contrast to the rest of India and had a very different brand of politics. Here, voters focused more on MP candidates and not much on the prime ministerial candidate.

Manohar Lal Khattar, the chief minister of Haryana, had said during a rally: 'Captain Amarinder doesn't want Rahul Gandhi to campaign in Punjab.' I don't know how true the claim was, but it was only because Amarinder Singh took the ownership of campaigning in Punjab that the Congress performed well in the state.

I was at a famous lassi shop 'Gyaan ki Lassi' where I spoke to a few people. They all believed that the Congress had a better chance as the sitting MP, Gurjeet Singh Aujla, had worked and they considered Hardeep Singh Puri as an outsider. They said that even if Hardeep Singh Puri was elected, he would be sitting in Delhi and people couldn't go to Delhi to share their problems.

BJP's sangathan (organization) was weak here, as local people mentioned, off the record, that the Punjab BJP Chief Shwait Malik himself did not want Hardeep Singh Puri to win, so that he could kickstart his own politics and receive an MP ticket in the next elections. Allegations of improper utilization of campaign funds by local party units were prevalent on the ground. Congress' sitting MP Gurjeet Singh Aujla had a good connect with the people as he remained accessible, especially to farmers.

Till the end it wasn't clear who was going to get a ticket from the BJP. Hence, amidst ineffective use of funds for campaigning, karykartas (workers) on the ground were demotivated to execute the campaign.

Gurdaspur

Once held by the BJP, Gurdaspur went to the Congress after the 2017 bypolls after the sitting BJP MP Vinod Khanna's demise. Congress' Sunil Jhakar defeated BJP's Swaran Salaria by around two lakh votes. Salaria became infamous after his sex scandal, leaving no other option than the Congress for voters. Salaria was given a ticket only based on his monetary capital base. The BJP failed to gain sympathy after Vinod Khanna's death.

Sunil Jhakar who hailed from Ferozpur lost the Ferozpur seat to SAD's Sher Singh Ghubaya in 2014 and hence didn't want to contest from there. While the party wanted him to contest from Ferozpur, Jhakar believed Gurdaspur would be a relatively safer seat for him. He realized that this time the SAD's candidate in Ferozpur was even stronger. It would be nearly impossible to beat Sukhbir Singh Badal. As Jhakar was the president, the party agreed to his choice of seat.

Continuing the legacy of giving the Gurdaspur ticket to a Bollywood celebrity, after some initial deliberations the BJP this time handed out the ticket to the popular actor Sunny Deol. Deol carried with him the image of a nationalist, mostly because of his movie *Gadar*. The actor's public image, therefore, complemented the image the BJP was trying to cultivate, especially after the Balakot air strikes. The youth found resonance with Sunny Deol and the crowd he managed to gather was speaking volumes about the possible mandate. His public appeal gave the BJP an edge in this head-to-head battle with the Congress. The BJP eventually won the seat with a margin of around 80,000 votes and a 7 per cent vote differential.

If I were to summarize the entire Punjab 2019 Lok Sabha elections I would like to point out some key analysis points:

- It wasn't a cadre-based election but a candidate-based election.
- Even when not in power, the SAD was still facing anti-incumbency, which it had created a few years ago.
- The youth and the wave of nationalism helped the BJP to gain a few seats, which almost looked impossible at the start.

- SCs were divided. While the Ravidas community voted for the BSP, the Valmiki community voted for the Congress. The BSP managed to get a considerable number of votes in multiple constituencies.
- AAP's depletion benefitted the Congress.
- In 2014, the AAP helped Bhagwant Mann win; in 2019, Bhagwant Mann helped the AAP get a lone seat.
- The RSS wasn't strong in Punjab and this was very evident.

JAMMU & KASHMIR

Jammu & Kashmir has a total of six constituencies—three under Jammu and three under Kashmir. Jammu consists of Jammu, Ladakh and Udhampur with Hindus in majority, while Kashmir has Srinagar, Baramulla and Anantnag with Muslims in majority. Srinagar has a considerable number of Sikhs too, who did not leave post the Kashmiri Pandit exodus in the early 1990s.

The primary political parties include the Jammu & Kashmir NC, the Congress Party, the BJP and the PDP.

Jammu Division

In 2014, the BJP had won all the three seats from Jammu, though the Ladakh seat was won with an extremely narrow margin. The margin of victories in Jammu and Udhampur were much higher.

Five years of BJP rule transformed local political equations. The year 2009 had witnessed more polarization than 2014 and hence fewer Muslims had looked to vote for the BJP then than in 2014. Let us look at the seat-wise analysis.

Jammu

This assembly constituency is considered as a stronghold of the BJP. Post Pulawama, the sentiment of nationalism was at its peak. The statement by the Congress leaders on Pulawama further diverted the voters away from them. Local population in Jammu is against terrorism and separatist narratives. The Balakot air strikes had consolidated people to vote for a strong nationalist government. The delivery of Central government schemes, particularly the Ujjwala Yojana, and the strong base of the RSS acted as catalysts, increasing the BJP's lead. Even though Dr Jitendra Singh was contesting from Udhampur, his positive image helped the BJP candidate from the Jammu constituency, Jugal Kishore Sharma. These factors helped the BJP to win the seat with an unprecedented lead of over 3 lakh votes.

Ladakh

The Ladakh constituency can be broadly divided into two regions—the Muslim-dominated Kargil and the Leh region with Buddhists and Hindus as dominant communities. Kargil constitutes around 65 per cent voters and the remaining 35 per cent are from Leh.

In 2014, the BJP won this seat by a margin of merely 36 votes. However, in 2019, two independent candidates—Sajjad Hussain and Asgar Ali Karbalai—also contested, both of whom were more popular than the Congress' candidate Rigzin Spalbar. In 2014, many Muslim voters had voted for the BJP, which wasn't the case in 2019. However, two independent candidates who acted as vote cutters for the Congress compensated for the loss, and made it easier for the BJP.

Udhampur

In 2014, BJP's Dr Jitendra Singh defeated Congress' Ghulam Nabi Azad with a margin of over 60,000 votes. Udhampur has assemblies with a relatively higher Hindu population. The Udhampur assembly has around 88 per cent Hindus, Kathua has 90 per cent, Kishtwar around 40 per cent and Ramban 28 per cent. As you move towards Kashmir, the demography changes and Muslim voters overshadow the Hindu voters in large numbers.

In 2019, the sitting MP, Jitendra Singh, was contesting against Vikramaditya Singh, the grandson of Maharaja Hari Singh who was the last reigning Maharaja of J&K. It was expected to be a three-cornered contest as the locally popular leader Lal Singh Chaudhary had started his own political outfit—the Dogra Swabhiman Sangathan Party. In 2014, Lal Singh Chaudhary had helped the BJP in shifting

Congress' votes on its side. Since he started his own political party this time, there was a possibility that he could prove to be stiff competition to the BJP.

However, several factors helped the BJP. The infamous Kathua rape case was understood as a loss to the BJP, but on the ground, the reality was different. The BJP managed to keep its votes intact. In the Doda assembly election, the BJP emerged stronger as several ground-level karykartas and booth-level workers from the Congress shifted to the BJP a few days ahead of the elections. Congress' leader Ghulam Nabi Azad did not campaign for the party at all. This severely dented the Congress' chances in the elections. With respect to development, people were satisfied—if not happy—with the incumbent government and the sitting MP, especially for providing good roads extending from Udhampur to Katra.

Kashmir Valley

The politics in Kashmir Valley is very different from the rest of India. I had to buy a new SIM card to remain connected to my team back in Delhi and it would take a day to get activated. We had no option but to extend our trip by a day. How I wished to see complete integration of Kashmir without any special provisions which alienated the people of the state from the rest of the country.

I was on my way to Anantnag in a shared car, when I got the opportunity to travel through India's longest road tunnel stretching over 9.28 km. The Chenani–Nashri Tunnel, also known as the Patnitop Tunnel, was inaugurated by Prime Minister Modi in April 2017. In stark contrast to the tunnel, the roads were in a really bad condition and we had a tough time travelling over almost 100 km.

Kashmir Valley witnesses a low voter turnout, which makes it difficult to predict the election outcome. However, the demography is such that results over the years have been the same more or less. After an alliance with the BJP, the PDP lost its voters and the contest was now between the Farooq Abdullah-led NC and the Congress.

Anantnag

PDP leader Mehbooba Mufti, who hails from Anantnag, could not find a suitable candidate to contest against NC and the Congress, and so she contested herself. The PDP sought and hoped for a low voter turnout. A high voter turnout would mean more people against the PDP and the opposite could have saved Mehbooba Mufti. Earlier only as much as 2–3 per cent voting happened here and the ECI decided to conduct re-elections in subsequent phases. The voter turnout did not increase substantially, and only 9 per cent voting took place the second time. However, most of these voters were disenchanted with Mehbooba Mufti and the PDP on its failure to effectively raise valley-centric issues with the centre. They considered her close to the centre and eventual preferred the NC over the PDP. Mehbooba was relegated to the third position and the Congress came second.

Srinagar

In Srinagar, Farooq Abdullah of the NC was the strongest candidate. I spoke to several people here and 9 out of 10 were against the PDP. It was purely a one-sided contest. The voter turnout of 15.6 per cent was more than enough for the NC to defeat the PDP with a margin of around 70,000 votes.

Baramulla

The voter turnout in Baramullar, at 38.9 per cent, was better than in Srinagar. PDP's decision to get into an alliance with the BJP worked against them. The alliance compulsion made the voters feel that PDP was not raising the constituency's issues. Mohammad Akbar Lone of the NC won convincingly with a margin of around 30,000 votes.

◆

After the abrogation of Article 370 on 5 August 2019, the politics of Jammu & Kashmir and Ladakh, now both Union Territories, has changed forever and it would be interesting to see how things pan out in the future—whether it leads to an emergence of new political faces or a change in political narrative by valley-centric parties, only time will tell.

9

UNCONQUERED SO FAR: SOUTH INDIA

South India has been a political greenfield investment for the BJP. Apart from Karnataka, the party has not been a major force in other south Indian states. While Karnataka has been a triangular fight between the Congress, JD(S) and BJP in the past, this time it was witnessing a bipolar battle. The Congress–JD(S) alliance was taking on the BJP. The latter has been traditionally strong in north Karnataka and the coastal areas, while the Congress dominated areas in Mysore. The JD(S) has its political clout largely around the Mysore and Mandya regions. This time the election in Karnataka was unique, as it was for the first time in recent past that the Congress and JD(S) were coming together in a Lok Sabha election to take on the BJP. Karnataka also had a very strong Modi impact, and the Congress–JD(S) state government in Karnataka was suffering.

In Kerala, the BJP was not a major player and the fight was between the Left and the Congress. The state in the past has also oscillated between the Left [CPI and CPI (M)], and the Congress. Post the Supreme Court's verdict on the Sabarimala temple case, there was renewed political interest in the state. Two states where regional parties dominated the political landscape were Andhra Pradesh and Telangana. The alliance with the Congress in Telangana had politically backfired for Chandrababu Naidu in Andhra Pradesh. The Congress Party did not gather favourable public opinion in Andhra Pradesh, especially after the creation of Telangana. The special package by the centre was a bone of contention, which also kept the BJP at a disadvantageous position in the state. Apart from the anti-incumbency factor in the assembly elections alongside the general elections in Andhra Pradesh, the support of Christians and SCs for Jaganmohan Reddy of YSRCP was visible. Anti-TDP and pro-Jagan narrative defined the politics in Andhra Pradesh. Telangana, on the other hand, witnessed a three-cornered contest between the AIMIM–Telangana Rashtra Samithi (TRS) alliance, the BJP and the Congress. The elections in Telangana were happening in the backdrop of the assembly elections where TRS won 88 seats out of 119. However, in the Lok Sabha elections, there were few seats where both the BJP and the Congress had the ability to give TRS serious competition. In fact, TRS founder K. Chandrashekar Rao's daughter, K. Kavitha, was facing a stiff competition in Nizamabad. Let us look at these states individually to identify prominent factors that played a deciding role in the 2019 verdict.

KERALA

Kerala had reached the epitome of the Left's decimation and served as a saviour for the Congress. In 2004, the Left had won 61 seats across India and since then it has been on the decline. In 2009, its seat tally reduced to 24 seats and by 2014 it was down to a mere 10 seats.

In recent years, the collapse of the Left ideology has been evident worldwide. Across the world, people are rejecting the Left doctrine and embracing the Right ideology of development-centric politics. Despite this global tide, the BJP had a lot of work to do in order to make a mark in Kerala politics. The party seems to have riled up active politics in the state with the Sabarimala issue. It was, however, the Congress that derived the maximum benefit in terms of seat share, winning 19 out of 20 seats.

The Left had swept the state in 2004, winning 18 out of 20 seats. Five years later, in 2009, its tally nosedived to four seats, but it then increased to eight seats in 2014. Even as it won four additional seats in 2014, the vote share of the Left reduced from 42 per cent in 2009 to 40 per cent in 2014, a reflection of its decline.

Until the 2019 Lok Sabha elections, the Left's political dominance could be seen in three states: West Bengal, Tripura and Kerala. While in West Bengal, the TMC led by Mamata Banerjee provided an alternative to people, Tripura witnessed an ideological battle between the Right and the Left, resulting in a clean sweep by the BJP. In Kerala, the Left vote base was slowly depleting and shifting to the BJP and the Congress. The Sabarimala issue had also hit a chord with the people.

To understand Kerala's politics, we must analyse the impact of the Ezhavas community who are also known as Ilhava, Irava, Izhava and Erava in the south of this region. By demography, the Ezava community constitutes nearly 22 per cent of the total population of Kerala. Historically, Ezavas are warriors (Kshatriyas). When Buddhism's influence started to grow in Sri Lanka, the Hindu community (Ezhava) moved to Kerala. Traditionally, the Ezhava community voted for the Left. V.S. Achyutanandan belonged to the Ezava community and is a popular Left leader in Kerala, who had consolidated the voters in the Left's favour. However, the Left's stand on the Sabarimala issue had made the community drift away from it.

If we talk about key constituencies, Palakkad and Alathur were witnessing a sharp decline of the Left. Rural constituencies had previously been strongholds of the Left with their strong cadre base there, but since 2009, the Left's vote share was slumping. Farmers involved in coffee farming and paniyas had been core voters of the Left. But this time, they displayed more proclivity to the Congress, as many promises made by the Left during the time of floods ended up being false hopes. The Left was accused of improper distribution of flood relief funds. They were incompetent in holding up their promise of home for flood-affected people, agriculture subsidy, relief fund, pension to aged people, and so on, and hence voters were now looking for an alternative, which the Congress was successful at providing.

The Sabarimala issue, as mentioned earlier, also acted as a catalyst. Ayappa devotees were upset with the Supreme Court's decision of allowing women of all age groups to enter the Sabarimala shrine. A significant chunk of the Left voters was unhappy with the Left's stand on the issue. The choice for them was between the Congress, which had a neutral stand, and the BJP which aggressively supported the devotees' position on the issue. Electorally, the Congress won, but the BJP also made gains in terms of the average vote share in the state.

Christians and Muslims formed the base vote for the Congress, and with them not taking a stand against the Sabarimala devotees' position, the Congress gained maximum from the anti-Left public sentiment in Kerala. The murder of RSS workers had united the BJP's cadre, but a low base vote was its biggest deficit in Kerala. Let us now look at a deeper analysis of the key constituencies.

Wayanad

One of the most talked-about constituencies of Kerala was Wayanad. Soon after the Congress realized that the contest in Amethi was going to be a close race, Rahul Gandhi filed a nomination from Wayanad, a constituency with a 60 per cent Muslims and Christian population. The Wayanad move was observed by many as an attempt to save the face of the then Congress President Rahul Gandhi, who was facing a tough fight from Smriti Irani in Amethi.

The Malappuram district of Wayanad constituency has three assemblies, namely Eranad, Nilambur and Wandoor which have over 70 per cent minority population. This may be the reason why the Congress considered it as a safe seat. Not to forget, Rahul Gandhi was also carrying with him the legacy of Rajiv Gandhi and Indira Gandhi.

During a rally in Kerala, Rahul Gandhi said that he won't attack the Left, thus clearing the air that they were not going to let the elections culminate into a Congress vs Left fight. Nationally, both were remotely part of the anti-BJP front. While in 2014 the minority votes got divided between the Left and the Congress, in 2019 the minority votes were unanimously going to the Congress. Minorities considered the Congress as their first preference. In 2014, there was anti-incumbency against the Congress nationwide. Thus, the minorities drifted to the Left in Kerala. The BJP was the last resort. In 2019, they saw the Congress as the party to take on the BJP nationally and amidst the Left depleting nationwide, they had no choice apart from the Congress.

While Kerala has a considerable number of Hindu voters, unlike in the northern states, these Hindu votes are not consolidated. When split, these Hindu votes get divided to mainly three parties: the Left, the Congress and the BJP who do not play a significant role in the elections in this region.

Thushar Vellapally, son of Vellapally Natesan who is a saint of the Ezhava community, was contesting against Rahul Gandhi. A businessman with no mass appeal, he failed to swing the Ezhava votes in favour of his party, the Bharath Dharma Jana Sena (BDJS), an NDA ally. The voters chose the Congress as their preferred party, having drifted away from the Left.

I remember speaking to a middle-aged man in the Kalpetta assembly of Wayanad. I asked who he thought would win. His immediate response was Rahul Gandhi. When prodded about the benefits of the predicted outcome, he had replied: 'We will have our constituency on the national map.'

Rahul Gandhi ended up winning by a vote share of 64.67 per cent, mostly from minority communities, and some Nairs and Ezhavas who rallied behind the Congress. P.P. Sunil of the CPI managed to get a vote share of 25 per cent while Thushar Vellapally (BDJS) could garner only 7 per cent votes.

Thiruvananthapuram

This constituency witnessed a close fight in 2014 when Shashi Tharoor managed to edge out a victory with a margin of 1.5 per cent vote share. It was widely believed that with Kummanam Rajasekharan contesting from the BJP, the fight would be even more challenging. However, contrary to popular perception, Tharoor swept with almost a 10 per cent vote share differential. Kummanam Rajasekharan was an ex-governor of Mizoram who resigned to contest the elections. On the ground, in the assemblies of Kovalam, Neyyattinkara and Parassala, Tharoor gained a massive lead. These assemblies were near the coast, and the fishermen community, Roman Catholics, Muslims and SCs were backing Tharoor as he was a Congress candidate. He carried a personal base vote in urban areas, especially the youth rallied behind him. Only in Nemom assembly, Rajasekharan could lead because of BJP MLA O. Rajagopal. O. Rajapgopal was also the 2014 Lok Sabha candidate from the BJP. Rajasekharan visited a few churches in the hope of attracting some Christian votes, but Rahul Gandhi contesting from Wayanad polarized Christians heavily in Tharoor's favour.

Alappuzha

This is the standalone constituency won by the Left in Kerala. The win in this constituency was attributed to the Left candidate A.M. Ariff who had been a two-time MLA from Aroor assembly in the Lok Sabha. His work on the ground was the talking point which helped him march across the victory line with a 10,000-vote differential. With senior Congress leader K.C. Venugopal not fighting the election, Shanimol Osman was the last choice. Venugopal had won this seat in the 2009 as well as 2014 elections. Campaigning by senior Congress leaders built the momentum in their favour, but a weak candidate choice relegated them to second position.

Apart from these three key constituencies, the Muslim League, a Congress ally, won two constituencies which had been their bastions—Malappuram and Ponnani—owing to more than 50 per cent Muslim population. BJP's vote share increased the maximum in Attingal and Pathanamthitta, but it could not convert them into victory seats. In both these constituencies, the BJP gained because of its stand on the Sabarimala issue, but as its minority base vote was lower than the Congress, it was the Congress which crossed the victory line. Post-Sabarimala, the Nair community which constitutes roughly 22 per cent of Kerala's population, also drifted away from the Left to the Congress and BJP.

Kerala was one state in the country which polled differently from other states. The voters did not want the BJP or a regional party, but voted with the Congress in mind.

KARNATAKA

Karnataka is one of the most important states of southern India as there is a shift in political power which is not limited to the precincts of any particular party or family. To understand Karnataka, let's divide the state into three broad categories, each with their peculiar geography and demography. First is north Karnataka, which is majorly dominated by the Lingayat community, followers of a Shaivite Hindu religious tradition. Second is south Karnataka, which has the Vokkaliga community in majority. A farmer community which is categorized under OBC in India's reservation system, the Vokkaligas has notable political power and dominance in the southern parts of Karnataka. Third is coastal Karnataka, which is majorly dominated by Hindutva politics.

Politically, Vokkaliga community members are the core voters of JD(S), whereas Kurbas, a Hindu caste with the native traditional occupation of shepherding, are the core voters of the Congress. The BJP has the Lingayats and other Hindus as its main voters.

As we know, the Congress and the BJP are pan-state parties whereas the existence of JD(S) is mainly in the Mysore (south Karnataka) region. In the 2018 assembly elections, 82 per cent of JD(S)'s seats came from 14 out of 28 Lok Sabha constituencies.

Karnataka's Lok Sabha election journey started soon after the state assembly elections where the BJP, despite emerging as the single largest party with 104 seats, could not form the government. I remember how, while predicting Karnataka elections in *Jan ki Baat*, the exit polls hit the bull's eye by predicting the BJP as the single largest party with 104 seats. Predicting Karnataka's outcome accurately was a point of inflexion for us, as we could accurately reflect the ground reality in our exit polls. JD(S) and Congress, two parties that had been each other's rivals, came together to form the government. The Congress wanted to keep the BJP away from power and was ready to go to any extent to ensure the same. The Congress even offered the chief minister's post to JD(S) even though the JD(S)'s tally was less than half of the Congress' tally.

During the assembly elections, Congress' Siddaramaiah and JD(S)' H.D. Deve Gowda had fought against each other. JD(S) President H.D. Kumarswamy had categorically said that there was no possibility of an alliance with the Congress. The Congress and JD(S) have stark ideological differences. After the Congress lost, Siddaramaiah was not holding any exclusive power anymore and as a result, D. Shivkumar and G. Parameshwara too got their hands over the controlling reins of Congress' Karnataka unit. This watering down was what changed the politics here. Siddaramaiah not being in power would mean reluctance from his side to even come out and campaign for the party and the same was seen later.

Similarly, the Congress disgruntled several of its local leaders by ignoring them. Seven-time Congress MLA and former minister Ramalinga Reddy wasn't given a ticket, which not only left the local karyakartas demotivated but also enraged them.

For the 2019 elections, the JD(S) and Congress underwent a prepoll alliance and the Congress had to succumb to JD(S)' demands. It gave away important seats to the JD(S) where the grand old party had been traditionally strong.

Throughout the 2019 elections one thing that was found consistent was how regional parties across India were becoming less and less relevant in the general elections. People were fast becoming aware that Lok Sabha elections involved choosing the prime minister of the country and votes should be given by keeping the larger issues like national security, the country's global image, economy, business, and so on in the forefront. Like in several other states, the popular regional party of Karnataka, JD(S) too was looking irrelevant in the state and it was in fact hampering the Congress' chances too.

Both the parties in alliance—Congress and JD(S)—proved to be antithetical to each other. The workers from both the parties were historic rivals. The same was seen in the 2019 election campaign, when the gathbandhan of karyakarkatas did not happen, and they lacked enthusiasm to campaign. Further, Lingayats were rallying oneway for the BJP because of Yediyurappa and the Congress' policy to divide Lingayats in its tenure. Even some of the core Kuruba Congress voters went to the BJP because of Modi. The Congress–JD(S) alliance was facing anti-incumbency in such a short period of time in government, and the BJP reaped its benefits in the 2019 Lok

Sabha polls. Karnataka, like Bihar, was at the top when it comes to ranking states based on the impact of the Modi wave.

Let's analyse some of the key constituencies of Karnataka.

Mandya

Mandya was going to witness one of the most awaited contests since the then chief minister and JD(S) President H.D. Kumaraswamy had fielded his son, Nikhil Kumaraswamy from this seat. Mandya has always been JD(S)' citadel. The BJP did not fight the elections from here and in fact helped the independent candidate, Sumalatha Ambareesh. Sumalatha's husband Ambareesh, a media personality and politician, was a three-time MP and a cult figure in Karnataka. He had initiated a lot of work and hence had a huge popularity. Nikhil Kumaraswamy hailed from the Hassan area and was considered an outsider in Mandya. Vokkaligas, the core voters of JD(S), split up as they did not wish to vote for an outsider. Women majorly supported Sumalatha, as they believed a woman could understand their problems better.

Apart from these two main factors that went against the JD(S), Mandya was also known for a strong JD(S) machinery. Despite unconfirmed reports of heavy money distribution near the voting day by some JD(S) supporters, Sumalatha won the constituency by more than 2 lakh votes. The BJP helped Sumalatha by mobilizing its workers for her campaign. I remember interacting with one of the locals while sipping coconut water on the roadside.

'What do you think? Does Nikhil have good chances?' I had asked.

He whispered, 'Ambareesh was a good man.'

I wondered why he is telling me about Ambareesh when the question is on Nikhil Kumaraswamy. Within moments many auto drivers in their mid-fifties surrounded me and started shouting pro-Sumalatha slogans. I could make out a huge undercurrent in favour of Sumalatha. People were fighting elections for Sumalatha and had already made up their mind. Apart from this, Siddaramiah had a good hold over Mandya. Wounds of loss at the hands of G.T. Devegowda of the JD(S) was still fresh in Siddaramiah's mind. He had a considerable hold in this area. The Congress got more than

5 lakh votes in Mandya in 2014. He was reluctant to extend support to Kumaraswamy's son in Mandya, as a revolt to what happened to him when he was defeated in Chamundeshwari by G.T. Devegowda in the Karnataka assembly elections.

Tumkur

Traditionally a Congress bulwark, Tumkur was won by either the BJP or the Congress in the last few elections. In a pre-poll alliance, JD(S) got this seat and with a tall leader like Deve Gowda contesting from here, the game was almost over for the BJP in this seat. Some local people I spoke to suggested that the BJP should not even bother campaigning. However, this idea did not resonate completely on ground as the BJP too had a good supporter base.

Three major factors turned people against the JD(S). The Vokkaligas were unhappy with the JD(S). They said that the party was now limited to one particular family. In addition, Amit Shah's road show helped the BJP gain ground in this constituency. Last but not the least was the Tumkur constituency where people were not just unhappy but also accused the JD(S) of diverting the water of the Tungabhadra River to Hassan, JD(S)'s home district.

I was at a famous idli shop at Tumkur where, as I ordered some *sheera* (a south Indian sweet dish), I spoke to a local who had come to the restaurant:

'What do you think? Who is stronger, Deve Gowda or the BJP?'

A man in his early sixties, he replied: 'Deve Gowda took our water to Hassan.'

The anger against Deve Gowda for drifting off the Tungabhadra water away from Tumkur to Hassan was evident. This resentment was visible among the Vokkaliga community. The Lambanis and the OBC communities were the vote base for the BJP, and Basavaraj managed to win the constituency by around 8,000 votes. The BJP organization in Karnataka was strengthened after the assembly elections under the party's national general secretary Muralidhar Rao and national general secretary (organization) B.L. Santosh. Even Deve Gowda's emotional appeal turned out to be a damp squid, and on voting day his booth-to-booth management was less effective than that of the BJP's. Had the BJP candidate campaigned more aggressively, the victory margin could have been bigger. The loss of JD(S)–Congress in their bastion of Tumkur was a reflection of the extent of the Modi wave in Karnataka.

Gulbarga

Yet another high-profile seat, Gulbarga had one of the tallest Congress leaders, Mallikarjun Kharge contesting. In 2014, Kharge had defeated the BJP candidate with a margin of around 75,000 votes, that too despite a brimming Modi wave. However, the scenario changed in 2019. While the SCs and Muslims were supporting the Congress, the BJP had Lambanis and Lingayats as its core voters.

People, especially those living in villages, had now become Modi supporters owing to various pro-poor schemes that were rolled out by the centre in the past five years. At the same time there were some anti-Kharge sentiments as well. Kharge had been an MP for eight terms, and was suffering from fatigue factor. The voters were looking for alternate faces. Dr Umesh Jadhav had reasonable clout in the constituency. He left the Congress to joine the BJP, and with him brought some Congress cadre too. There was some resentment against Kharge from the local Congress unit as he was accused of promoting his son at the cost of Congress workers. The youth across caste lines supported the BJP because of Modi. Even 25 per cent of SC youth drifted in the BJP's favour. The BJP was successful in converting anti-Kharge sentiments into votes and won the constituency by a margin of more than 80,000 votes and a vote share of 52 per cent.

Bangalore South

The Bangalore South constituency came in the news after the BJP ticket was unexpectedly given to the 28-year-old lawyer, Tejasvi Surya. It was widely expected that Ananth Kumar's wife would get the ticket from here. Ananth Kumar had been winning this seat since 1996. It was a comfortable seat for the BJP and maybe that was why the party did not hesitate in giving the ticket to a young face like Tejasvi Surya. At the same time, the party's leadership was also well aware that Ananth

Kumar's wife, Tejaswini, was not only capable but would likely receive sympathy votes as her husband, a very popular leader, had died due to pancreatic cancer just a few months before the general elections.

Tejaswini did not show any resentment for not being given a ticket and in fact campaigned for Tejasvi Surya who also visited her soon after being given the ticket. While the BJP was united (from booth-level karyakartas to Modi and Shah), the Congress was divided internally in many states.

In south Bengaluru, I boarded a state transport bus so as to get a wider view and realized that more than 90 per cent travellers in that bus were BJP supporters. There was a negative perception for the Congress–JD(S) alliance among people. Bangalore South historically has had a strong RSS presence and it is one of the strongest seats of the BJP in Karnataka. Tejasvi Surya, being young, excited first-time voters, who polled largely in his favour.

Apart from these seats where there was a contest, most of coastal Karnataka was outrightly in favour of the BJP. Areas of Udupi, Mangalore and the entire coastal belt had Hindutva brand of politics as the dominating narrative. Post Prime Minister Modi's public meeting in Mangalore, people lined up on the streets to catch a glimpse of him. This translated into one of the biggest unplanned roadshows of the campaign. Speaking to one of the persons standing and waiting to see Modi from a close distance, I enquired:

'Why are you waiting?'

He replied: 'Just to see PM Modi wave towards me.'

The Modi magic in Karnataka reached its optimum potential. The Congress–JD(S) alliance added to the Modi magic and the BJP could register its highest vote share of 51.4 per cent (up from 43 per cent in 2014) and won 25 out of 28 seats.

The Congress, despite forming a government in Chhattisgarh, Rajasthan, Madhya Pradesh and Karnataka, could not gauge popular public opinion in its favour in the Lok Sabha elections. The maturity of Indian voters is unmatched, and the voters' ability to take every election differently is a positive sign for Indian democracy.

TAMIL NADU

As I completed my Karnataka journey, I moved to Tamil Nadu. I expected the trends there to be similar to Karnataka, as the two states don't differ much in terms of demography and geography. However, my first interaction shattered all presumption and the perception built by mainstream media. This was my interaction with the cab driver driving me to my hotel. He revealed that he did not want Modi back, as he felt that Modi was against the Tamils and did not care about them.

Where in Karnataka 8 out of 10 people were knocked under the Modi wave, Tamil Nadu had a different wave altogether—9 out of 10 people did not want Modi back in power. A few major factors against the BJP were to do with how the sentiments of Tamil people were hurt when Prime Minister Modi did not turn up for a visit in the aftermath of Cyclone Gaja. They felt it was a sense of apathy towards the people of Tamil Nadu. People also claimed that not only did senior BJP leaders not visit but also held back from paying any support to the victims. The BJP, however, refuted these claims by saying that more than ₹500 crore had been given to the people of Tamil Nadu towards cyclone relief. As I ventured deeper into the villages of this state, I hardly found any place where people carried favourable sentiments for the BJP.

There were many factors which were more than telling and one of these was how the All India Anna Dravida Munnetra Kazhagam (AIADMK) was not only set to lose, but to lose very badly. The drama that followed Jayalalitha's demise pushed people to go against the party. The AIADMK had come across as a very power-hungry party that had not even spared the death of a leader like Jayalalitha, whom half the state of Tamil Nadu admired. Some people accused Shashikala of planning Jayalalitha's murder and of being a power grabber. People did not want the AIADMK back.

O. Panneerselvam and Edappadi K. Palaniswami also lost people's support. O. Panneerselvam, who had previously served as Jayalalitha's right hand, was not as strong a leader as her. Edappadi K. Palaniswami was considered an outsider and was not very popular. There was no clarity on who would become the chief minister after Jayalalitha's death and all the events that happened after her demise appeared to be nothing but drama in the public's eye.[27] On the other hand, the Dravida Munnetra Kazhagam (DMK) chief M.K. Stalin caught the right nerve of the people by promising a probe into Jayalalitha's death.

I was in Selum and took a rickshaw to travel local. I spoke to the rickshaw-puller who was from the Mukkulathor community. Traditionally an AIADMK supporter, the rickshaw-puller said he was going to vote for Stalin, as he had promised a probe into Jayalalitha's death. Also, he did not believe either in Palaniswami or Panneerselvam.

Another interesting factor which was no longer agreeing with the AIADMK was the support of Tamil-speaking Muslims. In 2016, Jayalalitha won despite a huge anti-incumbency against her and this was because she had the support of Tamil-speaking Muslims who constitute around 30–35 per cent of the total population. However, in 2019, with the BJP in power and AIADMK allying with the Paattali Makkal Katchi (PMK), Muslims were feeling unsafe and hence moved to the DMK.

In 2014, the media portrayed Tamil Nadu as a pro-BJP state because Radhakrishnan won. However, in reality there were no pro-BJP sentiments anywhere. The NDA did not work and it also failed to understand the caste equation here. Dalits supported AIADMK but as soon as the PMK, the party of Vanniyars, joined Dalits, they shifted to the DMK since Vanniyars have for long been rivals of the Dalits.

The AIADMK showed desperation to get maximum voters but it failed massively to bring them under one umbrella. Vanniyars and Dalits are rivals and the AIADMK's attempt to bring them together turned futile. Similarly, the AIADMK failed to get a majority of the dominant Muslim community to its side. Women too went against the AIADMK citing how the party had supported a rapist, and voting for the DMK or the Congress would be a rather better alternative. People predicted AIADMK's loss because it was forcefully inducting Hindutva

---

[27] In the end, it was O. Panneerselvan who succeeded Jayalalitha as the CM.

among the Tamil people, who identified themselves as seculars.

The Uri and Balakot air strikes did not have a big impact here and, in fact, people accused the central government of not negotiating with the Sri Lankan government to get their farmers released. As per locals, for Tamil people, Sri Lanka is a closer neighbour and the Modi government did not resolve issues effectively with the Sri Lankan government. This was seen as apathy on the part of the central government.

Hindutva backfired against the RSS, and the DMK capitalized on it and gave people a feeling that it was only the DMK which could enable people from various castes and religion to live together peacefully.

One thing that made the DMK stand ahead in the race was its social media presence. It was all the game of social media by the DMK that every youth parroted views on how they did not want the minority community to live under constant fear of getting lynched, when there were comparatively fewer cases of minority lynching in the state of Tamil Nadu.

On the other hand, NDA's state leadership looked weak and its social media strategy was damaging. NDA leaders were being mocked at and getting abuses hurled at them. This perception was successfully established by the DMK. People in Tamil Nadu were not just unhappy with the NDA but were determined to dethrone the AIADMK from the state and NDA from the centre. Tamil Nadu was certainly moving against the political wind blowing in the rest of the country. In fact, the AIADMK–BJP pre-poll alliance backfired for the AIADMK. Had the parties not aligned before elections, the AIADMK could have improved its tally.

An instance which proves the mainstream media is inconsistent and how it often wastes the public's and its own time was how they were trying to portray Kamal Hassan as one of the strongest leaders in Tamil Nadu. In reality, Kamal Hassan was not at all important and only a very small fraction of voters supported him. He had young educated voters as his core vote base and by making anti-Hindu statements, he lost Hindu votes. Muslims were less on his side, and hence he was left with the support of atheists who roughly constitute not more than 2–3 per cent of the total vote base.

One factor that proved fatal for the AIADMK was the party's breakaway faction, the Amma Makkal Munnetra Kazhagam (AAMK) led by T.T.V. Dhinakaran. The split led to the division of votes of the popular community of Mukkulathor between the AIADMK and the AMMK.

The recently held elections in Vellore explained the situation very well. After AMMK, MPK and Kamal Hassan did not contest, the DMK won. The presence of small parties was expected to eat into the votes of the DMK, but in contrast it was the DMK which ended up eating into the AIADMK's votes.

However, it will also be wrong to say that a majority of AIADMK supporters shifted to the DMK because traditional voters of the AIADMK abstained from voting, giving an edge to the DMK. Lack of trust in AIADMK's leadership and Jayalalitha's demise demotivated them.

Although the DMK capitalized on anti-Modi sentiments, this wasn't a sustainable approach since once the AIADMK consolidated its vote bank, the DMK would land in trouble. If you look at the past 20–25 years, whenever the AIADMK lost, it was predominantly because its core supporters had abstained from voting. Unlike the northern states of the country, the concept of swing voters doesn't fit here and the only way a party loses is when its core supporters abstain from voting.

Karunanidhi's death also stirred up a wave of sympathy support which benefited Stalin.

In the end, the DMK could sweep the state with 31 out of 39 seats and a vote share of 32 per cent.

TELANGANA AND ANDHRA PRADESH

Telangana and Andhra Pradesh have 17 and 25 Lok Sabha seats respectively. The politics of both these states is distinct from national-level politics, with the regional parties playing a more transcendent role.

Telangana

Owing to the Telangana movement, the Andhra Pradesh Reorganisation Act, 2014, also popularly known as the Telangana Act, bifurcated the state of Andhra Pradesh into Telangana and the residuary, Andhra Pradesh. With the Owaisi brothers being very vocal and undertaking polarization, the BJP is eyeing to play mainstream politics in the state with the aim to become the biggest opposition by 2024.

In the southern states of India, buying out votes in exchange for liquor has been a common phenomenon which has been executed really well by regional parties. Also, while Telangana has more of the pro-partition population, Andhra Pradesh has more anti-partition people. Hence their politics differ in this aspect.

The 2014 general elections were the last elections that a united Andhra Pradesh took part in, as less than a month after the polls the state was bifurcated into Andhra Pradesh and Telangana. Regional parties, the Telugu Desam Party (TDP) and the Yuvajana Sramika Rythu Congress Party (YSRCP), dominated the elections by winning 16 and 9 seats respectively whereas national parties like the Congress and the BJP had to be satisfied with just two and three seats respectively. The Owaisi-led AIMIM won one seat.

In 2019, after the bifurcation of the state when Telangana was stepping into the Lok Sabha elections for the first time as a state, TDP and YSRCP did not contest at all. This led to a redistribution of the votes to the three main parties in the contest: BJP, Congress and Telangana Rashtra Samithi (TRS). In a three-sided contest among these parties, the TRS got over 41 per cent vote share, the Congress around 29.48 per cent and the BJP 19.45 per cent. The BJP managed to get four seats whereas the Congress which had a higher vote share got only three seats, yet again establishing the fact that vote share and seats have no direct correlation. The Kalvakuntla Chandrashekhar (KCR) led TRS won nine seats to emerge as the strongest party in Telangana. Hindu consolidation in some constituencies had helped the BJP won four seats, which was also a pleasant surprise for the party. Apart from Hindu consolidation, the one difference between

Andhra Pradesh and Telangana was the impact of the Modi factor. Prime Minister Narendra Modi was the preferred national alternative in Telangana. People did not agree with the narrative of KCR of making TRS strong in order for Telangana to have a say in national politics. It also catalysed the BJP's upward march in constituencies where it had a base of 18–20 per cent. In Andhra Pradesh, supporting Jaganmohan Reddy in both state and national elections dominated as the narrative. The BJP lacked a base vote, and the Modi factor was not prominent in a state like Telangana.

Speeches of popular leaders resulted in polarizing the voters and in turn consolidating Hindu votes. The BJP and the Congress were not expected to gain any seats in these two states and the regional parties were all set to sweep the elections. TRS was pervading the elections and one of the silent yet most important factor that was working in its direction was Harish Rao, a mass leader who had the power to influence almost as much as half of the voters in Telangana. Chief Minister K. Chandrasekhar Rao wanted to project his son K.T. Rama Rao as the mass leader. The main reason behind projecting his son as the chief ministerial face had to do with the fact that some sources suggesting KCR was not well, and wanted to build his son's political career as soon as possible. Harish Rao getting sidelined by KCR was evident to his base core supporters, who then abstained from voting.

Unlike in other constituencies of the country, BJP's larger narrative of the Congress being anti-national did not work here as an ex-Indian Air Force personnel himself contested on a Congress ticket. In addition, the Opposition's narrative of 'democracy in danger' resonated with some voters and as a result the entire election turned out to be an absolute surprise.

There is a saying in Telangana that the person who provides you food and water should never be cheated. KCR's irrigation scheme under the leadership of Harish Rao paid big time and put KCR much ahead of his competitors. Farmers were unanimously voting for KCR.

Uttar Pradesh's chief minister, Yogi Adityanath, did multiple rallies in the state in 2018 and then again in 2019. In 2018, it was irrelevant as people were looking for a good CM candidate and no party other than TRS was able to provide them with one. However, in 2019 when there was an evident polarization, Yogi Adityanath's rallies seemed to have had a positive impact on voters.

Although KCR provided people with basic facilities such as good roads, water supply and electricity, at the same time he indulged in a lot of appeasement measures like handing out ₹1 lakh to Muslim girls on their wedding day and other similar incentives limited only to Muslims.

Let us analyse some key constituencies of Telangana before we move on to Andhra Pradesh.

Hyderabad

The common capital of Telangana and Andhra Pradesh, Hyderabad has over 65 per cent Muslims and in any constituency where Muslims are over 40 per cent, polarization unravels by itself. In Hyderabad where the AIMIM has a stronghold, polarization exists by default. However, there was a chance for other parties to take away the seat if Majlis Bachao Tehreek (MBT), founded by Mohammed Amanullah Khan as a result of differences with the then AIMIM president, Sultan Salahuddin Owaisi, contested. It would have led to a division of Muslim votes, thereby helping other parties which focus on Hindu voters. Since MBT did not contest the elections, Hyderabad was a one-sided affair with the AIMIM sweeping the seat easily.

Karimnagar

In the Karimnagar constituency there was polarization owing to reservation and the contesting BJP candidate was Bandi Sanjay Kumar who shifted to the BJP a few days before the elections. He brought along his core voters to the BJP with him.

In Telangana, an adivasi association had approached the apex court, seeking to declare the SC/ST Act, 1976, as illegal and unconstitutional owing to a mass influx of Banjaras in the state. Their claim was that the Banjaras were not originally a scheduled tribe and their migration from other states was adversely impacting the benefits available to the tribes of Telangana. A polarization was brewing here. The BJP won the constituency by a margin of more than 80,000 votes.

Malkajgiri

Malkajgiri is India's biggest constituency. A very interesting phenomenon which was seen in Makajgiri was how the ground-level workers of the BJP and Congress were coming together only to keep KCR in check. KCR was poaching Congress' MLAs, and stopping it was going to help the BJP gain some seats and the Congress some. The Congress had a sympathy wave growing in its favour among voters as KCR was poaching Congress MLAs, and as a result, the 'democracy is dying' narrative was working here for the Congress quite well. A strong base vote also helped the Congress edge out a victory with less than 10,000 votes.

Nizamabad

Nizamabad was the constituency with the highest number of candidates contesting and the reason behind this was only to get a mandate against KCR's daughter, Kalvakuntla Kavitha, who contested from here. There was a sentiment against K. Kavitha among the farmers who then decided to defeat her in the election.

The farmers had especially been demanding the government to fix an MSP for turmeric. The prices had been an issue for nearly a decade now, with the problem accentuating in the election year owing to a bumper turmeric harvest.

These farmers, primarily turmeric growers, had been seeking a just remuneration for their produce and demanding that the government set up a Turmeric Board. Unhappy on being sidelined, the farmers believed that filing over 100 nominations against a sitting MP would help highlight their cause nationally.

Around 175 turmeric and red sorghum (jowar) farmers had entered the Lok Sabha poll fray in Telangana to take on K. Kavitha in the Nizamabad Lok Sabha constituency.

These farmers together were set to hurt TRS big time and the ultimate gainer of this would be the BJP. As expected, the same happened and the farmers together got over 90,000 votes—around 30,000 more than the victory margin.

Arvind Dharmapuri himself was famous, but one thing that further strengthened his case was the then Home Minister Rajnath Singh's rally. Although people wanted KCR back, they wanted Modi back too. The Modi wave wasn't as strong here as it was in the rest of the country, but it was still considerable.

Adilabad

KCR in his speech had referred to the BJP and said, '*Ee Hindu Gaalu...bondu baalu...dikkumalina...daridrapu gaalu...desham lo aggi petale, gattar levale.*' It loosely translates in English to: 'These (self-proclaimed) Hindus are useless and disgusting... They want to stoke a fire in the country and belong in the gutter.'[28]

This speech of KCR polarized the elections and the rest of the work was done by the lone BJP MLA Raja Singh who had publicly claimed that he would not take an oath in front of a Muslim.

The presence of the Owaisi brothers further polarized the elections, and this time BJP was seemingly gaining as KCR too had made anti-Hindu remarks. He suffered electoral loss at the hands of the BJP by a margin of more than 55,000 votes.

Andhra Pradesh

Andhra Pradesh also witnessed the assembly elections alongside the Lok Sabha elections. However, voters were aware about the two distinct elections and while they wanted Modi at the centre, at the state-level their first preference was for regional parties. The political parties were Jaganmohan Reddy-led YSRCP, N. Chandrababu Naidu led-TDP, the BJP and the Congress Party.

In 2014, Chandrababu Naidu allied with the BJP and requested a special package for the state. This became his core election campaign issue and he managed to win 16 seats while Andhra Pradesh and Telangana were still one state. A few months before the 2019 elections,

---

[28]https://www.thenewsminute.com/article/ec-issues-notice-telangana-cm-kcr-derogatory-remarks-hindus-99807

Chandrababu Naidu parted ways from the BJP and accused the Modi government of not fulfilling his demand of special package for Andhra Pradesh.

Although the BJP contested separately, yet it wanted Jaganmohan Reddy-led YSRCP to gain as much as possible, as it would mean the depletion of the TDP. The revival of YSRCP would elevate the BJP to mainstream politics in Andhra Pradesh by capturing the Opposition space. In 2019, YSCRP won 22 out of 25 seats with a massive 20 per cent increase in vote share, whereas the TDP had to suffer a loss of over 11 per cent vote share. The BJP's decision to contest separately cost it a significant loss of over 7 per cent vote share and two seats. In fact, the BJP and the Congress polled lesser votes than NOTA. NOTA received 1.5 per cent votes in 25 Lok Sabha seats, whereas BJP could attract 0.96 per cent voters and the Congress performed marginally better at 1.29 per cent.

There was anti-Naidu sentiments too as the TDP did not work much in the state and Naidu's alignment with the Congress further damaged his reputation. Core voters of TDP—SCs and Christians—found YSRCP as an alternative, as the voters knew that the Congress or the BJP were anyway not going to win. Hence, a big chunk of TDP's core voters shifted to YSRCP.

Jaganmohan Reddy's father and former chief minister of Andhra Pradesh, Y.S. Rajasekhara Reddy had a very good image among the people of the state and Jaganmohan Reddy's 3,648 km-long padyatra, covering more than 130 out of the 175 assembly constituencies in the state worked in his favour. His father had earlier defeated TDP chief, N. Chandrababu Naidu in 2004 after undertaking a similar walkathon.

The people of Andhra Pradesh were against the partition of the state, believing it to be an injustice to them. Since the state's partition happened under a Congress government, there was naturally a sentiment brewing against the party. Chandrababu Naidu's alignment with the Congress was set to hurt him.

In both these states, people did not find any resonance with the idea of a hung assembly and wanted a government with a clear majority.

CONCLUSION: THE WAY FORWARD

Right after the conclusion of the 2019 general elections, while there is yet to be a widespread acceptance for the humongous mandate received by Prime Minister Modi among different sets of people, one thing that is undeniable is how the baseline of Indian politics has been completely transformed—moving from caste, class and religion to the narrative of development and nationalism. There is negligible to no existence of linear math between vote shares and seats in the general elections. Vote shares for specific leaders in numerical terms do not always convert into seats. Voters are aware enough to raise local issues in assembly elections and vote on national matters during general elections. A new era in politics backed by voters' awareness has put the all time-tested ways of politics to trial.

The 2014 mandate for the BJP was based on hope, but 2019 was based on the public's hope turning into tangible ground reality in the preceding five years. It was as if a five-year courtship was now culminating into a marriage. The 2019 mandate was based on the performance of the BJP in its first term, a term which elevated the party to the image of a national party that had widened its social base. During the first term, demonetization and GST were two of the boldest moves of the Modi government in its bid to fight against corruption. Encouraged by the mandate received for a successive term, Prime Minster Modi took yet another set of bold decisions right at the beginning of the second term. As soon as Amit Shah took charge of the Home Ministry, India saw pending decisions being taken up within the first six months of the government's tenure. Be it the issue of Triple Talaq or abrogation of Article 370 in Kashmir or the Citizenship Amendment Bill—while the media as well as the public had speculated some steps likely to be taken up by the Modi government, nobody had predicted the BJP would take up such absolute steps and completely nail these long-standing issues.

With regard to Kashmir, the BJP government did not stop at the abrogation of Articles 370 and 35A but also took steps to ensure the trifurcation of the state. Travelling on-ground across India, I discovered around 70 per cent of the country's population approved of the decision, and there was a resounding support for Modi on the decision, except in some Muslim-dominated pockets of south India.

On 9 November 2019, the apex court of the country gave its verdict on the most awaited Babri Masjid demolition case—the case which many believed was pretty much written with a permanent marker on the BJP's manifesto as it kept making an appearance in every election. The constructing of the Ram temple in Ayodhya had been on BJP's agenda since long. In fact, because it had been part of the manifesto for so long, the party has also been accused by some quarters of not being sincere with the issue and keeping it alive only to get Hindu votes. The Supreme Court order in favour of building of the Ram temple in Ayodhya has now put those accusations at rest.

With the Citizenship Amendment Bill (CAB), which gives citizenship to persecuted religious minorities, the Modi government fulfilled another poll promise. The Bill was a long-pending issue and had been a topic of discussion since independence. Right from the first Prime Minister Jawahar Lal Nehru to Indira Gandhi, to Rajiv Gandhi to Manmohan Singh, all have spoken in favour of the Bill. In the Rajya Sabha in 2003, Manmohan Singh had asked the then Deputy Prime Minister L.K. Advani to pass the Bill to protect the rights of the persecuted minorities in Bangladesh.[29]

However, soon after the Bill was passed in the Rajya Sabha in December 2019, the country witnessed protests against the Bill. Rumours were spread that the Bill will marginalize the Muslims of India and they might have to move to other countries. The government took too long to address the issue and to clarify that the Bill has absolutely nothing to do with the Muslims of India. Meanwhile, the protests turned violent in West Bengal, Assam and

---

[29]https://www.opindia.com/2019/12/citizenship-amendment-bill-manmohan-singh-2003-statement/

Delhi. The students of Jamia Millia Islamia too were part of the protest, but with outsiders (that is, not students of the university) joining in, the protest took a violent turn.

Home Minister Amit Shah, in a debate, clearly said that the government is not going to back down and CAB will be implemented exactly the way it has been passed in the houses of Parliament. Delhi and West Bengal have their assembly elections in 2020 and 2021 and the CAB will act as one of the most important factors. While the Opposition is saying it is unconstitutional, the government said it doesn't violate any Article or Section of the Constitution.

By solving long-pending issues like Article 370, the BJP on one hand has built an initial favourable opinion, but on the other hand has eliminated topics which had garnered votes for it in the past. For reaching its next target of making India a $5 trillion economy, more work needs to be done on the economic front. The 2024 general elections will definitely be fought on entirely different issues but one cannot deny that matters like the Ram temple, Article 370 and the CAB will certainly influence the election outcome for ages to come.

MPs elected by the people are the ones who eventually chose the country's prime minister. But now people voted keeping in mind the prime minister of their choice, who handpicked the best in his party as the people's representatives. In many cases, people even went ahead with electing a parliamentarian, even if they held animosity towards him or her, only because they had faith in Modi and believed that he is working for the best in the interest of the nation.

No one form of media (newspaper, print, TV, social media) today has control on the narrative or can play a single-handed role in shaping public opinion. With politicians building their own direct communication channels with people through various mobile network platforms and social media, building a political narrative has become a more democratic exercise. People have also realized that not everything that the media says is the 'gospel truth' and have started cross-verifying each and everything. Even when it comes to politicians, only legitimate demonization is publicly acceptable; attempts at fabrication of facts are outrightly rejected by the public.

Modi has changed the rules of success in Indian politics. On the ground, people view him as a leader who has the right intention. This is why people praised him despite standing in long queues at the time of demonetization or facing initial difficulties during GST's transitional phase. Even when he went through with solving the Kashmir issue, people believe that even if some time in the future the lid came off and there were any disturbances in the country, Modi has the capability of binding the country together.

Regardless of low GDP numbers or widespread talks of an economic slowdown, the public considered Modi as the best choice for the country, and his effective delivery of social schemes (housing, toilet, health insurance, gas) overshadowed the 'slowing down of economy' narrative. Even if businessmen faced problems with GST, they still rallied behind Modi. Even if the youth was struggling with unemployment, they believed that it would only be Modi who could provide them with a bread to break. Modi, in short, had built a pro-people bond with the masses. This has been his X factor.

Another change in the political baseline that was observed was how people from various parties, ideologies and backgrounds started joining the BJP. The hard pill that the saffron party has to swallow here has got to do with the realization that its mandate is only in the name of Modi. The public recognized his work and thus voted for him. Taking in people with antithetical ideologies or ways might seem to be a gain in the short term, but would only prove to cause political harm to the party in the long term.

Another thing the public believed was that Modi and Shah could solve issues at the grassroots level. After the 2019 elections, Amit Shah emerged as a popular name—the second leader in line after Modi who was talked-about on the ground—and this was perhaps the reason why he was made the home minister.

Looking ahead, a critical need of the hour is to develop an Opposition which is oriented towards nationalist-consciousness. India deserves people in the Opposition who serve the public despite not being in power. The Congress Party needs to reinvent itself in order to stay relevant in post-Modi era politics.

If the Congress' strategy involves staying off the rails and waiting out for the BJP to lose its charm, it might take time but you never know, things may work for it in the distant future. But if it is in a haste to rise up to power again, then the party needs to focus on rebranding itself as an Opposition which is looked at as nationalist.

The depletion of family politics, be it the BSP or RJD, was also something novel in the current Modi era. Also, it would be extremely difficult for parties to get votes in the name of caste, sympathy or entitlement in the general elections in the future, even though these factors may still play a reduced but important role in state elections. As local as an election gets, the greater the dominance of these factors, and as national as an election gets, these factors start taking a backseat.

As soon as the BJP won, it headed out on its conquest for the southern states where it has been running a successful membership drive in Andhra Pradesh. Even in West Bengal, a high number of people joined the BJP. This only shows how focused the party is and any national party which wants to beat the BJP at its game has to be on its foot 24x7. Their leaders have to be seen more on the ground. The BJP, on the other hand, needs to revisit its strategy in the states, and has to be cautious of over using the 'Modi factor' in state elections. It needs to analyse the takeaways from its performance in state elections. Post the 2019 Lok Sabha elections, the BJP cannot feel that the edge that it has in an era where politics has shifted from the left of centre ideological politics towards the right of centre ideological politics for granted or as a cushion.

Ticket distribution too plays an important role in the elections. Be it an MLA or MP, a strong face has to be seen. But these representatives have to work for the public and it will be their work which will define their party's longevity.

Modi was—and still is—a big political factor in India and his image after 2019 and in the months to come has become more like that of a global leader. His gesture of patting US President Donald Trump's hand, for example, left an indelible impression on a local young villager, who had hardly seen his country's prime minister play an assertive role in world politics. Besides global powers, even Muslim countries were on Modi's side and this message has seeped well into the minds of the people from the countryside.

In the coming days, what can be inferred by observing the current way of things is how the Congress has shifted its focus on launching Priyanka Gandhi with the UP elections. When it comes to Delhi, so far it looks like it would be a BJP vs AAP fight.

Another interesting observation is how the Opposition has corrected its mistake of always opposing the prime minister. Though the BSP initially opposed Modi, it also came out to support the abrogation of Article 370. Arvind Kejriwal, who has been quite vocal in his anti-Modi stance, has altogether stopped attacking Modi. Politicians have realized that attacking Modi directly or personally will not help them if they sought to gain political capital

Only a nationalist conscious and committed Opposition will be able to give the BJP a tough fight in the coming years and the 2021 West Bengal and 2022 Uttar Pradesh assembly elections will set the road for political narrative ahead of the 2024 Lok Sabha elections.

ACKNOWLEDGEMENTS

There was a time when I would take interviews on the streets of Delhi with unwavering passion in my heart to contribute to society through my work. From those initial days to travelling across India to predict election results, and writing this book—my journey has been rather eventful for a 28-year-old! I am thankful to God, my parents Rajni and Dilip Bhandari, sisters Shilpa and Shubhra, friends and people who have blessed me through the years.

I would also like to thank the young team of *Jan ki Baat* who tirelessly worked on the ground with me to execute my mission to reflect the accurate voice of the people of India. I also thank Arnab Goswami, the managing director of Republic Media Network, who has supported me since my initial days. He believed in me and gave me a big platform to reach out to people, and he has always been a true well-wisher. I would also like to thank Lord Meghnad Desai who encouraged me to write this book. Vinay Sharma has been with me constantly in the book-writing process, and his continuous research support was important in shaping the book. Suhail Mathur, from The Book Bakers, has been on speed dial. The team at Rupa Publications has also been very supportive and they have been gracious to me despite my missing the deadlines on a few occasions.

Above all, I want to thank the people of India, who gave their time and interacted with me—their interactions helped simplify political and election analysis in general, and the 2019 general elections in particular. My conversations with people on the ground were intriguing, and they opened my mind to the different layers that govern how the Indian voter thinks.

Lastly, and most importantly, I am grateful for the journey itself—travelling to more than 400 Lok Sabha constituencies has been an unforgettable learning experience for me and has made me a more optimistic and positive person.

INDEX

Aam Aadmi Party (AAP), xiv, 127, 128, 129, 130, 132, 133, 134, 135, 137, 138, 139, 140, 141, 142, 179, 182, 183, 185, 217
Abdullah, Farooq, 34, 188
Adityanath, Yogi, 7, 14, 20, 21, 22, 23, 26, 27, 28, 36, 207, 208
Advani, L.K., 61, 119, 120, 213
All India Majlis-e- Ittehadul (AIMIM), 67, 100, 109, 110, 111, 112, 191, 206, 208
All India United Democratic Party (AIUDF), 144, 146, 147, 148, 149, 150, 151, 152
Andhra Pradesh Reorganisation Act, 2014, 206
Anna Dravida Munnetra Kazhagam (AIADMK), 202, 203, 204, 205
Anti-incumbency, 24, 69, 74, 81, 87, 95, 96, 97, 109, 110, 111, 112, 116, 148, 154, 162, 169, 179, 182, 185, 190, 193, 197, 203
Article 35A, 213
Article 370, 169, 189, 212, 214, 217
Asom Gana Parishad (AGP), 144, 145, 147, 149, 152
Assam Agitation (1979–85), 144
Azad, Ghulam Nabi, 187

Babri Masjid demolition case, 213
Badal, Sukhbir Singh, 180, 182, 184
Bahujan Samaj Party (BSP), xiii, 1, 2, 5, 8, 10, 12, 22, 23, 24, 25, 28, 29, 33, 65, 143, 164, 169, 183, 185, 216, 217
Balakot air strikes, xiv, 7, 64, 75, 78, 83, 85, 86, 121, 123, 129, 150, 169, 171, 174, 176, 182, 185, 186, 204
Balyan, Sanjeev, 8, 9
Banerjee, Mamata, 33, 34, 35, 36, 37, 38, 39, 40, 41, 42, 43, 44, 45, 46, 47, 48, 49, 51, 52, 55, 58, 59, 60, 192
Bihar Minor Mineral Rules, 2017, 64
Biju Janata Dal (BJD), 160, 161, 162, 163, 164, 165, 166, 167
Bypoll, 1, 4, 11, 21, 22, 23, 91, 99, 132, 138, 184

Chauhan, Shivraj Singh, 50
Citizenship Amendment Bill (CAB), 47, 213, 214
CPI (M), 35, 48, 154, 155, 156, 190

Das, Raghubar, 94
defamatory remarks, 136
Democracy, 66
Demonetization, 39
Dravida Munnetra Kazhagam (DMK), 203, 204, 205
Drug menace, 181

Election Commission of India (ECI), 11, 34, 40, 188
Exit poll, 23
Fadnavis, Devendra, 100, 115
farmers' agitation, 102, 107
farmers' distress, 102, 121, 122, 123, 124
Forest Rights Act, 2006, 102

Gandhi, Priyanka, 132
Gandhi, Rahul, 14, 17, 21, 27, 34, 67, 105, 109, 113, 128, 129, 136, 137, 145, 146, 159, 169, 184, 193, 194, 195
gathbandhan, xiii, 2, 5, 8, 10, 11, 12, 17, 19, 22, 24, 26, 27, 28, 30, 31, 32, 33, 61, 67, 102, 110, 143, 197
Gehlot, Ashok, 82, 83, 84, 85
Goods and Services Tax (GST), xiv, 13, 39, 118, 119, 121, 177, 212, 215
Gorkha Janmukti Morcha (GJM), 56
Gorkhaland Agitation, 56
government welfare schemes, 50, 53, 98

Hindustani Awam Morcha (HAM), 62
Hindutva, 89, 94, 97, 107, 114, 196, 201, 203, 204
Hooda, Deepender Singh, 171

Indigenous Peoples Front of Tripura (IPFT), 154

Jaitley, Arun, 139, 183
Jammu & Kashmir National Conference (NC), 169, 186, 188, 189

Jan Lokpal Bill, 127
Janata Dal (Secular) JD(S), 169, 190, 196, 197, 198, 199, 200, 201
Janata Dal United (JDU), 61, 62, 65, 67, 70, 71, 72, 76, 77, 78
Jat agitation, 168, 170
Jayalalitha, 202, 203, 205
Jharkhand Mukti Morcha (JMM), 93, 94, 95
Jharkhand Vikas Morcha (JVM), 93, 94, 95

Kairana exodus, 4, 8
Kalvakuntla Chandrasekhar Rao (KCR), 206, 207, 208, 209, 210
Kathua rape case, 187
Kejriwal, Arvind, 127, 129, 217
Kharge, Mallikarjun, 34, 200
Khattar, Manohar Lal, 171, 172, 183
Koregaon Bhima violence, 106
Kumar, Nitish, 61, 62, 63, 64, 67, 70, 73, 74, 76, 77

Lal, Devi, 170, 171, 173
Lok Janshakti Party (LJP), 61, 62, 66, 69, 73

mahagathbandhan, 61, 65, 66
Mahatma Gandhi National. Rural Employment Guarantee Act (MGNREGA), 66
Marandi, Babulal, 93
Maratha reservation, 102
Mayawati, 1, 2, 12, 18, 25, 26
Mufti, Mehbooba, 188

Naidu, Chandrababu, 34, 190, 210, 211

Nanar oil refinery, 115
Narayan, Jayaprakash, 63
National Register of Citizen (NRC), xiv, 47, 145, 146, 147, 153, 157
national security, 4, 16, 42, 101, 108, 137, 197
nationalism, 7, 21, 62, 75, 83, 84, 85, 86, 88, 93, 121, 123, 125, 150, 168, 169, 170, 171, 172, 173, 176, 177, 181, 185, 186, 212
nationalism wave, 7, 84, 86, 93, 123, 169, 172, 177, 181
Nationalist Congress Party (NCP), 99, 100, 103, 104, 105, 106, 107, 108, 110, 111, 112, 113, 116, 117, 157
Naxalites, 73
Nirmal Gram Puraskar (NGP), 110
Nishad Party, 22
North-East Democratic Alliance (NEDA), 145, 146, 149
Nyuntam Aay Yojana (NYAY), 66, 74, 123

Owaisi (Asauddin, Sultan Salahuddin), 67, 206, 208, 210

Paswan, Ram Vilas, 61, 69
Patidar movement, 120, 121, 125
Patnaik, Naveen, 160, 161, 162, 164, 165, 166, 167
patriotism, 81, 125, 170
Pawar, Ashok, 173
Pawar, Sharad, 34, 104, 106
Peoples Democratic Party (PDP), 169, 185, 188, 189
Pilot, Sachin, 82, 86
Pradhan Mantri Awas Yojana, 88

Pradhan Mantri Ayushman Yojana, 88
Pradhan Mantri Kisan Samman Nidhi, 108, 122
Pradhan Mantri Kisan Samman Nidhi (PM-KISAN) Yojana, 122
Pulwama attack, 64, 86, 97, 123, 129, 150, 169, 170, 181

Rafale, 16, 78, 136, 137
Raje, Vasundhara, 80, 81, 86
Ram temple, 213, 214
Rashtriya Lok Dal (RLD), 8, 66
Rashtriya Lok Samata Party RLSP, 62, 69
Rashtriya Loktantrik Party (RLP), 84
Rashtriya Swayamsevak Sangh (RSS), 23, 89, 90, 113, 114, 117, 151, 185, 186, 193, 201, 204
Reddy, Jaganmohan, 191, 207, 210, 211
Reservation, 102
Rohingya Muslims, 146, 148, 149, 151

Sabarimala, 190, 191, 192, 193, 195
Samajwadi Party (SP), xiii, 1, 2, 3, 5, 8, 10, 14, 18, 22, 23, 24, 28, 29, 33, 143, 169
Sarkar, Manik, 154, 155
Sarma, Himanta Biswa, 145, 149, 150, 154
Shah, Amit, 1, 34, 37, 40, 47, 80, 99, 103, 119, 120, 122, 126, 145, 158, 199, 212, 214, 215
Shiromani Akali Dal (SAD), 168, 179, 180, 181, 182, 183, 184, 185
Shiv Sena, 99, 100, 101, 102, 103,

104, 105, 108, 109, 110, 111, 112, 113, 114, 115, 116, 117, 118, 119, 125
Singh, Amarinder, 168, 180, 184
Soren, Shibu, 93, 94
Stalin, M.K., 34, 203
Sule, Supriya, 103, 104, 105, 106
Swachh Bharat Abhiyan, 88

Telangana movement, 206
Telangana Desam Party (TDP), 191, 206, 210, 211
Telangana Rashtra Samithi (TRS), 191, 206, 207, 208, 209

Thackeray, Uddhav, 99, 101, 115
the Left, xiii, 35, 60, 167, 190, 191, 192, 193, 194, 195
Trinamool Congress (TMC), xiii, 33, 34, 35, 36, 37, 38, 39, 40, 41, 42, 43, 44, 45, 46, 47, 48, 49, 50, 51, 52, 55, 56, 57, 59, 60, 192
Triple Talaq, 75, 141, 212

Yadav, Akhilesh, 2, 18, 22, 34
Yadav, Lalu Prasad, 64, 78
Yadav, Mulayam Singh, 2, 29, 30
Yuvajana Sramika Rythu Congress Party (YSRCP), 191, 206, 210, 211